The Complete Speaker's Index

to Selected Stories

for Every Occasion

The Complete Speaker's Index
to Selected Stories
for Every Occasion

Jacob M. Braude

PRENTICE-HALL, INC.

Englewood Cliffs, N. J.

PRINTED IN THE UNITED STATES OF AMERICA
16452 — B & P

DEDICATION

I lovingly dedicate this volume
to my grandchildren
Michael, Matthew and Catherine Lynn—
life's precious but not taxable dividends.

What This Book Can Do for You

This book was compiled with a double thought in mind. With the thought that even if you were never called upon to make a speech or write an article, you can still have a wonderful time entertaining yourself by dipping into the pages that follow in spare moments or when you feel the need to escape from the pressure of daily life and its many problems.

Where else in a single volume can one learn that the only thing that perfect mates come in is shoes and gloves, and that marriage is three parts love and seven parts forgiveness of sins, or that a marriage is happy when the couples are as deeply in love as they are in debt, or that a man taking a wife is either adding another milestone towards his eventual success or another millstone towards his ultimate defeat?

How many other comparable volumes tell you that the average woman likes to be put on a pedestal, but not quite out of reach, and that all women, according to Winston Churchill, are professional? At least he told us that he himself never met an amateur.

And what man isn't interested in reading about the facets of success in life and to learn that the road to success is always under construction, and the secret of success is known only to those who have not succeeded? These are but a few of the pithy sentiments you will find in the following pages.

Reading this volume for simple entertainment or as escape literature gives you but a single idea of its usefulness. You will find it to be a reference book of invaluable assistance when called upon to prepare a speech, write an article, deliver a dissertation or engage in animated conversation.

There are three areas in which the following pages can be

especially useful to the amateur or professional writer or speaker. In the first place, it contains a number of illustrative anecdotes, and there is nothing better or more convincing than to tell the right story at the right time. What speaker has not at some time or other felt the need to electrify his audience when he stood in danger of losing it and what author has not felt the same under similar circumstances?

Henry Ward Beecher, the famous preacher, had a genius for bringing the most somnolent audience back to life. One July morning he rode into a West Virginia town which was widely known in lecture circles as "Death Valley"—for the reason that any speaker unfortunate enough to have an engagement to lecture there wilted and curled up when he faced the town's stupid and indifferent audience.

Beecher was duly warned. That afternoon, when he was being introduced, half the audience was already dozing. Beecher rose from his chair and, wiping his brow with a large handkerchief, strode to the front of the platform.

"It's a God-damned hot day," the clergyman began.

A thousand pairs of eyes goggled and an electrical shock straightened the crowd erect. Beecher paused, and then, raising a finger of solemn reproof, went on, "That's what I heard a man say here this afternoon."

He then proceeded into a stirring condemnation of blasphemy and, needless to say, took his audience with him.

What could be more devastating when one is offered a compromise which, in fact, is no compromise at all? Then tell the story about George M. Pullman and his founding of the community which now bears his name, at what was once the outskirts of Chicago.

It was during the early part of 1880 that The Pullman Company purchased more than four thousand acres of prairie land adjoining Lake Calumet, some twelve miles south of the business district of Chicago. On this tract there were constructed shops and a town to house 8500 people.

Solon Spencer Beman, a New York architect, was the master builder of this model town, and as it was nearing completion, he was so proud of his achievement, of its public buildings, residences, paved streets, parks, playgrounds, sewage system, and water supply, that he went to Mr. Pullman one day and suggested that he thought it would be quite appropriate to name the city "Beman," after its architect.

Mr. Pullman was quick to admit that Beman was a pretty name, but in reply he said, "Beman, we both had something to do with this. It was my original idea and I put up the money for it. You did a fine job in laying out the plans. I will compromise with you. We will use the first syllable of my name and the second syllable of your name and we'll call the city 'Pullman'."

What could be more effective?

The pages that follow also contain some overall themes which in and of themselves, when properly strung together, could well furnish the entire body of a talk or article. If you are called upon to deliver a patriotic address and you need something with which to begin and something with which to finish, by referring either to the categories as they appear in alphabetical order or to any one of three indices in the tail-end of the book, you may come upon America-Americanism; Patriotism; United States Flag; Democracy, and countless other titles. If it happens to be a commencement address that you are called upon to deliver, ample available material will be found under such titles as Leadership; Citizenship; History; Progress, and Crime Prevention.

For preachers and ministers there are categories under Church; Church attendance; Church collections; Christmas; Sin; Marriage; Divorce and Righteousness.

For the businessman there is Capital-Labor; Management; Employer-Employe; Salesmanship and the like.

Take the word prejudice, which you will find as being down on something you're not up on. That could well be the text of an entire treatise, and the material necessary to give it volume and substance is all contained in this book.

Now, it's one thing to know that what one is looking for is to be found within the covers of a book and another thing to be able to find it when you need it. A reference book is only as good as its index. In fact, Horace Binney once remarked that the best book in the world would owe the most to a good index, and the worst book, if it had but a good single thought in it, might be kept alive by it. Lord Campbell once commented that so essential did he consider an index to be to every book that at one time he had proposed to bring a bill into Parliament to deprive an author who published a book without an index of the privilege of copyright and, moreover, to subject him for his offense to a pecuniary penalty.

The comprehensive Subject Index in this book can best be utilized by using it in conjunction with the categories under which the items appear. There will be occasions when you will recall having come upon a particularly appropriate passage but may not be able to lay your finger on it because you cannot recall the category under which it is listed. Many of the items lend themselves to being listed under any one of three or four different captions.

Under such circumstances, if you should recall one or two key words either in the item or the story or the joke, all you need do is to use those key words, look under the Subject Index for each of them, and then find the identical numbers. Having done that, you will have the number of the item you are seeking.

For instance, you recall the story about the young man who said he hated to have a "shall" and a "shall not" flung at him every minute because it was so arbitrary, and that it dealt with an arbitrary signpost that appeared somewhere along a road. All you need do is to look up in the index under "Arbitrariness" and then under "Signpost" and you would find that in each instance appears No. 828. That would be your cue to the item number that tells the story that you are seeking.

On the other hand, you may recall the author of an item but not the category under which it is listed. In such case you would have but to turn to the index relating to author and source, and there your want would be satisfied.

As you continue to work with the volume, you will find for yourself other useful ways in which the book can be put to great use. I leave you with this thought and wish you happy reading and enjoyable hunting.

Contents

The Complete Speaker's Index

to Selected Stories

for Every Occasion

Ability

1.   The greatest ability is dependability.

2.   The wicked are always surprised to find ability in the good.
—Luc de Clapiers Vauvenargues

Absence

3.   He that fears you present will hate you absent.
—Thomas Fuller

4.   Absence is to love what wind is to a fire; it puts out the little, it kindles the great.
—Roger de Bussy-Rabutin

5.   Absence, like death, sets a seal on the image of those we have loved; we cannot realize the intervening changes which time may have effected.
—Oliver Goldsmith

Absent-mindedness

6.   G. K. Chesterton, the English author, was hopelessly absent-minded. When he became engaged to be married, he was eager to share the happy news with his mother, to whom he was devoted. He went home and wrote her a long letter. Mrs. Chesterton was touched by her son's devotion, as she knew how much effort he had put into the letter. She knew because she lived in the same house and was in the room with him while he wrote it.

7.   Albert Einstein had a pair of carpet slippers that were as dear to his heart as his violin. Mrs. Einstein had to watch him constantly lest he wander down to the village in his bedroom slippers. Of course, in Einstein's case, absent-mindedness was a contributing factor. You hardly

1

Abstinence

wonder at the bedroom-slipper story when you remember that he once received a check for $1,500 from a foundation and used it for months as a bookmark. Then he lost the book.

Abstinence

8. Abstinence is as easy to me as temperance would be difficult.
—Dr. Samuel Johnson

9. The temperate are the most truly luxurious. By abstaining from most things, it is surprising how many things we enjoy.
—William Gilmore Simms

Abuse

10. There are two things you are sure to meet with which you need never pay any attention to—abuse and flattery. The first can't harm you and the second can't help you.

Accomplishment-Accomplishments

11. A man seldom knows what he can do until he tries to undo that which he has done.

12. There is nothing more disgraceful than that an old man should have nothing to produce as a proof that he has lived long except his years.
—Seneca

Accounting

13. Old accountants never die, they just lose their balance.

14. Anyone can keep accounts, but it takes an accountant to make them complicated.

Achievement-Achievements. See also Accomplishment

15. Never look back at the many you have passed, but always look forward to the man ahead of you. He's the man you have to beat.

16. Our business in life is not to get ahead of others but to get ahead of ourselves—to break our own records, to outstrip our yesterdays by our today, to do our work with more force than ever before.
—Stewart B. Johnson

Action

17. We learn to do neither by thinking nor by doing; we learn to do by thinking about what we are doing.
—George D. Stoddard

18. I am only one, but I am one. I cannot do everything, but I can do something. What I can do, I ought to do. And what I ought to do, by God's grace, I will do.

19. Better that we should err in action than wholly refuse to perform. The storm is so much better than the calm, as it declares the presence of a living principle. Stagnation is something worse than death. It is corruption also.
—William Gilmore Simms

20. It is good policy to strike while the iron is hot; it is still better to adopt Cromwell's procedure, and make the iron hot while striking. The master-spirit who can rule the storm is great, but he is much greater who can both raise and rule it.
—Elisha L. Magoon

21. Once during World War I, railroad crossties were sorely needed at the front. An officer sent this wire to General Charles G. Dawes who headed the General Purchasing Board: *"Exigent we have crossties. Move heaven and earth to get them by Saturday."* Dawes telegraphed back the same day: *"Raised hell and got them today."*

Adolescence

22. Snow and adolescence are the only problems that disappear if you ignore them long enough.

23. Growthwise, up to the age of twelve boys are about a year behind the girls; during the ages twelve to seventeen the boys are gradually catching up; and from seventeen on it's neck and neck.

Advancement

24. The best way to grow is to outgrow your job.

—HAL STEBBINS

25. The way to get ahead is to start now. If you start now, you will know a lot next year that you don't know now and that you would not have known if you had waited.

Adversity

26. Prosperity is no just scale; adversity is the only balance to weigh friends.

—PLUTARCH

27. It is often better to have a great deal of harm happen to one than a little; a great deal may rouse you to remove what a little will only accustom you to endure.

—LORD GREVILLE

28. Men think God is destroying them because he is tuning them. The violinist screws up the key till the tense cord sounds the concert pitch;

but it is not to break it, but to use it tunefully that he stretches the string upon the musical rack.

—Henry Ward Beecher

29.   Adversity is a medicine which people are rather fond of recommending indiscriminately as a panacea for their neighbors. Like other medicines, it only agrees with certain constitutions. There are nerves which it braces and nerves which it utterly shatters.

—Justin McCarthy

Advertising

30.   *A tip to advertisers:* Tell them what they want to know—not what you want to say.

31.   "Build a better mousetrap, and the world will beat a path to your door." Thus, more or less, runs the ancient saw, and indeed, the world will probably do it—that is, if it knows you are selling mousetraps and knows how to get to your door. If it doesn't, you may just be sitting there with a gradually mounting mountain of mousetraps. Advertising is important.

32.   If you want to write effective advertising, this is the way to do it: stick to the facts, relate the facts to individual wants and needs, be interesting and even entertaining, but, in all you do, prepare the reader or the auditor for the ultimate experience he will have with the product. Trying to achieve good advertising any other way is placing your trust in magic. Any writer who sets out to deceive the public must first deceive himself— by believing that anything but the facts can, in the long run, prevail.

—Walter Weir, *Truth in Advertising
and Other Heresies* (McGraw-Hill)

Advice

33.   The only foolproof way to give advice is to ask people what they think they should do.

Affectation

34. How is it possible to expect mankind to take advice when they will not so much as take warning?

—Jonathan Swift

35. The person who is too stubborn to take advice is rarely quite as stubborn as the person who insists that he take it.

Affectation

36. All affectation is the vain and ridiculous attempt of poverty to appear rich.

—Johann Kaspar Lavater

Age

37. No wise man ever wished to be younger.

—Jonathan Swift

38. It's not how old you are that counts, but how you are old.

—Marie Dressler

39. The first forty years of life give us the text: the next thirty supply the commentary.

—Arthur Schopenhauer

40. To be seventy years young is sometimes much more cheerful and hopeful than to be forty years old.

—Dr. Oliver Wendell Holmes

Aging

41. The best thing for grey hair is a sensible head.

42. Those long, long days of youth soon become those short, short days of age.

43. About the time one learns how to make the most of life, the most of it is gone.

44. Those who love deeply never grow old; they may die of old age, but they die young.

—ARTHUR WING PINERO

45. One trouble with growing older is that it gets progressively tougher to find a famous historical figure who didn't amount to much when he was your age.

46. To grow old and never know it is to achieve the greatest possible success in life, next to growing old and never having your friends suspect it.

—ELBERT HUBBARD

47. Nobody grows old by merely living a number of years. People grow old by deserting their ideals. Years wrinkle the skin, but to give up enthusiasm wrinkles the soul.

48. Some fifty years ago psychologists thought that man's mental powers reached their peak at the age of 25 and then began a gradual decline. The latest findings show that a man reaches his peak mentally somewhere around the age of 35 and maintains the same level until well past 70.

—MAXWELL MALTZ

49. Our cerebral processes do not automatically shut themselves off in the sixties. Doing something constructive every day, even in a very small way, keeps the mind alert.

Alaska, State of

Michelangelo worked until he was 89. The thought of packing up at 65 probably never entered his head. For posterity it was just as well. A contemporary of his, Titian, pressed on with his painting until compulsorily retired by the plague in his 100th year.

Picasso, with 80 years well behind him, thought up a new method of painting. Eiffel, the man who built the tower, published a work on aeronautics at the age of nearly 90. And the late Sir Harry Lauder kept right on to the end of the road. Not bad advice, either.

Alaska, State of

50.   Here is an apt suggestion for the Alaskan State Song: "Freeze A Jolly Good Fellow."

51.   Residents of the other 49 states can brag all they want about their fair cities, but to an Alaskan, there's no place like Nome.

Alaska-Texas. See Texas-Alaska

Ambition

52.   It is by attempting to reach the top at a single leap that so much misery is produced in the world.

—WILLIAM COBBETT

53.   The modesty of certain ambitious persons consists in becoming great without making too much noise; it may be said that they advance in the world on tiptoe.

—VOLTAIRE

America—American—Americanism

54.   In America it's coffee breaks. In Britain it's "absent-tea-ism."

55.   Loyalty . . . is a realization that America was born of revolt, flourished in dissent, became great through experimentation.

—HENRY STEELE COMMAGER

56.   The American tradition has always dictated that it is far better to debate an important matter without settling it than to settle it without debating it.

57.   Be Americans. Let there be no sectionalism, no North, South, East or West; you are all dependent one on another and should be one in union. Observe justice and good faith toward all nations; have neither passionate hatreds nor passionate attachments to any; and be independent politically of all. In one word, be a nation; be Americans, and be true to yourselves.

—GEORGE WASHINGTON

Ancestry

58.   It is of no consequence of what parents any man is born, so that he be a man of merit.

—HORACE

59.   A man can't make a place for himself in the sun if he continues to take refuge under the family tree.

60.   There is no king who has not had a slave among his ancestors, and no slave who has not had a king among his.

—ATTRIBUTED TO HELEN KELLER

61.   Who brags about his great forbears
Would steal the praise that should be theirs.

—FROM THE HINDUSTAN

Anger

62.　An angry man opens his mouth and closes his eyes.

—CATO

63.　To be angry is to revenge the fault of others upon ourselves.

—ALEXANDER POPE

64.　He that will be angry for anything, will be angry for nothing.

—CAIUS CRISPUS SALLUST

65.　Anger causes us often to condemn in one what we approve of in another.

—PASQUIER QUESNEL

66.　The size of a man can be measured by the size of the thing that makes him angry.

—J. K. MORLEY

67.　For every minute that you are angry, you lose 60 seconds of happiness.

—RALPH WALDO EMERSON

68.　Speak when you're angry and you'll make the best speech you will ever regret.

69.　Recorded words are fetters;
　　　When angry, don't write letters.

—CHINESE PROVERB

Anticipation

70.　Some people not only expect the worst—they even go out and look for it.

71.　There would be few enterprises of great labor or hazard undertaken, if we had not the power of magnifying the advantages which we persuade ourselves to expect from them.

　　　　　　　　　　　　　　　—Dr. Samuel Johnson

Anxiety

72.　Better be despised for too anxious apprehensions than ruined by too confident a security.

　　　　　　　　　　　　　　　—Edmund Burke

73.　The beginning of anxiety is the end of faith, and the beginning of true faith is the end of anxiety.

　　　　　　　　　　　　　　　—George Mueller

Appearance—Appearances

74.　You can't always judge by appearances—the early bird may have been up all night.

75.　I have always observed that to succeed in the world we must be foolish in appearance, but in reality wise.

　　　　　　　　　　　　　—Charles de Secondat Montesquieu

Appreciation

76.　When you are sitting on top of the world give a thought occasionally for the ones who are carrying it on their shoulders.

77.　In proportion as our own mind is enlarged, we discover a great number of men of originality. Commonplace people see no difference between one man and another.

　　　　　　　　　　　　　　　—Blaise Pascal

Approbation

78.   If silence lends consent, the number of men who have voted "aye" on a proposition they did not approve of is legion.

—Leon L. Watters

79.   Whenever you commend, add your reasons for doing so; it is this which distinguishes the approbation of a man of sense from the flattery of sycophants and admiration of fools.

—Richard Steele

Architect—Architects—Architecture

80.   It's remarkable what a good architect can do. He can make an old house look better just by talking about the cost of a new one.

81.   Today, the idealistic stone mason, who said he was not just laying stone but building a cathedral, would be fired for not knowing it was only a garage.

82.   Architecture is the printing press of all ages, and gives a history of the state of the society in which it was erected, from the cromlech of the Druids to those toyshops of royal bad taste,—Carlton House and the Brighton Pavilion. The Tower and Westminster Abbey are glorious pages in the history of time, and tell the story of an iron despotism, and the cowardice of unlimited power.

—Lady Morgan

Argument—Arguments

83.   The best way to win an argument with a woman—take her side.

84.   Some argue to prove a point; others to prove themselves.

12

85. To argue with a fool is like carrying a lantern before a blind man.

—De Gaston

86. Never argue at the dinner table, for the one who is not hungry always gets the best of the argument.

—Richard Whately

87. It is never good for a wise man to argue with a fool. Bystanders don't always know which one is which.

88. There would be fewer arguments if we tried to determine what's right instead of who's right.

Art—Artist—Artists

89. The artist doesn't see things as they are, but as he is.

90. Each time I sell a painting it is like an operation, like feeling a limb amputated.

—Pablo Picasso

91. Art is the reaching out into the ugliness of the world for vagrant beauty and the imprisoning of it into a tangible dream.

—George Jean Nathan

92. A man who works with his hands is a laborer. A man who works with his hands and his brain is a craftsman. But a man who works with his hands and his brain and his heart is an artist.

93. The aim of every artist is to arrest motion, which is life, by artificial means and hold it fixed so that a hundred years later, when a stranger looks at it, it moves again, since it is life.... This is the artist's way of scribbling "Kilroy was here" on the wall of the final and irrevocable oblivion through which he must someday pass.

—WILLIAM FAULKNER

94. Leonardo da Vinci, according to the *Encyclopedia Britannica*, worked at the portrait of Signora Zanobi del Giocondo, the sitter for the Mona Lisa, during some portion of four successive years, causing music to be played during the sittings that the rapt expression might not fade from off her countenance.

95. In the Great Hall of Chequers, where the British Prime Minister resides, hangs an old masterpiece by the Flemish painter, Peter Paul Rubens. It illustrates the fable of the lion caught in a net and the mouse that freed him by gnawing the bonds.

The painting has been admired by a succession of Prime Ministers. But during the Churchill regime, something about the Rubens mouse jarred Sir Winston's artistic sensibilities.

Finally, Churchill, an amateur painter himself, could stand it no longer. He called for his brush and easel, and determinedly retouched the mouse in the masterpiece.

Art, Modern

96. Modern paintings are like women. You'll never enjoy them if you try to understand them.

97. The artist was showing his pictures to a friend. "Now here's a picture; one of my best, too. When I started out I had no idea what it was going to be."

His friend looked puzzled. "Tell me, after you got through, how did you find out what it was?"

Aspiration—Aspirations. See also **Ambition**

98. Few of us can measure up to what we hope to be, but as long as we keep our hopes high we won't be ashamed of what we are.

99. Without high aspirations man would not have progressed much in the unfoldment of his civilization on this planet. As far back as the days when men lived in caves, there were those in the group who believed that life could be better. If this had not been so, man would never have moved out of that existence.

Atheism

100. Atheism is a disease of the soul, before it becomes an error of the understanding.

—ATTRIBUTED TO *Felix Frankfurter*
IN *Wisdom* MAGAZINE

101. They that deny a God destroy man's nobility; for certainly man is like the beasts in his body; and if he is not like God in his spirit, he is an ignoble creature.

—FRANCIS BACON

Atomic Age

102. Scientists are still debating whether or not splitting the atom was a wisecrack.

103. In this atomic age, we don't celebrate the arrival of the New Year but rather our survival of the Old Year.

Attire. See also **Wearing Apparel**

104. Change of fashions is the tax which industry imposes on the vanity of the rich.

—SEBASTIEN CHAMFORT

105. No man is really well-dressed who does not wear a friendly expression on his face.

106. The hostess gown was invented to keep one from running down the party to the wrong person.

107. The influence of costume is incalculable; dress a boy as a man and he will at once change his own conception of himself.

—Bayle St. John

108. Children are often very observant without understanding cause and effect. One little fellow watched with a worried and anxious look on his face while his father proceeded to change from a business suit to a tuxedo. Finally he could stand it no longer and burst out, "Daddy, don't wear that suit. It always gives you a headache the next morning."

Audience—Audiences

109. Eloquence is in the assembly, not in the speaker.

—William Pitt

110. We can't all be heroes, for someone has to sit on the curb and clap as they go by.

—Will Rogers

Authorship

111. How vain it is to sit down to write when you have not stood up to live.

—Henry David Thoreau

112. No author can be as moral as his works, as no preacher is as pious as his sermons.

—Jean Paul Richter

113. I can never understand how two men can write a book together. To me that's like three people getting together to have a baby.

—Evelyn Waugh

114. It is the part of prudence to thank an author for his book before reading it, so as to avoid the necessity of lying about it afterward.

—George Santayana

115. Writing a book was an adventure. To begin with it was a toy, an amusement; then it became a mistress, and then a master, and then a tyrant.

—Winston Churchill

116. There are two kinds of writers, those who are and those who aren't. With the first, content and form belong together like soul and body; with the second, they match each other like body and clothes.

—Karl Kraus

117. Every book is, in an intimate sense, a circular letter to the friends of him who writes it. They alone take his meaning; they find private messages, assurances of love, and expressions of gratitude, dropped for them in every corner. The public is but a generous patron who defrays the postage.

—Robert Louis Stevenson

Automation

118. The purchasing agent faces his toughest decision when he negotiates to buy the machine designed to replace him.

119. Automation has in no way and to no degree reduced the need for human effort; it has merely altered the specifications. The requirement today is less muscle and more skill, and it takes effort both to supply and absorb the amount of training needed.

—Maurice R. Franks

120. A professor was obligated to hold a series of weekly classes some 400 miles from his home. He grew weary of making that weekly trip, so he just sent tape recordings of his lectures each week. Being in the distant city a few weeks later, he dropped by to see how his classes were getting along. Looking through the glass door, he saw and heard the tape recorder faithfully playing back his lecture, but in the seats where the students should have been sitting there were only tape recorders taking down his lecture.

—Byrl A. Whitney

Avarice

121. The lust of avarice has so totally seized upon mankind that their wealth seems rather to possess them than they possess their wealth.

—PLINY

122. Avarice, in old age, is foolish; for what can be more absurd than to increase our provisions for the road, the nearer we approach to our journey's end.

—CICERO

Average—Averages

123. In baseball, a game won today will count as much as the last game of the season, so far as the averages go. And this applies to you and me in our day-to-day work.

—WILLIAM FEATHER

124. Averages can be somewhat deceptive. Witness the case of the statistician who drowned while wading across a river with an average depth of two feet.

125. If a man stands with his left foot on a hot stove and has his right foot in a freezer, the statistician would say that on the average he is comfortable.

Bachelorhood

126. There are two kinds of bachelors: Those too fast to be caught, and those too slow to be worth catching.

—VELMA ARMSTRONG

Bargain—Bargains

127. Buying a cheap article to save money is like stopping the clock to save time.

Beauty

128. What Mother Nature giveth, Father Time taketh away.

129. The French artist, Pierre Auguste Renoir, suffered a great deal from an old malady, rheumatism. It was particularly painful for him to continue painting, which he did seated in a chair.

One day a friend passed while he was forcing himself to work. Noting Renoir's obvious pain, the friend exclaimed, "You have done enough already Renoir. Why do you continue to torture yourself?"

The artist looked at him for a long moment and replied, "The pain passes, but the beauty remains."

130. It is said that beauty is in the eye of the beholder. It is that capacity of mind, which appreciates the quality, color, and form of all life. Beauty is in the ear of the listener, too, for infinite variety of colorful sound is all around us. Beauty is the expression of God's bountiful harmony. Depression and doubt flee in the presence of nature's beauty. We see beauty in the so-called ugly face when we look for it. To develop within ourselves an appreciation of the beautiful and colorful is to have an awareness of the Presence of God.

Behavior

131. There's no right way for doing something wrong.

132. Laws control the lesser man ... right conduct controls the greater one.

Belief—Beliefs

133. No man believes his creed who is afraid to hear it attacked.
—WENDELL PHILLIPS

134. Give us clear vision that we may know where to stand and what to stand for—because unless we stand for something, we shall fall for anything.

Bible, The

135. Most of the events we find recorded in the *Bible* occurred in an area about 400 miles long and 80 miles wide.

136. The skeptic Voltaire once said: "In 100 years the *Bible* will be a forgotten book found only in museums." When the 100 years were up, the home in which he had made his pronouncement was occupied by the Geneva Bible Society.

137. The *Bible* has given us the most marvelous record of family life of any civilization on earth. . . . The *Bible* never grows old. We grow old. Our houses grow old. Our businesses become outdated. Our wardrobes change quickly. But the *Bible,* a study of man's relationship to God, never changes. That's why the way of life of the family of Israel has survived the centuries. Faithful records of the family life of other civilizations contemporary with the *Bible,* the Babylonian, the Hittite, even the Greek, have perished, but the family record of Israel is alive and vital today.

—Edith Deen

Bird—Birds

138. Protect the birds! The dove brings peace and the stork brings tax exemptions.

139. The unerring sense of direction with which birds are able to migrate between places thousands of miles apart has long been a source of wonder to scientists. Only very recently have experiments shown that birds, like sailors, steer by the sun. Though generally able to keep perfectly on course, they sometimes are confused on cloudy days. Scientists also determined night flying birds steer by the stars. They did this by placing birds in a planetarium where stars could be projected to show how they would appear in any latitude and longitude. The complex set of instincts which enables birds to use the sun and stars to direct them to places where they have never been before seems to be completely inborn.

Blame

140. The girl who can't dance says the band can't play.

—JEWISH PROVERB

141. When a man points a finger at someone else, he should remember that four of his fingers are pointing at himself.

142. It was the traditional ninth inning with the score tied, two out, and the bases loaded. On the next pitch the batter knocked an easy roller to the shortstop. It should have been a sure out, but the shortstop threw the ball into the stands.

Leaving the field the pitcher flung his glove into the grass and began to berate the shortstop for losing the game. At this point the manager stepped in and asked one simple question:

"Who loaded the bases in the first place?"

Boastfulness

143. The man who has a right to boast doesn't have to.

144. If people knew what an inspiring thing it is to hear a man boasting, so long as he boasts of what he really has, I believe they would do it more freely and with a better grace.

—ROBERT LOUIS STEVENSON

Book—Books

145. A book is the only immortality.

—RUFUS CHOATE

146. A book should be luminous, but not voluminous.

—CHRISTIAN NEVELL BOVEE

147.   A used copy—if the right person has used it—is far more valuable than a new book.

—CURTIS HIDDEN PAGE

148.   Books are but waste paper unless we spend in action the wisdom we get from thought.

149.   Without books God is silent, justice dormant, natural science at a stand, philosophy lame, letters dumb and all things involved in Cimmerian darkness.

—RICARDO BARTHOLIN

150.   A book is an ambassador of goodwill. It signifies a hope for the future and a faith in the present. And if it is an old book, it also pays honor to the past. A book is not given cynically; and it is seldom given without at least some thought for its intrinsic value. It goes out in the honest belief that it will be a personal and intimate source of pleasure to the giver and to the receiver alike.

Boredom

151.   Insincerity isn't especially commendable, but often it rescues a dull evening.

152.   It is to be hoped that, with all the modern improvements, a mode will be discovered of getting rid of bores; for it is too bad that a wretch can be punished for stealing your pocket handkerchief or gloves, and that no punishment can be inflicted on those who steal your time, and with it your temper and patience, as well as the bright thoughts that might have entered into your mind (like the Irishman who lost the fortune before he had got it), but were frightened away by the bore.

—LORD BYRON

Borrow—Borrowing

153.   A friend not in need is a friend indeed.

154. Before borrowing money from a friend, decide which you need more.

155. If a dollar saved is a dollar earned, a dollar borrowed is a dollar spent.

156. If I had the inclination and ability to do the cruelest thing upon earth to the man I hated, I would lay him under the necessity of borrowing money of a friend.

—EDWARD MOORE

Bravery

157. A hero is no braver than the ordinary man, but is braver five minutes longer.

—RALPH WALDO EMERSON

158. The bravery founded upon the hope of recompense, upon the fear of punishment, upon the experience of success, upon rage, upon ignorance of dangers, is common bravery, and does not merit the name. True bravery possesses a just end, measures the dangers, and, if it is necessary, the affront, with coldness.

—FRANÇOIS DE LA NOUE

Brevity

159. The man of few words doesn't have to take so many of them back.

160. When Peter Studebaker joined his brothers in the operation of the Studebaker company in 1863, he signed a contract with Clem Studebaker, company president, that is a classic in simplicity. In full it read: "I, Peter Studebaker, agree to sell all the wagons my brother Clem can make. I, Clem, agree to make all he can sell."

Bribery

161. The finest gems come in small sizes:
The 10 Commandments contain 297 words.
The Declaration of Independence has 300 words.
Lincoln's Gettysburg Address has 266 words.
The Preamble to the Constitution has 117 words.
The Lord's Prayer has 67 words.
The Golden Rule has 12 words.

Bribery

162. Men are more often bribed by their loyalties and ambitions than by money.

—ROBERT JACKSON

163. Of all the valuable things that money can't buy, the most valuable is a man who can't be bought.

Brotherhood

164. There will never be a brotherhood of mankind as long as one brother has something another thinks he should have.

165. Brotherhood is an outstretched hand, met and clasped by a hand outstretched. It is being one's brother's keeper. It is as old as man, as eternal as man, as vital as man. And since man is its keeper, brotherhood is *of* the people, *by* the people, *for* the people, so that in its living action it becomes the purest form of democracy.

166. A British soldier had gone through the terrible ordeal of Dunkirk during World War II. A friend asked him when he was safely back in England: "What did it feel like out there on the beach at Dunkirk, with the sea in front of you, the German army behind you, and the German bombers overhead?" He answered: "It was a strange feeling I had. I felt that every man on the beach was my brother."

—HAROLD E. BUELL

24

167. Some missionaries were talking with an African Christian named Lutete, owner of the hotel where they were staying. They stopped talking to watch an airplane pass overhead. Then Lutete said, "One day I took an airplane ride that made me very happy. For the first time I saw the world as God sees it. Looking down from the air, I could see houses and people, but I couldn't tell where the white people lived and where the Africans lived. I thought, it is like that with God. . . . He doesn't see whether we are black, white, red, brown or yellow. He sees us as His children."

Bureaucracy

168. Of all forms of government, those administered by bureaus are about the least satisfactory to an enlightened and progressive people. Being irresponsible, they become autocratic, and, being autocratic, they resist all development. Unless bureaucracy is constantly resisted it breaks down representative government and overwhelms democracy. It is the one element in our institutions that sets up the pretense of having authority over everybody and being responsible to nobody.

—CALVIN COOLIDGE

169. Trying to get a straightforward answer from some bureaucrats is like the problem of the old lady who took her canary back to the bird store because it stopped singing. When she first bought it, it sang sweetly enough. And then suddenly it lapsed into a silent, brooding melancholy.

The dealer's explanation was very simple, "Your bird wants a mate."

"Is my bird a male or female?" the old lady asked.

"Really, I can't say," replied the dealer. "You'll have to find that out for yourself."

"But how can I tell?"

"Why, very easily. All you have to do is get two worms, a male and a female, and put them both in the cage. If your bird is a male it will eat the female worm; if it is a female it will eat the male worm."

"But how can I tell a male worm from a female worm?" persisted the old lady.

"Madam," replied the dealer, politely but firmly, "this is a bird store. You will have to get that information from a worm dealer."

Business

170. The science of business is the science of service.
—ARTHUR FREDERICK SHELDON

171. Most of the money a businessman calls profits is merely money that has not been wasted.
—A. V. BURDINE

172. Thought, not money, is the real business capital, and if you know absolutely that what you are doing is right, then you are bound to accomplish it in due season.
—HARVEY S. FIRESTONE, *Men and Rubber, The Story of Business*

173. Ten Commandments of Business:
1. Love your work—it pays.
2. Handle the hardest job first each day.
3. Do not fear criticism—criticize yourself often.
4. Be glad and rejoice in the other follow's success—study his methods.
5. Do not be misled by dislikes—acid ruins the finest fabrics.
6. Be enthusiastic—it is contagious.
7. Be fair, and do at least one decent act every day.
8. Honor the chief—there must be a head to everything.
9. Have confidence in yourself, and make yourself fit.
10. Harmonize your work—let sunshine radiate and permeate.

Calendar

174. There's a lot to learn from the calendar. It plans its work a year ahead—never complains—always finishes on time and you don't have to wind it up.

175. In the Roman calendar, ascribed to Romulus, the year was divided into ten months. The last, or tenth month, was called December.

Although etymologically incorrect, this name was retained when two more months were added to the calendar, and December became the twelfth month. The Saxons called it winter-monath, and heligh-monath (holy month) because of Christmas.

Capacity

176.   The real tragedy is the tragedy of the man who never in his life braces himself for his one supreme effort, who never stretches to his full capacity, never stands up to his full stature.

—Arnold Bennett

177.   Greatness, in the last analysis, is largely bravery—courage in escaping from old ideas and old standards and respectable ways of doing things.. This is one of the chief elements in what we vaguely call capacity.

—James Harvey Robinson

Capitalism

178.   Capitalism is the only system in the world founded on credit and character.

—Hubert Eaton

179.   Capitalism is a way of organizing society for productive enterprise which takes risks in order to preserve ideals.

—Lester DeKoster

Capital—Labor

180.   Sometimes labor is on top and sometimes capital is, but there is never any doubt as to who is in the middle.

181.   The trade-unionist has the same limitation imposed upon him as the capitalist. He cannot advance his interests at the expense of society.

—J. Ramsay MacDonald

Capitulation

182. Any doctrine which preaches the oneness of management and labor—whether it stresses their unity in a party, class, race, nation or even religion—can be used to turn the worker into a compliant instrument in the hands of management. Both Communism and Fascism postulate the oneness of management and labor.... Our sole protection lies in keeping the division between management and labor obvious and matter-of-fact. We want management to manage the best it can, and the workers to protect their interests the best they can. No social order will seem to us free if it makes it difficult for the worker to maintain independence from management.

—Eric Hoffer

Capitulation

183. Smile at the wrongs thou canst not right,
    Kiss the hand thou darest not bite.

—From the Chinese

184. It is often shorter and better to yield to others than to endeavor to compel others to adjust themselves to us.

—Jean de La Bruyère

Card-playing

185. People who play bridge for fun count the evening's pleasure sufficient winnings.

186. A certain professor of psychology says that a good poker player could successfully handle any sort of executive job. Maybe so, professor, but what would a good poker player want with a job?

Carelessness

187. However long and hard the climb to the top may be, the bottom is only one careless misstep away.

188.   I am more powerful than the combined armies of the world. I have destroyed more men than all the wars of the nation. I massacre thousands of people in a single year. I am more deadly than bullets and I have wrecked more homes than the mightiest of guns.

I steal in the United States alone over $500,000,000 each year. I spare no one and I find my victims among the rich and poor alike; the young and the old; the strong and the weak. Widows and orphans know me to their everlasting sorrow.

I loom up in such proportions that I cast my shadow over every field of labor. I lurk in unseen places, and do most of my work silently; you are warned against me yet you heed me not. I am relentless, merciless and cruel.

I am everywhere—in the home, on the streets, in the factory, at railroad crossings; on land, in the air, and on the seas.. I bring sickness, degradation and death—yet few seek me out to destroy me. I crush, I maim, I devastate; I will give you nothing and rob you of all you have.

I am your worst enemy. I am CARELESSNESS!

Cause—Causes

189.   That cause is strong which has not a multitude, but one strong man behind it.

—JAMES RUSSELL LOWELL

190.   A human being is happiest and most successful when dedicated to a cause outside his own individual, selfish satisfaction.

—DR. BENJAMIN SPOCK

Caution

191.   All is to be feared where all is to be lost.

—LORD BYRON

192.   *Advice from an old carpenter:* Measure twice and saw once.

Censorship

193.　Blessed are the censors for they shall inhibit the earth.

194.　How do the censors manage to keep from being themselves corrupted by reading all the books and seeing all the pictures they say will corrupt the rest of us?

Certainty

195.　It's not the things you don't know that get you into trouble, but the things you know for sure.

196.　The longing for certainty and repose is in every human mind. But certainty generally is illusion, and repose is not the destiny of man.
—Justice Oliver Wendell Holmes

Chain reaction

197.　Mallet strikes chisel . . . chisel splits the wood.
—Chinese proverb

198.　Chain reaction in our contacts with people can spread sunshine—or grief—a lot farther than most of us realize. I saw a cartoon strip the other day that ought to hang on the walls of a lot of offices—and in a lot of homes. The president in an angry mood bawled out the superintendent. The superintendent found fault with the foreman. The foreman took it out on the workers. The workers took it out on each other, and then went home, snapped at their wives. The wives scolded the kids and the kids scolded the dog! Far fetched? Not so much. Think what the day is like when the big boss—and everyone else—smiles instead of snaps.

Chance

199.　Many shining actions owe their success to chance though the general or statesman runs away with applause.
—Henry Home

200. Chance is a term we apply to events to denote that they happen without any necessary or foreknown cause. When we say a thing happens by chance, we mean no more than that its cause is unknown to us, and not, as some vainly imagine, that chance itself can be the cause of anything.

Change

201. Time without change produces only age.

202. We are reasonably accustomed to change in these fast-moving times, but often it is the rapidity of the change which startles and sometimes unnerves us. There simply doesn't seem to be sufficient time between changes to make the necessary adjustments.

203. Great economic and social forces flow with a tidal sweep over communities that are only half conscious of them. Wise statesmen are those who foresee what time is bringing, and endeavor to shape institutions and to mold men's thought and purpose in accordance with the change that is silently surrounding them.

—Viscount John Morley

204. Deploring change is the unchangeable habit of all Englishmen. If you find any important figures who really like change, such as Bernard Shaw, Keir Hardie, Lloyd George, Selfridge or Disraeli, you will find that they are not really English at all but Irish, Scotch, Welsh, American or Jewish. Englishmen make changes, sometimes great changes. But, secretly or openly, they always deplore them.

—Raymond Postgate

Changelessness

205. If you have always done it that way, it probably is wrong.
—Charles F. Kettering

206. Teenagers can take consolation that there is nothing new about the trouble they may cause their parents. In the Istanbul Municipal

Museum is the Presse Papyrus, 6,000 years old, the oldest piece of known writing in existence. The first sentence reads: "Alas, things are not what they used to be. Everyone wants to write a book and children are no longer obedient to their parents."

—H. W. Aers

Character

207. A man should be upright, not be kept upright.

—Marcus Aurelius

208. Character is always lost when a high ideal is sacrificed on the altars of conformity and popularity.

—Dr. William Arthur Ward, Texas
Wesleyan College, Fort Worth

209. Character is the capacity to conduct one's self with restraint in times of prosperity and with courage and tenacity when things do not go well.

—James V. Forrestal

210. We are very much what others think of us. The reception our observations meet with gives us courage to proceed or damps our efforts.

—William Hazlitt

211. The noblest contribution which any man can make for the benefit of posterity is that of a good character. The richest bequest which any man can leave to the youth of his native land is that of a shining, spotless example.

—John Winthrop

212. Perhaps one of the strongest and most effective influences making for noble character is the lurking thought that someone, somewhere, is expecting something worthwhile of us. If we could trace the circumstances and instances surrounding many of this world's finest achievements we might be surprised to find that the impulse which made them possible lay back of someone's great expectation.

Charity

213.   The truest charity is the effort to correct the cause for the need of charity.

214.   We often excuse our own want of philanthropy by giving the name of fanaticism to the more ardent zeal of others.
                                                              —Henry Wadsworth Longfellow

215.   When I die, I should be ashamed to leave enough to build me a monument if there were a wanting friend above ground. I would enjoy the pleasure of what I give by giving it alive and seeing another enjoy it.
                                                              —Alexander Pope

Charm

216.   Charm is a way of getting the answer yes without having asked any clear questions.
                                                              —Albert Camus

217.   Justice Tom C. Clark of the United States Supreme Court used to tell the story of how on several occasions he stood in a receiving line alongside Speaker Sam Rayburn and noticed as the young ladies came along they invariably planted a kiss on the Speaker's cheek. Unable to understand why his long-time friend should be the beneficiary of such special preferential treatment he asked, " How come?"
        "You either got it or you ain't," was the Speaker's reply.

Child—Children

218.   A child is an angel dependent on man.
                                        . .—Count Joseph Marie de Maistre

33

Childhood

219. Alarm clock: a small device used to wake up people who have no children.

Childhood

220. Childhood shows the man, as morning shows the day.
—John Milton

221. When grown people speak of the innocence of children, they don't really know what they mean. Pressed, they will go a step further and say, well, ignorance then. The child is neither. There is no crime which a boy of 11 had not envisaged long ago. His only innocence is, he may not yet be old enough to desire the fruits of it. His ignorance is, he does not know how to commit it.
—William Faulkner

Child-training

222. In bringing up a child, think of its old age.
—Joseph Joubert

223. The surest way to make it hard for your children is to make it soft for them.

224. The training of children is a profession where we must know how to lose time in order to gain it.
—Jean Jacques Rousseau

225. A child who has not been taught the meaning of the word "no" by the time he is four years old has spent four years in the academic school of crime.

226. Education commences at the mother's knee, and every word spoken within the hearing of little children tends toward the formation of character. Let parents bear this ever in mind.
—Hosea Ballou

227.   An infallible way to make your child miserable is to satisfy all his demands. Passion swells by gratification; and the impossibility of satisfying every one of his demands will oblige you to stop short at last, after he has become a little headstrong.

—HENRY HOME

228.   President William Howard Taft, a doting father, showered every luxury on his children. On one occasion, a friend took him to task for being so extravagant.

"Don't you think it is unwise," said the friend, "to spend so much money on mere youngsters?"

"Not at all," replied Taft. "I figure if I give them every luxury now, they won't be spoiled by it later on."

229.   In the home there can be no harmony and progress without discipline. The authority is in the hands of the parents and they must learn to use discipline judiciously in training their children. If coddling prevails and the children are allowed to do as they please and, worse than all, try to teach the parents, then surely that family is not heading toward happiness and success. It is certain the members of that home will go from bad to worse unless their ways are mended.

230.   You may give them your love but not your thoughts,
For they have their own thoughts.
You may house their bodies but not their souls,
For their souls dwell in the house of tomorrow, which you cannot visit, not even in your dreams.
You may strive to be like them, but seek not to make them like you.
For life goes not backward nor tarries with yesteryear.

—KAHLIL GIBRAN

231.   A youngster is somewhat like a pendulum of a clock. If we hold a pendulum far to one side then suddenly let go of it, it swings just as far to the opposite side. Sometimes it swings wildly; not only sideways but forward and backward when not properly released. So it is with the training of a child. He needs to be disciplined so that he remains in an even swing or expression of life. But he must be allowed to swing—to express! A discipline which constantly represses him can be maintained only so long. When he reaches his teens, he is apt to break loose from it and swing in the opposite direction. . . . This slight pulling away is actually a good sign. The youngster is very much in the normal swing of life. And though his parents may be all too aware that he has not yet reached the goal toward which they have been guiding him . . . he is showing clearly that he is reaching out for it.

—WILLA FOGLE

Christianity

232. The world is equally shocked at hearing Christianity criticized and seeing it practiced.

—D. ELTON TRUEBLOOD

233. The trouble with some of us today is that we want to live the good Christian life, tomorrow.

234. The Christian is not a man who is better than someone else, but one who is better than he would be if he were not a Christian.

235. No one is without Christianity, if we agree on what we mean by the word. It is every individual's . . . code of behavior by means of which he makes himself a better human being than his nature wants to be . . . its symbol . . . is man's reminder of his duty inside the human race. Its various allegories are the charts against which he measures himself and learns to know what he is.

—WILLIAM FAULKNER

Christmas

236. To the child, Christmas is wondrous because it is so new; to his grandfather Christmas is wondrous because it is old.

237. We keep Christmas rightly by being merry, for Christmas is our remembrance that we have had a sign. In the light of Christmas stars we know that we do not walk alone. ... That is why we move the stars indoors to shine from a tree, and it is why we say to one another, "Merry Christmas!"

—Booth Tarkington

238. Christmas is many things. It is a star shining brightly to guide Magi from the East to the baby Jesus. It is shepherds gazing with awe and wonder at the heavenly visitors who announced the birth of the King of Kings. It is peace in a world of war and unrest, joy in a time of bewilderment and sorrow, hope in a situation of anxiety and apprehension. But most of all Christmas is the Son of God cradled in the arms of Mary, God's great gift of salvation and reconciliation to all mankind.

239. *In Brazil* the Christmas fiesta season is solemnly heralded by an open air Mass on Christmas Eve. Under the brilliant sky, in mid-summer weather, a colorful altar is set up in the cathedral church-yard, where the worshippers reverently pray and chant religious hymns, in a fiesta atmosphere of banners and religious trappings. After devotions the families have Christmas Eve supper in their homes.

240. *In China* Christmas is the climax of many days of Advent preparation. Before church on Christmas Eve, the people dress in their most colorful costumes, carry their best lanterns, and parade up and down the winding streets singing Christmas carols to the accompaniment of a mandolin. This singing is stopped by the burst of firecrackers, announcing the midnight Mass, at which the people yearly recognize the gift of the trust of children. Chinese children call their tree the "Tree of Light" instead of a Christmas tree. Their tree has no candles but is decorated with brilliant paper flowers, colored paper chains, and cotton snowflakes.

241. *In England* on Christmas Eve the yule log is brought inside and placed in the big fireplace. According to custom, each person in the family must sit upon the log and salute it before it is lighted to assure good luck for the household in the new year. Religious services predominate the English Christmas celebrations. Processions of carolers gather under the lofty arches of great cathedrals at midnight on Christmas Eve to sing the old and cherished hymns.

242. *In Germany* toy-giving is an important part of Christmas. The immortal carol, "Silent Night, Holy Night"—Kris Kringle—hand-carved toys and the Christmas tree are only a few of the many contributions to the joyous Christmas season made by the Germany of yesteryear. The greatest of the contributions is the "Tannenbaum"—the Christmas tree.

243. *In Holland* in order to provide food and water for St. Nick's good white horse on Christmas Eve, the little children stuff their clean wooden shoes with hay and carrots and place them on the window sills. A dish of water is set alongside them. The children are up early on Christmas morning to see what has been left them, and they are always pleasantly surprised to see that the hay and carrots have been replaced with small gifts, toys and surprises.

244. *In Italy* the Christmas scene is set with a profusion of pretty flowers and graceful olive trees. Their Santa Claus is the beneficent old witch, "Befana," who, clothed in rags, rides from house to house on a broomstick, leaving presents beside the hearth for the children. The "Precipio," truly symbolic of the Italian Christmas, is found in every home, with tiny statuettes of the Holy Family, angels, shepherds, and Wise Men grouped about a miniature manger.

245. *In Norway* the families are busy many weeks beforehand, making gifts and preparing food. According to tradition, church bells are heard chiming in all the cities of Norway, calling the people to five o'clock church on Christmas Eve—December 24th—when the Christmas celebration really begins. One of the most charming customs of Norway is the remembrance of the animals and birds, since they were the only ones present at the birth of the Holy Babe. The farm animals and cattle are most carefully tended, and are given extra portions of food.

246. *In Poland* when the first star appears in the evening sky on December 24, Fast Day is ended and the Christmas supper begins. Straw is placed under the table, dishes, and tablecloth, and one chair is left vacant for the Holy Child. Symbolizing peace on earth is the Peace Wafer, procured from the priest and given to the head of the family to break and share with the guests. While the wafer is being eaten, wishes for the coming year are exchanged. The Polish Christmas centers around the songs which are a combination of the religious and secular sentiments of the people, sung in memory of the Savior's birth.

247. *In Spain,* according to an old tradition, the Magi are said to journey to Bethlehem every year. And so, on Epiphany Eve, the children are laden with gifts as they wait at the city gates to meet the Kings. They look for the group in the sunset, but soon the glorious vision fades away and the children turn homeward, believing the Kings to have passed behind the mountain. Spanish children have no Christmas tree and do not hang up stockings on Christmas Eve. Instead, they practice a custom called "nacimiento," which means hiding slippers and shoes for Balthasar and the Wise Men to fill with goodies.

248. Christmas gifts are in keeping with Christmas traditions. On the first Christmas the three Wise Men brought their gifts of gold, frankincense and myrrh. The legends of St. Nicholas began in the early centuries of Christianity. While our American Santa Claus is comparatively modern, his name really comes from St. Nicholas. It was the poem of Clement C. Moore, "The Night Before Christmas," which made him into the jolly old elf so popular today.

No one desecrates Christmas by the exchange of gifts, however extravagant or unwise some of them may be. For in reality there are two Christmases in our modern times. There is the Christmas of the religious world and there is the Christmas of the secular world.

One of the truly fine things about Christmas in the United States is this—those who wish to make the day primarily one of religious observance are free to do so. Those who choose to make it one of the finest, most generous, and friendly holidays of the year have equal freedom. The ideal of course is to make it both, and as long as freedom lives in America, millions of people living here will do just that.

Church

249. The world at its worst needs the church at its best.

Church attendance

250. Persons used to shun the church because of its stern descipline. Now they neglect it because of its soft requirements.

—HUGH ELMER BROWN

Church attendance

251. Empty pews mean empty lives.

—ARNOLD GLASOW

252. Blessed is the man who can hear an alarm clock on Sunday as well as on Monday.

253. To neglect the church on the Sabbath is to break an appointment with God.

—DR. WILLIAM ARTHUR WARD,
TEXAS WESLEYAN COLLEGE, FORT WORTH

254. *On a church bulletin board in California:* "Come to worship every Sunday and avoid the Easter rush."

255. "How many people attend your church?" one pastor asked another. The minister thought a moment, and then replied, "Sixty regular, 250 C and E."

"What's C and E?" the other wanted to know.

Came the prompt answer, "Christmas and Easter."

256. When a minister called on a member of the church who had been lax in his attendance during the hot summer, he asked him gently if he had played golf the previous Sunday. The man indignantly denied it and then produced a panful of fish from the refrigerator to prove it.

257. One very optimistic minister had the habit in his opening prayer each Sunday of thanking God for the weather. On a particularly cold, icy, windy, slushy Sunday morning, the few people who had ventured out wondered how the minister could possibly refer to the weather in his morning prayer with any sense of gratitude. To their surprise, he said in the beginning of his prayer, "Dear God, we thank Thee that Thou dost send us so few Sundays like today."

258. It is related that a teamster once visited Rabbi Yitzhak to ask him about a problem which troubled him greatly. It seems that his work often made it impossible for him to attend the services in the synagogue, and he thought that, perhaps, he ought to change his job. The Rabbi asked: "Do you carry poor passengers free of charge?" "Yes," replied the teamster. "Then," said the Rabbi, "you serve the Lord in your occupation just as faithfully as I do when I am in the synagogue."

—Bishop Gerald Kennedy

Citizenship

259. Mere passive good citizenship is not enough. Men and women must be aggressive for what is right, if government is to be saved from those who are aggressive for what is wrong.

—Robert M. LaFollette

260. The citizen of today is not the voiceless, faceless man of the modern anti-Utopias. He can influence government at every level— directly by participation in honest local politics and by choosing men of integrity to represent him at higher levels, indirectly by the views he holds, the courage with which he holds them, the letters he writes to his elected representatives, the lobbies—interested or disinterested—he supports, even with the replies he makes to pollsters.

—Barbara Ward

City—Cities

261. Many cities have grown so fast their outskirts no longer cover their extremities.

—Frank ·Rathbun

Civic duty

262.   If you would be known, and not know, vegetate in a village; if you would know, and not be known, live in a city.

—CHARLES C. COLTON

Civic duty

263.   Some folks figure they are civic-minded just because they complain about the town clock, watch the home team on TV and vote against the school bonds.

—HAROLD COFFIN

264.   Participation in community affairs not only affords outlets for creative interests; it plays important roles in bettering local conditions, in molding the character of the community, and in contributing warmth to its personality. While thus engaged the doer acquires a growing sense of belonging. The resultant recognition and increasing respect from others brings added stature as a solid citizen.

Civilization

265.   Civilization can be measured by the degree of helplessness that results when the electric power goes off.

266.   When Albert Schweitzer revisited Europe after his long sojourn in Africa, one of his admirers asked him, "Well, what do you think of civilization?"

"It's a good idea," replied Schweitzer. "Somebody ought to start it."

Cleverness

267.   Cunning is the art of concealing our own defects, and discovering other peoples' weaknesses.

—WILLIAM HAZLITT

Coercion

268. No man can be coerced into doing his best work. He can only be inspired to do it.

—SANDIE STEVENS

269. *Chairman of the Board to other members:* "Of course, it's only a suggestion, gentlemen, but let's not forget who's making it."

Coincidence

270. A teacher asked her pupils to give examples of coincidence. There was a prolonged moment of silence. Then a youngster in the back of the room spoke up: "My father and mother were married on the same day."

College

271. College deans never die; they just lose their faculties.

272. College doesn't give you an education—it gives you schooling only.

273. The important degree for the college graduate is the degree to which he is willing to work to make himself a success.

Commencement exercises

274. From high-school senior to college freshman is quite a letdown.

275. A well-known businessman says his success was due to luck. That certainly makes it hard on speakers at commencement exercises.

Committee—Committees

276.   A committee of five consists of the one who does the work, three who pat him on the back, and the one who brings in the minority report.

Communism

277.   Communism began by incarcerating the few to free the many, and then enchained the many to protect the few.

—Dagobert D. Runes

278.   The guiding principle of socialism is: "From each according to his ability, to each according to his work." The guiding principle of communism, the more advanced phase, is: "From each according to his ability, to each according to his needs."

—Isolak Stepanyan

279.   Communism is at war with the whole human race. It is based on the blasphemy that a human being is just a particle of matter, without independent mind or spirit. It seeks to destroy the family as an institution. It seeks to wipe out religion. It seeks to blot out the human conscience and to distort all concepts of right and wrong.

—Thomas J. Dodd

Comparison—Comparisons

280.   In argument, similes are like songs of love: they much describe; they prove nothing.

—Matthew Prior

281.   The superiority of some men is merely local. They are great because their associates are little.

—Dr. Samuel Johnson

Compensation

282. I am absolutely convinced that no wealth in the world can help humanity forward, even in the hands of the most devoted worker in this cause. The example of great and pure individuals is the only thing that can lead us to noble thoughts and deeds. Money only appeals to selfishness and irresistibly invites abuse.

—Albert Einstein

283. As there is no worldly gain without some loss, so there is no worldly loss without some gain. If thou hast lost thy wealth, thou hast lost some trouble with it; if thou art degraded from thy honor, thou art likewise freed from the stroke of envy; if sickness hath blurred thy beauty, it hath delivered thee from pride. Set the allowance against the loss, and thou shalt find no loss great; he loses little or nothing who reserves himself.

—Francis Quarles

Complaint—Complaints

284. No one complains about the way the ball bounces when he catches it.

285. Things cannot always go your way. Learn to accept in silence the minor aggravations, cultivate taciturnity and consume your own smoke with an extra draught of hard work, so that those about you may not be annoyed with the dust and soot of your complaints.

—Sir William Osler

Compliment—Compliments—Complimentary

286. A compliment is a gift, not to be thrown away carelessly unless you want to hurt the giver.

—Eleanor Hamilton

287. Some persons never say anything bad about the dead—or anything good about the living.

45

288. One of the finest compliments that can be paid to any man is to say, "He kept his tears to himself and shared his laughter with others."

Compromise—Compromises

289. The poorest judges of distance are all those fellows who voluntarily agree to meet you halfway.

290. Compromise is odious to passionate natures because it seems a surrender; and to intellectual natures because it seems a confusion.

—George Santayana

291. The real problem in politics, particularly for those with ideological loyalties, is to sense when *not* to compromise. In a situation where some are arguing that $2 + 2 = 6$, while others assert the sum is 4, there can always be found the "moderates" who want, in the interests of harmony, to split the difference and settle for 5. If one begins with the assumption that all determinations are relative, this is understandable, even commendable: All good pragmatists will rally around $2 + 2 = 5$ as a "focus of consensus," and condemn with equal vigor the "extremists" who maintain that $2 + 2 = 6$ *and* those who stand firm behind 4.

—John P. Roche

Conceit

292. What is the first business of one who studies? To part with self-conceit. For it is impossible for anyone to begin to learn what he thinks he already knows.

—Epictetus

293. I'm certain that a man's best friend is his conceit. The average man has such a high opinion of himself that he feels he has to live up to a high standard. Consequently the conceited man thinks harder, works harder, plays harder, and is happier than the man who lacks conceit.

—R. Cameron

Condescension

294.   People who look down on others may be living on a bluff.

295.   There is nothing more likely to betray a man into absurdity than condescension.

—Dr. Samuel Johnson

Conference—Conferences

296.   Conference: an organized way of postponing a decision.

297.   If a conference lasts a long time, it must end in peace; no one can keep on defying his enemies all day.

—Alfred Duggan

Confidence

298.   Misplaced confidence is seldom found again.

299.   Confidence is a thing not to be produced by compulsion. Men cannot be forced into trust.

—Daniel Webster

300.   To confide, even though to be betrayed, is much better than to learn only to conceal. In the one case, your neighbor wrongs you; but in the other you are perpetually doing injustice to yourself.

—William Gilmore Simms

Conformity

301.   The rewards of conformity are mediocrity and monotony.

—Arnold H. Glasow

Conscience

302. For to do anything because others do it, and not because the thing is good, or kind, or honest in its own right, is to resign all moral control and captaincy upon yourself, and go posthaste to the devil with the great number.

—Robert Louis Stevenson

Conscience

303. He who has no conscience makes up for it by lacking it.

—Stanislaus J. Lec

304. The most painful wound in the world is a stab of conscience.

—John Ellis Large

305. Conscience is, in most men, an anticipation of the opinion of others.

—Sir Henry Taylor

306. If you should escape the censure of others, hope not to escape your own.

—Henry Home

307. He who sacrifices his conscience to ambition burns a picture to obtain the ashes.

—Asian proverb

308. Some persons follow the dictates of their conscience only in the same sense in which a coachman may be said to follow the horses he is driving.

—Richard Whately

Conservative—Conservatism

309. No man can be a conservative until he has something to lose.

—James P. Warburg

310. A conservative is a man who will not look at the new moon, out of respect for that "ancient institution," the old one.

—Douglas Jerrold

Considerateness

311. It is not enough to forgive our enemies. We must also be tolerant toward our friends and considerate of our families.

312. Henry Ford once put up this sign above the front door of a cottage he and Mrs. Ford were temporarily occupying: "Please use the back door. There is a nest of young phoebes in one corner of the porch, and a robin's nest in the other corner."

Years before, an example in kindness had been set for him by his farmer-father. Coming upon a very crooked furrow one day, young Ford asked, "Why isn't this furrow straight like all the others you plow, Dad?"

The elder Ford took his son by the hand and led him to the spot of earth he had avoided. There, in the grass, was a bird's nest.

—Jack Kytle

Consistency

313. The man who spends one-half of the day in studying what is just, and the other half in practicing what is so, shows a knowledge of consistency.

—J. A. James

314. Consistency is a verbal criterion, which cannot be applied to the phenomena of life. Taken together, the various activities of a single individual may "make no sense," and yet be perfectly compatible with biological survival, social success and personal happiness.

—Aldous Huxley

Contempt

315. None but the contemptible are apprehensive of contempt.

—Francois de La Rochefoucauld

Contentment

316.   If you see a man tamely submit to contemptuous treatment, be certain he merits it; an innocent, independent mind will keep arrogance at a distance.

—Joseph Bartlett

Contentment

317.   Enjoy your own life without comparing it with that of another.

—J. A. N. C. Condorcet

318.   If you don't enjoy what you have, how could you be happier with more?

319.   Taking things as they come does not wear one out so fast as dodging them.

320.   The ideal is to be poor enough always to have something to strive for and rich enough not to have to.

321.   To live content with small means; to seek elegance rather than luxury, and refinement rather than fashion; to be worthy, not respectable, and wealthy, not rich; to study hard, though quietly, talk gently, act frankly; to listen to stars and birds, to babes and sages with open hearts; to bear all cheerfully, do all bravely, await occasions, hurry never, in a word, to let the spiritual, unbidden and unconscious, grow up from the common, is what many of us would like.

—William Henry Channing

Controversy—Controversies

322.   When a thing ceases to be a subject of controversy, it ceases to be a subject of interest.

—William Hazlitt

323.   Lincoln was once chased by a bull through the meadow and around a haystack. Finally he caught up with the bull from behind, caught him by the tail, and the bull ran off across the meadow. Whereupon Lincoln exclaimed, "Why are you running? Who started this, you or I?"

Conversation

324.   When holding a conversation, it is a good idea to let go of it occasionally.

325.   Conversation is like a boat—if everybody crowds on the same side, it sinks. It needs balance to keep afloat.
—MARJORIE S. PITHER

326.   The average value of conversations could be enormously improved by the constant use of four simple words: "I do not know," or of Louis XIV's favorite remark: "I shall see."
—ANDRÉ MAUROIS

Cooperation

327.   The production of wealth is not the work of any one man, and the acquisition of great fortunes is not possible without the cooperation of multitudes of men.
—PETER COOPER

Correction—Corrections

328.   To free a man from error is to give, not take away.
—ARTHUR SCHOPENHAUER

329.   All are not friends who flatter—
All are not enemies who correct.

51

Cosmetics

330.   Cosmetics were used by women in the Middle Ages. Women in the middle ages still use them.

331.   Powder and paint were first brought into Europe from the East by the crusaders, and reached their most extravagant use in the eighteenth century. Indeed it is recorded that in 1770 a bill was introduced in Parliament which would have enacted that:

"All women who shall, from and after such Act, impose upon, seduce and betray unto matrimony any of His Majesty's subjects, by scents, paints, cosmetic washes, artificial teeth, false hair, Spanish wool, iron stays, hoops, high-heeled shoes, bolstered hips, shall incur the penalty of the law in force against witchcraft and like misdemeanors, and that the marriage, upon conviction, shall stand null and void."

Cost of living. See Living, High cost of

Courage

332.   Facing danger is not courage unless one knows the danger faced.

333.   A brave man thinks no one his superior who does him an injury; for he has it then in his power to make himself superior to the other by forgiving it.

—Alexander Pope

334.   The truest courage is always mixed with circumspection; this being the quality which distinguishes the courage of the wise from the foolhardiness of the rash and foolish.

—Jones of Nayland

52

335. The kind of courage which makes popular heroes is the kind we hear most about, but the courage which enables individuals to triumph over the wearisome trials of life is the kind that does more good for more people.

336. Fortunately for themselves and the world, nearly all men are cowards and dare not act on what they believe. Nearly all our disasters come of a few fools having the "courage of their convictions."

—COVENTRY PATMORE

Courtesy

337. The courteous learn their courtesy from the discourteous.

338. Courtesy is a pleasing form of kindness. It springs from the heart. If the mind prompts the action, it is not courtesy for courtesy does not reason. It is born of an instinctive desire to be kind and helpful. It is possible to develop a veneer of politeness that may, for a time, pass for courtesy, but like other counterfeits, it will never last long or go far.

339. An old man, successful in his business life, in his social life, just successful in all ways, told a young writer that he own at least half of his million-dollar fortune, not to ability, but to courtesy.

"I try to be nice to everybody," he explained. "No matter how cranky people are, how distant, how disagreeable, I follow the rule of unfailing courtesy. It's hard sometimes, but it is always profitable—and that's what counts."

"Profitable in what way?" the writer asked although he knew the answer all the time.

"In this life, especially if we are selling, as I have always been," the man replied, "there is no profit whatever in enemies. All the profit is in people who like you and who therefore want to show their liking by doing something nice for you. I am sure that for every dollar I earned as a salesman from ability and skill, I earned another because I was so nice to everybody that everybody wanted to do me a good turn."

—CHARLES B. ROTH

Covetousness

340. He deservedly loses his own property who covets that of another.

—PHAEDRUS

341. Those who give not till they die show that they would not then if they could keep it any longer.

—BISHOP HALL

Cowardice

342. It is vain for the coward to fly; death follows close behind it; it is by defying it that the brave escape.

—VOLTAIRE

Crime—Crimes

343. Most crime is closely tied to certain flaws and inconsistencies in our way of life and effective control ultimately depends upon how much we are willing and able to change, to give up perhaps, while still honoring our civil liberties and without breaking our basic democratic framework.

Crime prevention

344. Better build schoolrooms for "the boy," than cells and gibbets for "the man."

—ELIZA COOK

345. Solon, the wise man of Athens, was asked how crime could possibly be abolished in any state.

"It will be abolished," said he, "when those who are not wronged feel the same indignation as those who are."

Crime—Punishment

346. Heaven will permit no man to secure happiness by crime.
—VITTORIO ALFIERI

347. Punishment is not the answer to the problems of crime, it answers only the call for revenge.
—DAGOBERT D. RUNES

348. A community is infinitely more brutalized by the habitual employment of punishment than by the occasional occurrence of crime.
—OSCAR WILDE

Critic—Critics—Criticism

349. Critics are brushers of other men's clothes.

350. If you can't stand the heat, get out of the kitchen.
—HARRY S. TRUMAN

351. No man has a right to criticize, who has not earned that right.

352. The man who refuses to hear criticism has no chance to evaluate it.

353. A prince, criticized by his subjects, should never attempt to justify himself to them.
—NAPOLEON I

354. The most noble criticism is that in which the critic is not the antagonist so much as the rival of the author.
—BENJAMIN DISRAELI

55

Cruelty

355. The severest critics are always those who have either never attempted, or who have failed in original composition.

—William Hazlitt

356. The men and women that are lifting the world upward and onward are those who encourage more than criticize.

—Elizabeth Harrison

357. If men of wit and genius would resolve never to complain in their works of critics and detractors, the next age would not know that they ever had any.

—Jonathan Swift

358. A young man who thought more highly of himself than he ought to think was standing in front of a taxidermist store. In the window was an owl which had attracted many sightseers. Anxious to display his knowledge, he said with a pompous air, "Well, if I couldn't stuff an owl better than that, I would quit the business. The head isn't right. The pose of the body isn't right. The feet are not placed right."

But before he could finish his judgment, the owl turned his head and winked at him. The crowd laughed and the critic moved on.

Cruelty

359. Cruelty is no more the cure of crimes, than it is the cure of sufferings. Compassion, in the first instance, is good for both. I have known it to bring compunction when nothing else would.

—Walter Savage Landor

Curiosity

360. Knock at the door before you enter upon your neighbor's privacy; and remember that there is no difference between entering into his house and looking into it.

—Jeremy Taylor

361.   Desire and curiosity are the two eyes that make women beautiful or fossils interesting; and the man may squander his estate and come to beggary, but if he keeps these two amulets he is still rich in the possibilities of pleasure.

—ROBERT LOUIS STEVENSON

Custom—Customs

362.   There is no tyrant like custom, and no freedom where its edicts are not resisted.

—CHRISTIAN NEVELL BOVEE

363.   It is an old Chinese custom that a Chinese shake his own hand when he meets a friend. The implication is, of course, that he is congratulating himself on being so lucky as to meet so fine a person.

364.   A world traveler was dining with some friends one evening and he was discussing the feminine sex as he had seen it around the globe.

"The world's ideas about modesty are certainly unusual and varied," he said. "For instance, in Turkey, if a girl is surprised in her bath, she will cover her face every time. And a Chinese woman will invariably hide her feet under the same circumstances. But the white woman..."

"Yes, go on," urged a listener.

"Well," exclaimed the speaker, "a white woman will always keep the bathroom door locked!"

Cynic—Cynics—Cynicism

365.   The only deadly sin I know is cynicism.

—HENRY STIMSON

366.   A cynic is worse than a fool. The fool lacks insight but has faith; the cynic lacks both, though his cloak of impudence covers this emptiness.

—DAGOBERT D. RUNES

Danger

367. Trust him little who smilingly praises all alike, him less who sneeringly censures all alike, him least who is coldly indifferent to all alike.
—Johann Kaspar Lavater

Danger

368. A danger is never overcome without danger.
—Publilius Syrus

369. We triumph without glory when we conquer without danger.
—Pierre Corneille

370. Danger feared is folly, danger faced is freedom.
—V. Raymond Edman

Death

371. There is no death! What seems so is transition.
—Henry Wadsworth Longfellow

372. It is not the fear of death that saddens people, but the love of life.
—Dagobert D. Runes

373. One may live as a conqueror, a king, or a magistrate; but he must die as a man.
—Daniel Webster

374. It is one of God's blessings that we cannot foreknow the hour of our death; for a time fixed, even beyond the possibility of living, would trouble us more than doth this uncertainty.
—James the Sixth

375. To me there is something thrilling and exalting in the thought that we are drifting forward into a splendid mystery—into something that no mortal eye has yet seen, no intelligence has yet declared.

—Edwin Hubbell Chapin

376. Death to a good man is but passing through a dark entry, out of one little dusky room of his Father's house into another that is fair and large, lightsome and glorious, and divinely entertaining.

—Adam Clarke

377. Death is the wish of some, the relief of many, and the end of all. It sets the slave at liberty, carries the banished man home, and places all mortals on the same level, insomuch that life itself were a punishment without it.

—Seneca

378. Living is death; dying is life. We are not what we appear to be. On this side of the grave we are exiles, on that citizens; on this side orphans, on that children; on this side captives, on that freemen; on this side disguised, unknown, on that disclosed and proclaimed as the sons of God.

—Henry Ward Beecher

379. The bitterest tears shed over graves are for words left unsaid and deeds left undone. "She never knew how I loved her!" "He never knew what he was to me!" "I always meant to make more of our friendship!" "I did not know what he was to me till he was gone!" Such words are the poisoned arrows which cruel death shoots backward at us from the door of the sepulchre.

—Harriet Beecher Stowe

Debt

380. Debt is the secret foe of thrift, as vice and idleness are its open foes. The debt habit is the twin brother of poverty.

381. Many of us would be delighted to pay as we go, if we could only catch up from paying as we've gone.

Debtor—Creditor

Debtor—Creditor

382. A slight debt produces a debtor; a heavy one an enemy.

—PUBLILIUS SYRUS

383. Every time you lend money to a friend you damage his memory.

384. It is a sure sign of an improved character if you like paying debts as much as getting money.

—GEORG CHRISTOPH LICHTENBERG

385. Which is really the good neighbor—the one who lends freely or the one who pays back promptly?

Decadence

386. Revolutions are perhaps successful less often because the revolutionists are powerful or cunning than because the old institutions have decayed too much to withstand the new pressures. Men all too often put new wine into old bottles, with unhappy results.

—DON K. PRICE

Deception

387. The greatest of all cunning is to seem blind to the snares which we know to be laid for us. Men are never so easily deceived as while they are endeavoring to deceive others.

—FRANCOIS DE LA ROCHEFOUCAULD

388. Deceit and falsehood, whatever conveniences they may for a time promise or produce, are, in the sum of life, obstacles to happiness. Those who profit by the cheat distrust the deceiver; and the act by which kindness was sought puts an end to confidence.

—DR. SAMUEL JOHNSON

60

Decision—Decisions

389.   Patience may often be merely the inability to make a decision.

390.   That should be considered long which can be decided but once.

—PUBLILIUS SYRUS

391.   It's wiser to sleep over a decision than to lie awake worrying about the one you made.

—ARNOLD H. GLASOW

392.   The percentage of mistakes in quick decisions is no greater than in long-drawn-out vacillations, and the effect of decisiveness itself "makes things go" and creates confidence.

—ANNE O'HARE MCCORMICK

393.   When making a decision of minor importance, I have always found it advantageous to consider all the pros and cons.

In vital matters, however, such as the choice of a mate or a profession, the decision should come from the unconscious, from something within ourselves.

In the important decisions of our personal life, we should be governed, I think, by the deep inner needs of our nature.

—SIGMUND FREUD

394.   *Sixteen ways to dodge decisions:*
1. Take flight into detail;
2. Counsel infinite delay of action;
3. Delegate the problem to a committee;
4. Look for the answer in the "book";
5. Induce the boss to commit himself on how to handle the problem;
6. Give an answer in doubletalk;
7. Delegate the problem to a subordinate;
8. Indicate that all problems must be considered in serial order;
9. Have a "study" made to "get all the facts";
10. Arrange to be called out of town;

61

Defamation

11. Call in an expert to "make sure we're on solid ground";
12. Deny that any problem exists;
13. Take flight into illness;
14. Take flight into the bottle;
15. State the problem belongs in someone else's province;
16. Simply put on one's hat and go home.

Defamation

395. Defamation and calumny never attack where there is no weak place; they magnify, but they do not create.

—Lord Chesterfield

Defeat—Defeatism

396. You are never so near victory as when defeated in a good cause.

—Henry Ward Beecher

397. People who achieve happiness and success are those who refuse to accept the idea of defeat. They know it is the thought of defeat that causes defeat, so they go to work and organize victory out of mistakes.

Defense—Defensiveness

398. If a cause be good, the most violent attack of its enemies will not injure it so much as an injudicious defense of it by its friends.

—Charles C. Colton

399. Faith is a defense against anxiety; joy is a defense against hostility; self-awareness is a defense against guilt feelings; courage is a defense against pain; creative work is a defense against boredom; hope is a defense against despair; and love is a defense against loneliness.

—Russell L. Dick

Definition—Definitions

400. A large part of the discussion of disputants comes from the want of accurate definition. Let one define his terms and then stick to the definition, and half the differences in philosophy and theology would come to an end, and be seen to have no real foundation.

—TRYON EDWARDS

Delay

401. In delay we waste our lights in vain, like lamps by day.

—WILLIAM SHAKESPEARE

402. If thou intendest to do a kind act, do it quickly, and then thou mayest expect gratitude.

—AUSONIUS

Delusion—Delusions

403. There's payday for everyone, even for the fellow laboring under a delusion.

404. No man is happy without a delusion of some kind. Delusions are as necessary to our happiness as realities.

—CHRISTIAN NEVELL BOVEE

Demand and supply. See **Supply and demand**

Democracy

405. Schools need not preach political doctrine to defend democracy. If they shape men capable of critical thought and trained in social attitudes, that is all that is necessary.

—ALBERT EINSTEIN

406. Democracy takes into account the factor to which communism seems to be invincibly obtuse: the unsearchable depths of the mind and spirit of man, who will forever thwart the attempts of dogma and ideology to predict him or to hem him in.

—ADLAI E. STEVENSON

407. Primarily, democracy is the conviction that there are extraordinary possibilities in ordinary people, and that if we throw wide the doors of opportunity so that all boys and girls can bring out the best that is in them, we will get amazing results from unlikely sources. Shakespeare was the son of a bankrupt butcher and a woman who could not write her name. Beethoven was the son of a consumptive mother, herself daughter of a cook, and a drunken father. Schubert was the son of a peasant father and a mother who had been in domestic service. Faraday, one of the greatest scientific experimenters of all time, was born over a stable, his father an invalid blacksmith and his mother a common drudge. Such facts as these underlie democracy. That is why, with all its discouraging blunders, we must everlastingly believe in it.

—HARRY EMERSON FOSDICK

408. Democracy is a way of life that looks easy but is difficult. In these confused times, when people feel tempted to blame someone as responsible for the world's ills, one has to remember the fact that no one, living or dead, can do for us the job of being free. Our forefathers knew what they were about. They knew that fighting for and winning liberty was not the end, but only the beginning. We may despair of democracy, but we also may look around the world and see no other system that is working, working in the sense that under it humans are developing a long-range capacity to behave with cooperative intelligence as free individuals.

Dependability

409. In a sense, nothing simply does itself. Someone has to do everything that is done ... sooner or later someone has to make *final* decisions. The sincerest satisfactions in life come in doing and not in dodging duty; in meeting and solving problems, in facing facts, in being a dependable person. And one of the great discoveries in life is finding a dependable person.

—RICHARD L. EVANS IN *Within These Walls*

410.   A certain man with whom I do business often calls me up on the telephone and asks what I have to say regarding a certain matter about which he has written to me. Several times I have said, "I have not received any such letter," and he replies, "Why, I gave it to my office boy three hours ago." But it had not arrived. This is a small thing, but it just illustrates the point. What I want in my office, and what you all want about you, are men whom you do not have to tell to do a thing and then have to ask the next day, "Have you done what you were told to do?"
—John D. Rockefeller, Jr.

Despair

411.   In all things it is better to hope than to despair.
—Johann Wolfgang von Goethe

412.   Beware of desperate steps. The darkest day, live till tomorrow, will have passed away.
—William Cowper

Desperation

413.   When you get to the end of your rope, tie a knot and hang on.
—Franlin D. Roosevelt

Destiny

414.   Man proposes, but God disposes.
—Thomas à Kempis

415.   Why ask my answer, strong-armed unbeliever?
What answer can the mutton give the cleaver?
—Hindustan proverb

416.   There's a big difference between a mere desire to do a thing, and a burning passion to do it—a determination to accomplish it at any cost. A mere desire is like warm water in a locomotive—it will never produce steam. It takes fire and force and enthusiasm to generate the things that propel the successful character.

417.   A famous athletic coach once said that physical ability is only half of the equipment necessary for a champion. The other half is heart. He did not mean the anatomical heart: he meant the determination, the courage, the will to win which is also called "heart." He told of having coached men during his long career who never stood out on any team because they only had the bodies of champions. Their hearts were second-string.

He illustrated his point with the fable of the Mouse and the Magician. The Mouse squeaked about the house in constant fear of the neighborhood cats. Taking pity on him the Magician made him a Cat. Immediately he began to suffer with fear of dogs, so the Magician made him a Dog. Then he began to fear tigers, and the Magician changed him into a Tiger. Now in the form of a tiger, he began to fear the hunters. In disgust the Magician shouted, "Out with you! Be a mouse again! You have only the heart of a mouse."

If you want to be a champion in any sport or profession or business career, you must develop the mental attitude that gives you heart. Without heart, all your skills and abilities will fail to win you the recognition you desire.

—Nuggets

Diet—Dieting.   See also **Overweight**

418.   Eat less to live longer to eat more.
—Dr. Frederick J. Stare

419.   Most dieters are thick and tired of it.

420.   Cutting down, not out, is the secret of weight control.
—Dr. Frederic J. Stare

421.   For the sake of health, medicines are taken by weight and measure; so ought food to be, or by some similar rule.
—Rev. P. Skelton

Difference—Differences

422.   If you can't tell the difference, what difference does it make?

423.   If men would consider not so much wherein they differ, as wherein they agree, there would be far less of uncharitableness and angry feeling in the world.

424.   America has believed that in differentiation, not in uniformity, lies the path of progress. It acted on this belief; it has advanced human happiness, and it has prospered.

—Louis D. Brandeis

425.   Little people make much of the little which makes them different from one another, but to the aeons eternalizing the universe, man differs from man as barely as a dust grain varies from a dust grain.

—Dagobert D. Runes

426.   Our institutions were not devised to bring about uniformity of opinion; if they had been we might well abandon hope. It is important to remember, as has well been said, "the essential characteristic of true liberty is that under its shelter many different types of life and character and opinion and belief can develop unmolested and unobstructed."

—Charles Evans Hughes

Difficult—Difficulty—Difficulties

427.   The greater the difficulty the more glory in surmounting it. Skillful pilots gain their reputation from storms and tempests.

—Epicurus

428.   *It is difficult*
        To forget
        To forgive
        To excuse
        To take advice

Dignity

> To avoid mistakes
> To admit one's faults
> To be unselfish
> To save
> To be charitable
> To be considerate
> To get out of a rut
> To make a little go a long way
> To be strong in adversity
> To control oneself
> To be able to start from scratch
> To be in form—always
> To keep at it
> To think first and then act
> —but it pays!

Dignity

429. Many a man labors under the delusion that standing on his dignity will enable him to see over the heads of the crowd.

430. Place confers no dignity upon some men; like a balloon, the higher they rise the smaller they look.

—George Denison Prentice

Diplomacy

431. To say nothing, especially when speaking, is half the art of diplomacy.

—Will Durant

432. A diplomat is a gentleman who can tell a lie in such a manner to another gentleman (who is also a diplomat) that the second gentleman is compelled to let on that he really believes the first gentleman, although he knows that the first gentleman is a liar, who knows that the second gentleman does not believe him, yet both let on that each believes the other, while both know that both are liars.

Direction

433.   Every life is unsatisfactory until its owner has made up his mind what he means to do with it.

434.   It is often said that the direction in which one moves and the pace at which one moves are more important than the place at which one stands at the moment.

—WILBUR LARSON

Disappointment—Disappointments

435.   For everything you have missed you have gained something else.

—RALPH WALDO EMERSON

436.   Disappointment in the matter of friendship arises chiefly, not from liking our friends too much, but from an overestimate of their liking for, or opinions of us.

—CHARLOTTE BRONTÉ

Discipline

437.   Who will not be ruled by the rudder must be ruled by the rocks.

438.   A little boy was playing near a giant tree in his own backyard. His father stood watching him, when suddenly he saw something that galvanized him into action. "Fall on your face, son, NOW!" he shouted. This his son did. "Crawl to me as fast as you can," the father ordered. His son scrambled awkwardly toward him and was soon lifted from the ground and clasped to his father's bosom. Then he looked toward the tree, and there he saw a giant python snake, its wicked head darting here and there in search of the meal that had escaped it. But for obedience that boy would have lost his security.

—E. E. CLEVELAND

Discontent

439.   Discontent—there are two kinds in the world: the discontent that works and gets what it wants, and the kind that wrings its hands and loses what it has. There's no cure for the first but success, and there is no cure at all for the second.

—C. H. CAMPBELL

Discord

440.   I passed a building undergoing repairs. On one side workmen were removing large quantities of bricks which had crumbled away. Why, I mused, had some bricks disintegrated and not others?

"Fifty years ago, when the building was erected," said the foreman, "there came a day when the laborers at the brickyard had trouble with one another. And now, long years after the failure of those men to work together for a single day, a moral is written in crumbling brick."

How like the untold story of human life! For life is not built as a solid mass, but of individual days cemented by motives, hates, and loves.

—WALDEMAR W. ARGOW

Discovery

441.   It is not the finding of a thing, but the making something out of it after it is found, that is of consequence.

—JAMES RUSSELL LOWELL

442.   Knowledge once gained casts a faint light beyond its own immediate boundaries. There is no discovery so limited as not to illuminate something beyond itself.

—JOHN TYNDALL

443.   Opportunities today are more plentiful than ever before. Each new thing that is discovered in the world does not cut down by one the sum of discoveries to be made. It rather opens up a whole new vista of discovery and development in a new direction.

—JANE LYON

Discretion

444. If thou art a master, be sometimes blind; if a servant, sometimes deaf.

—THOMAS FULLER

Dishonesty

445. Crooked sticks make crooked shadows.

446. Who purposely cheats his friend would cheat his God.

—JOHANN KASPAR LAVATER

447. Dishonesty is a forsaking of permanent for temporary advantages.

—CHRISTIAN NEVELL BOVEE

Disobedience

448. Disobedience in the eyes of anyone who has read history is man's original virtue. It is through disobedience that progress has been made, through disobedience and through rebellion.

—OSCAR WILDE

Distrust

449. Distrust is a defensive principle; they who have much to lose have much to fear.

—EDMUND BURKE

450. Confidence may be risky, but it is nothing like so risky as mistrust.

—ARNOLD J. TOYNBEE

Divorce

451. Divorce is not the enemy of marriage, it is its ally.

—JOSEPH COLLINS

Doctor—Patient

452.　I believe in divorce because again and again we must have in marriage, as in every other experience of life, a decent corrective of mistake and tragedy.

—John Haynes Holmes

Doctor—Patient

453.　When I was 40, my doctor advised me that a man in his forties shouldn't play tennis. I heeded his advice carefully and could hardly wait until I reached 50 to start again.

—Hugo Black

454.　While in the hospital for the birth of her son, a woman shared a room with a young mother whose obstetrician was very reserved and businesslike. On one of his visits, trying to make conversation, she said, "Doctor, they certainly keep you busy, don't they?"

"Yes," he said quietly, without looking up from his notes, "I have too many men working for me."

Dog—Dogs

455.　A dog is the only thing on earth that loves you more than you love yourself.

—Charles Darwin

456.　If a dog will not come to you after he has looked you in the face, you ought to go home and examine your conscience.

—Woodrow Wilson

457.　Every animal lover knows that the status of dogs varies widely from country to country the world over: the Chinese eat them, Arabs kick them, Frenchmen and Americans dote on them, and in Britain there is mounting evidence that they may one day be given the vote.

458.   You can't buy loyalty, they say;
I bought it, though, this very day;
You can't buy friendship, firm and true
I bought sincerest friendship, too;
And truth and kindness I got,
And happiness, Oh, such a lot!
So many joyous hours to be
Were sold with that commodity.

I bought a life of simple faith,
And love that will be mine till death,
And two brown eyes that I could see
Would not be long in knowing me.
I bought protection. Bought a guard
Right now and ever afterward.
Buy human friendship? Maybe not!
You see, it was a dog I bought.

—Anonymous

Do-it-yourself

459.   There's a new un-do-it-yourself kit for do-it-yourselfers.

460.   *One housewife to another:* "My husband is absolutely no good at fixing anything, so everything at our house works."

Double-dealing

461.   It is generally the fate of a double-dealer to lose his friends and keep his enemies.

Doubt—Doubts

462.   The only limit to our realization of tomorrow will be our doubts of today.

—Franklin D. Roosevelt

73

Drinking

463. The trouble with the world is that the stupid are cocksure and the intelligent full of doubt.

—BERTRAND RUSSELL

464. Doubt is like the dark. A room may be dark because the sun is not shining—or it may be dark because the windows are dirty. One cannot turn on the sun, but one can wash the windows.

Drinking

465. He who drinks on credit gets doubly drunk.

—BULGARIAN PROVERB

466. What is said when drunk has been thought out beforehand.

—FLEMISH PROVERB

467. One expedient to find peace is through alcohol. Strange as it may seem, I believe most of the alcohol drunk in this world is drunk for no other reason. It dulls the sensibilities of the mind. It offers us an escape from the reproaches of conscience and from the hard conditions of reality. It dissolves our inhibitions, our fears and our sense of inferiority, while all the while riveting these fetters on us more tightly. If alcohol only kept its promises, it would be a true friend to man. Unfortunately, the only promise it keeps is the promise of our ruin.

—ELWOOD WORCESTER

Duty—Duties

468. The rewards of duty are not rest from labor, but greater tasks.

—KARL FOLLEN

469. So long as men do their duty, even if it be greatly in a misapprehension, they will be leading pattern lives; and whether or not they come to lie beside a martyr's monument, we may be sure they will find a safe haven somewhere in the providence of God.

—ROBERT LOUIS STEVENSON

Easter

470.   To the earliest Christians, Easter—not Christmas—was the all-important holiday. Relatively little notice was taken of the anniversary of Christ's birth. As far as the Gospels are concerned, Jesus commanded men to remember not His birth but His death. Therefore, Easter is considered the most ancient and most important festival of the Christian year.

471.   Why is the hare associated with Easter and why are Easter eggs colored or wrapped in colored paper? The hare was sacred to the ancient goddess of spring, Eastre, from whom the word Easter is derived, says an authority on folklore. Julius Caesar reported that this animal was especially venerated in Britain. Ordinary people were not supposed to eat hare's flesh as it was under the special protection of the goddess. It was also believed in Northern Europe that the hare made a nest in springtime in which it laid colored eggs—the egg being an ancient symbol of rebirth of the sun. In superstitious belief, color was a protective magic against evil spirits.

Easy money.   See **Wealth**

Education

472.   It is not what is poured into the student, but what is planted, that counts.

—Eugene P. Bertin

473.   Modern education to some parents is being able to blame the teacher for their son's failure.

474.   Education is what you have left over when you subtract what you've forgotten from what you have learned.

475.   In one way only does American education prepare for success —it tries to tell us how to reach it; but it rarely shows us what to do with it.

—John Erskine

476. As an apple is not in any proper sense an apple until it is ripe, so a human mind is not in any proper sense a human being until it is educated.

—HORACE MANN

477. It was in making education not only common to all, but in some sense compulsory for all, that the destiny of the free republic of America was practically settled.

—JAMES RUSSEL LOWELL

478. The essence of education is incompletion. A person who has completed his education is no longer educated. A measure of education is the awareness of an increasing number of things that lie ahead of you.

—LAWRENCE B. PERKINS

479. The ability to learn is not as important as the inclination to use knowledge for social good. Better an average boy with honorable aspirations than a brilliant boy bent upon evil. The keen mind of the latter is a greater menace to society.

480. In all probability, the highest tax we pay is not the *ad valorem,* or income, or excise, or sales tax. The highest tax we pay is the "ignorance tax." Each generation has this choice: Spend its resources voluntarily and in reasonable amounts for the education of the boy *or* less voluntarily but in larger amounts for the ignorance of the man.

—CHARLES F. CARROLL

481. Education is really not a process of instilling something in us from the outside. Its true purpose is to reveal something already latent within us. True education is more than imparting knowledge. It is the arousing and awakening in ourselves of inherent wisdom which will illumine the mind.

—REV. OBADIAH HARRIS

482. The old stereotype of schooling that assumed that you "mastered a subject" is now obsolete. You can, hypothetically, learn all of physics up until yesterday and will be lagging behind by tomorrow. Today we must conceive of the educated person, almost exclusively, as the one who comes out of school eager and able to go on teaching himself.

—M. L. Story

483. We used to think that education was something which happened to you when you went to school. We thought that teachers educated, that books educated, that school plants educated. Now we know that education is a life process; that all experience, in some measure, educates; and that the purpose of the school is to guide this experience which the individual learner undergoes, only the experience which he makes a part of himself and which, to some degree, makes him a different person, truly educates.

—Dean Lobaugh

484. Every man has two educations—that which is given to him, and the other, that which he gives to himself. Of the two kinds, the latter is by far the more valuable. Indeed, all that is most worthy in a man, he must work out and conquer for himself. It is that which constitutes our real and best nourishment. What we are merely taught seldom nourishes the mind like that which we teach ourselves.

—Jean Paul Richter

Effort

485. No great intellectual thing was ever done by great effort; a great thing can only be done by a great man, and he does it *without* effort.

—John Ruskin

486. Work done with little effort is liable to yield little results. Every job can be done excellently or indifferently. Excellence necessitates effort—hard, sustained, concentrating effort. So, if you are sleeping over your job instead of sweating over it, overhaul yourself.

—B. C. Forbes

487. The purpose of struggle is to give strength. When life is too easy, and we do not have to work hard to acquire the things we want, we

Egotism

grow soft. We should thank Providence that man must earn his bread by the sweat of his brow. In this modern day that does not necessarily mean physical labor. It can mean mental labor, too. For there is such a thing as "sweating out" the solution to a problem with pencil or computer as well as sweating from physical exertion.

Egotism

488. There was never a man so empty as the man who is full of himself.

489. When all is summed up, a man never speaks of himself without loss; his accusations of himself are always believed, his praise never.
—Michel E. de Montaigne

Eloquence

490. True eloquence consists in saying all that is proper and nothing more.
—François de La Rochefoucauld

491. True eloquence consists in saying just enough; brevity improves eloquence, action is its life.

492. There is as much eloquence in the tone of the voice, in the eyes, and in the air of a speaker as in his choice of words.
—François de La Rochefoucauld

Employer—Employe

493. No matter whose payroll you are on, you are working for yourself.

494. If the boss calls you down, be grateful; the probabilities are you should have been fired.

—Elbert Hubbard

495. The man who knows how will always find a job, but the man who knows why will always be the boss.

496. If you suspect a man, don't employ him; if you employ a man, don't suspect him.

497. The man who laughs at the boss' jokes does not necessarily have a sense of humor, but he surely has a sense of direction.

498. For every executive afraid to delegate responsibility, there are ten employes who refuse to accept it.

—Arnold H. Glasow

499. He stopped grousing when his boss sent him this memo: "Be thankful for problems, for if we didn't have them you wouldn't be here, and if they were less difficult someone with less ability would have your job."

500. Two domestic employes were talking over their problems in connection with their work. Said one to the other, "The lady I work for says I should always warm the plates for our dinner guests. But that's too much work. I just warm hers, and she never knows the difference."

501. In the early days of the printing industry itinerant printers roamed the country looking for any plant that needed extra help. Some were capable; some were not. The procedure for hiring and firing was amazingly simple. The boss drove a nail into the wall for the new man to hang his coat on when he went to work. If the boss didn't want him any longer, he pulled the nail out of the wall. An itinerant printer knew it was time to move on when his nail was gone.

Employment

502. The devil never tempted a man whom he found judiciously employed.

—Charles H. Spurgeon

503. One test of how much you love your job is this: Which seems longer—the week or the weekend?

504. There are just two kinds of employes in any business—those who are on the way up, and those who are on the way out.

505. It is better to take a job a little too big for you and grow into it, than to take a job a little too small for you and be squeezed out of it.

506. The proper mental attitude goes a long way toward helping anyone find satisfaction in his job. It may not be exactly the job he wants; it may not be the job he intends to spend the rest of his life on; but while it is his job, life can be a lot more pleasant if he gets all the satisfaction possible out of doing it.

The proper mental attitude can be simply stated as the desire to do whatever one has to do to the best of one's ability.

To do this a person has to make up his mind to like his work. No one can do his best on a job which he considers drugery. Thinking so makes it so, and it is often easier and more practical to change one's thinking about his work than to change jobs.

—*Nuggets*, February 1963

Endurance

507. What can't be cured must be endured.

—William Langland

508. There is nothing in the world so much admired as a man who knows how to bear unhappiness with courage.

—Seneca

Enemy—Enemies

509. There is no little enemy.

—BENJAMIN FRANKLIN

510. Your worst enemies are the friends you have treated as others treat you.

511. Our enemies are our friends whom we have never taken the trouble to understand.

512. An enemy often teaches a man more than his friends do, and makes him work harder.

—J. FRANK DOBIE

513. About the most flattering thing we can say about our enemies is that we know where they stand.

—DOUGLAS MEADOR

514. Everyone needs a warm personal enemy or two to keep him free of rust in the movable parts of his mind.

—GENE FOWLER

515. If you have some enemies, you are to be congratulated, for no man ever amounted to much without arousing jealousies and creating enemies. Your enemies are a very valuable asset as long as you refrain from striking back at them, because they keep you on the alert when you might become lazy.

Engineer—Engineers—Engineering

516. Thousands of engineers can design bridges, calculate strains and stresses, and draw up specifications for machines, but the great engineer is the man who can tell whether the bridge or the machine should be built at all, where it should be built and when.

—EUGENE G. GRACE

Ennui

517. Possibly the creative engineer is happy because he is constantly thinking how he can better the work he is doing. He is urged forward by a delightful dissatisfaction. He may design a great machine, watch it take form in the shops, set it up again in a manufacturing plant, rejoice in its superiority to all other machines of its kind ever made, and then he will start wondering what improvements he can add to the next machine he builds.

Ennui

518. Ennui is the desire of activity without the fit means of gratifying the desire.

—George Bancroft

519. Ennui, perhaps, has made more gamblers than avarice, more drunkards than thirst, and perhaps as many suicides as despair.

—Charles C. Colton

520. Ennui is a French word for an English malady, which generally arises from the want of a want, and constitutes the complaint of those who have nothing to complain of.

—Paul Chatifield

Enterprise

521. The method of the enterprising is to plan with audacity and execute with vigor; to sketch out a map of possibilities, and then to treat them as probabilities.

—Christian Nevell Bovee

522. What passes in the world for talent or dexterity or enterprise is often only a want of moral principle. We may succeed where others fail, not from a greater share of invention, but from not being nice in the choice of expedients.

—William Hazlitt

Enthusiasm

523. Enter into the spirit of life, into the joy of living, and into the usefulness of being alive. For no one will grow tired and old if he has faith and enthusiasm.

—ERNEST HOLMES

524. Every man is enthusiastic at times. One man has enthusiasm for thirty minutes—another has it for thirty days, but it is the man who has it for thirty years who makes a success in life.

—EDWARD B. BUTLER

525. The word enthusiasm comes from the ancient Greek— meaning *God within You!* How do you become enthusiastic? There is just one simple rule: To become enthusiastic, ACT enthusiastic! Apply this magic ingredient . . . during the next thirteen weeks, and be prepared to see astonishing results. It may easily revolutionize your entire life!

—FRANK BETTGER

Envy

526. Envy is the first concession to inadequacy.

—DOUGLAS MEADOR

527. There are many roads to hate but envy is one of the shortest of them all.

528. If the grass is greener on the other side of the fence, you can bet the water bill is higher.

529. Don't mind the fellow who belittles you; he's only trying to cut you down to his size.

530. Before we passionately desire anything which another enjoys, we should examine into the happiness of its possessor.

—François de La Rochefoucauld

531. If we only wanted to be happy it would be easy, but we want to be happier than other people, which is almost always difficult, since we think them happier than they are.

—Charles de Secondat Montesquieu

532. To diminish envy, let us consider not what others possess, but what they enjoy; mere riches may be the gift of lucky accident or blind chance, but happiness must be the result of prudent preference and rational design.

—Charles C. Colton

533. It is the better part of wisdom not to fret our souls overmuch over the apparent advantages which others may enjoy. Envy is a canker which corrodes the soul and poisons the wellsprings of life and happiness.

—B. C. Forbes

Epitaph—Epitaphs

534. The tombstone tells when you died, not how you lived.

535. Here lies an atheist, all dressed up and no place to go.

536. *On a celebrated cook:*
Peace to his hashes.

537. *Inscription on bopster's gravestone:*
Don't dig me, man—I'm gone!

538. Here lies the body of John Mound,
Lost at sea and never found

539.   On my tomb, if ever I have one, I mean to get these words inscribed: "He clung to his paddle."

—Robert Louis Stevenson

540.   Here lie the bodies of two sisters dear;
One's buried in Ireland, the other lies here.

541.   So live that your fellow man will not get a good laugh out of the inscription on your tombstone.

542.   *Epitaph on a scolding wife by her husband:*
Here my poor Bridget's Corpse doth lie,
She is at rest, —and so am I.

543.   Here lies Estrella, who transported a large fortune to heaven in acts of charity, and has gone thither to enjoy it.

—Italian epitaph

544.   Here lies the body of Harry Hershfield.
If not, notify Ginsberg and Co., Undertakers, at once.

—Harry Hershfield, epitaph suggested
by himself.

545.   *On a Mr. Button:*
Oh! Heavens and Earth, Oh! stars and poles;
That graves should be but button-holes.

546.   *Lines on a man named Owen Moore:*
Owen Moore has run away,
Owin' more than he could pay.

547.   *On a former organist and choirmaster:*
Time and Stephen are both even:
Stephen beat Time, but Time beat Stephen.

548. Here lies interr'd beneath these stones
The beard, the flesh and eke the bones
Of Wrexham's clerk, old Daniel Jones.

549. *On Thomas Kemp, who was hanged for stealing sheep:*
Here lies the body of Thomas Kemp
Who lived by wool, but died by hemp.

550. Here lies the body of John Partridge, who died 13th of May.
What, shoot a partridge in the month of May!
Call you that sportsmanlike? eh. Death? eh.

551. What we gave, we have;
What we spent, we had;
What we left, we lost.
—Epitaph on the grave of
Earl of Devon, 1419

552. Here lies in peace old Thomas Gordon
With mouth like a cave and teeth accordin'.
Oh, friend, step lightly on the sod,
For if he yawns, you're gone, by God!

553. Here lies the form of my sweet love,
Who passed from earth to realms above,
She clipped the shell of this earthly sin,
And hatched herself a cherubim.

554. Tom Smith is dead, and here he lies,
Nobody laughs and nobody cries;
Where his soul's gone, or how it fares,
Nobody knows, and nobody cares.
—Epitaph on Tom Smith of
Newbury (England), 1742

555.   A coffin-maker I was long
      And many a coffin made,
But now confined in coffin strong,
      I've left the coffin trade.

556.   Beneath this stone in hope of Zion
Doth lie the landlord of the "Lion":
Resigned unto the Heavenly will,
His son keeps on the business still.

557.   This is the grave of Mike O'Day
Who died maintaining his right of way.
His right was clear, his will was strong,
But he's just as dead as if he'd been wrong.

558.   Here lies the mother of children seven,
Four on earth and three in Heaven,
The three in Heaven preferring rather
To be with mother than stay with father.

559.   Two brighter babes you would not see
Than God Almighty gave to we;
But they were overtaken with ague fits
And here they lie, as dead as nits.

560.   While sojourning on earth, he filled up the measure
      Of time that to mortals is given
So well, that he's gone to inherit the treasure
      That in life he exported to heaven.
              —TAKEN FROM THE TOMBSTONE OF ONE
                WHO WAS FAMED FOR HIS DEEDS OF CHARITY

561.   Reader, pass on, nor waste your time
On bad biography and much worse rhyme:

For what I am this crumbling clay immures,
And what I was is no affair of yours.

562.　Here lieth the body of William Pears
Beneath these great Cathedral stairs.
His name was Jones: it was not Pears:
It was put down to rhyme with stairs.

563.　Gaily I liv'd, as Ease and Nature taught,
And spent my little Life without a Thought,
And am amaz'd that Death, that Tyrant grim,
Should think of me, who never thought of him.
—Abbé Regnier

564.　Dust from dust at first was taken,
Dust from dust is here forsaken;
Dust with dust will here remain,
Till dust from dust shall rise again.

565.　*Epitaph to a Body*
He died of nothing. Life's full cup
　　He dared but sip, lest it should spill;
Death dashed it down into the dark,
　　And he is nothing still.
—Lizette W. Reese

566.　Here lies in a horizontal position the outside case of Thomas Hind, clock and watchmaker, who departed this life wound up in the hope of being taken in hand by his maker, thoroughly cleaned, repaired and set a-going for the world to come.

567.　He was—
But words are wanting to say what.
Think what a man should be,

Though a lawyer:
He was that.

568. *On a brewer:*
Poor John Scott lies buried here,
    Although he was both 'ale and stout:
Death stretched him on the bitter bier:
    In Paradise he "hops" about.

569. *On the builder of the Exchange at Newcastle-on-Tyne:*
Here lies Robert Trollop
Who made yon stones roll up:
When Death took his soul up,
His body filled this hole up.

570. *For Suzanne Lenglen, the famous tennis player:*
When Death cried "Game and Set,"
    Suzanne complained: "A Let,"
But Death would not be cheated;
So here she lies defeated.
                              —KENSAL GREEN

571. Here lies Pierre Victor Fournier, inventor of the Everlasting Lamp, which consumes only one centime's worth of oil in an hour. He was a good father, son and husband. His inconsolable widow continues his business in the Rue aux Trois. Goods sent to all parts of the City. Do not mistake the opposite shop for his.

572. *A tombstone in an Arizona cemetery carries this epitaph:*
Here
Lies
Lester Moore
Four Slugs
From a .44
No Les
No Moore

573. *Here lies John Higgs*
A famous man for killing pigs;
For killing pigs was his delight
Both morning, afternoon and night.
Both heats and colds he did endure
Which no physician ere could cure.
His knife is laid: his work is done:
I hope to Heaven his soul has gone.

574. One of the most peculiar of all epitaphs appears in a Rotterdam, Holland, graveyard on a stone inscribed:
Here lies
Tom Klaes
The greatest smoker in Europe
He broke his pipe
July 4th, 1872
Mourned by his family and
All tobacco merchants
STRANGER, SMOKE FOR HIM

575. *On a blacksmith:*
My Sledge Hammer's now declin'd,
My Bellows, too, have lost their wind;
My fire's extinct, my Forge decayed,
And in the dust my Vice is laid.
My Coals are spent, my Iron's gone,
My last Nail's drove, my Work is done;
Whene'er my passing bell shall toll,
The Lord my God receive my soul.

576. There was an old woman who always was tired,
She lived in a house where no help was hired;
Her last words on earth were: Dear friends, I am going
Where sweeping ain't done, nor churning nor sewing;
And everything there will be just to my wishes,
For there they don't eat, there's no washing of dishes;
And though there the anthems are constantly ringing,
I, having no voice, will get rid of singing.

Don't mourn for me now and don't mourn for me never,
For I'm going to do nothing for ever.

577. Beneath this stone, facetious wight,
Lies all that's left of Poor Joe Wright;
Few hearts with greater kindness warmed,
Few heads with knowledge more informed;
With brilliant wit and humour broad
He pleased both peasant, squire and lord.
At length old Death with visage queer
Assumed Joe's trade of auctioneer
Made him the lot to practice on,
With Going! going! going! and anon
He knocked Joe down,
So poor Joe's gone.

Equality

578. The idea of bringing all on an equality with each other has always been a pleasant dream; the law cannot equalize men in spite of nature.

—Luc de Clapiers Vauvenargues

579. So far is it from being true that men are naturally equal, that no two people can be half an hour together, but one shall acquire an evident superiority over the other.

—Dr. Samuel Johnson

580. In the Declaration of Independence our forefathers held as a self-evident truth that "all men are created equal." Even in 1776 it is unlikely that the signers of the Declaration intended to give these words the literal and out-of-context meaning that some people today try to ascribe to them.

However beautiful the concept of equality may be, we have only to look about us to see that all men are not equal to one another.

Some are born into homes of plenty, others into homes of want. Doors that open eagerly for the few may be closed brusquely for the many. Opportunities generously offered to some may not even be made known to those less fortunate.

Escape

Some men are born with better minds than others. Certainly there is a natural inequality between an Edison or an Einstein and some lowly illiterate who never learned to read or to count.

Some men are born with better bodies than others. What awkward batter striking out in a sandlot game would claim equality with Babe Ruth or any of those stalwarts who seek today to break his homerun record?

Some men are born with greater emotional stability than others. There is little equality between the man who cracks up and must be cared for in an institution and the one who is able to adjust to whatever crisis life may thrust upon him.

And yet, in spite of obvious inequalities, all men are created equal in many ways. They are equal in their right to live their lives to the best of their abilities. They are equal in their rights to be generous and kind and helpful to others. They are equal in their right to believe in a better world both here and hereafter, and equal in their right to work in their own modest way to help bring that better world closer to reality.

Perhaps that may be something of what the authors of the Declaration of Independence were thinking about when they held that all men are created equal. They well knew that God created a world in which so many men are so unequal in so many ways.

—*Nuggets*, JULY 1962

Escape

581. They change their clime, but not their mind, who rush across the sea.

—HORACE

582. Too many people go through life running from something that isn't after them.

583. A man is always pursued by what he runs away from, and can always make a friend of what he stands up to.

—ROBERT HICHENS

Eternity

584. This minute, too, is part of eternity.

—DUNCAN STUART

Evasion—Evasiveness

585. Evasions are the common shelter of the hard-hearted, the false and impotent, when called upon to assist; the real great alone plan instantaneous help, even when their looks or words presage difficulties.

—Johann Kaspar Lavater

Evil

586. To overcome evil with good is good, to resist evil by evil is evil.

—Mohammed

587. Never let a man imagine that he can pursue a good end by evil means, without sinning against his own soul. The evil effect on himself is certain.

—Robert Southey

Example—Examples

588. None preaches better than the ant, and she says nothing.

—Benjamin Franklin

589. No reproof or denunciation is so potent as the silent influence of a good example.

—Hosea Ballou

590. There is a transcendant power in example. We reform others unconsciously when we walk uprightly.

—Anne Sophie Swetchine

591. Men trust rather to their eyes than to their ears; the effect of precepts is therefore slow and tedious, whilst that of examples is summary and effectual.

—Seneca

592. The pulpit only "teaches" to be honest; the marketplace "trains" to overreaching and fraud; and teaching has not a tithe of the efficiency of training. Christ never wrote a tract, but he went about doing good.

—Horace Mann

593. In colonial days the more experienced woodsmen chipped bits of bark off forest trees to mark the trails for others. Today, in a sense, we adults are trail blazers for our youngsters. And the trails we blaze must mark commendable conduct in ourselves, if we want their conduct to be commendable, too.

If we seek merely swollen, slothful ease and ignoble peace, if we shrink from the hard contests where men must win at the hazard of their lives and at the risk of all they hold dear, then bolder and stronger peoples will pass us by, and will win for themselves the domination of the world.

—Theodore Roosevelt

Excessiveness

594. More than one cigar at a time is excessive smoking.

—Mark Twain

595. The more a man looks at a thing, the less he can see it, and the more a man learns a thing the less he knows it.

G. K. Chesterton

Excuse—Excuses

596. An excuse is worse and more terrible than a lie; for an excuse is a guarded lie.

—Alexander Pope

597. Time wasted thinking up good excuses would be better spent avoiding their need.

Executive—Executives

598. A wise executive employs optimists to produce results and pessimists to appraise them.

599.   *What is an Executive?*

He is called by many names: the boss, top management, head man, chief, president, vice president, treasurer, owner, partner, chairman, his initials, or just plain Tom or Bill. Each day he lives with problems and every day he's on the lookout for solutions. A good executive is understanding, fair, a cajoler, coordinator, arbitrator, listener, and decider. In addition he is efficient, hard-working, patient, impatient, aggressive, ambitious for himself and his firm.

His constant companions are work, too little time, budgets, taxes, inventory, ideas, new products, production, employe relations, profit and loss charts, marketing, advertising, and company dollars. No one knows better than he the meaning of pressure. He is second-guessed, loved, appreciated, tolerated, respected, blamed, praised, understood, misunderstood, needling and needled, but never ignored.

The executive knows the loneliness of management. For there comes a time for decision. Despite all the counsel from associates above and below, it is he who says *yes or no.* He can't afford to err in judgment, whether it be selection of personnel or the kinds of raw materials that go into the product. He is always responsible.

The good executive is the voice for his company—both written and spoken. Thus, he is a reader, student, speaker, moderator, writer . . . as well as the subject of a speech or article. He is the product of business and means business. What he does can produce a ripple or tidal wave of activity.

Although his collar is white and his shoes are polished, he knows the meaning of long hours and hard work. For this he has learned: To get a better job, *keep doing a better job.* That's how executives are made.
—Copy by F. X. Timmons for
the *Wall Street Journal.*

Exercise, Physical

600.   Some people would never get any exercise at all if they didn't have to walk to their cars.

601.   The only exercise some people get is jumping to conclusions, running down their friends, sidestepping responsibility and pushing their luck.

Experience

602. To many men experience is like the stern lights of a ship, which illume only the track it has passed.

—SAMUEL T. COLERIDGE

603. Don't judge a man's future by his past—experience may have taught him a lesson.

604. Experience is a poor guide to man, and is seldom followed. What really teaches a man is not experience, but observation.

—HENRY L. MENCKEN

605. A mother glows when her teenage daughter is the pick of the crop among the boys, but the father is often disturbed.

—WILLIAM FEATHER

606. The youth gets together his materials to build a bridge to the moon, or perchance a palace or temple on the earth, and at length the middle-aged man concludes to build a woodshed with them.

—HENRY DAVID THOREAU

Extreme—Extremes

607. Push right to the extreme and it becomes wrong: press all the juice from an orange and it becomes bitter.

—BALTASAR GRACIÁN

608. The greatest flood has the soonest ebb; the sorest tempest the most sudden calm; the hottest love the coldest end; and from the deepest desire ensues the deadliest hate.

—SOCRATES

Fact—Facts

609. I often wish that I could rid the world of the tyranny of facts. What are facts but compromises? A fact merely marks the point where we have agreed to let investigation cease.

—Bliss Carman

610. Charles F. Kettering, of General Motors, when illustrating the value of having the facts and knowing what to do with them, said: "The French Government spent 500 million dollars in the Panama Zone, and did not get a canal; we spent 400 million dollars, and did get a canal. Why did our engineers succeed while the French engineers failed? Because of just one fact which our engineers knew, but which the French did not know. Our engineers knew that mosquitoes carry malaria and yellow fever. These two diseases were what made the Panama Zone uninhabitable, so our engineers cleaned out the mosquitoes, and then proceeded to dig the canal."

Failure

611. Not failure, but low aim, is a crime.

—Ernest Holmes

612. Who bravely dares must sometimes risk a fall.

—Tobias George Smollett

613. There are a lot of good ways to become a failure, but never taking a chance is the most successful.

614. No man is ever defeated until he is defeated in spirit. He may know failure after failure, but failure is not final defeat.

615. Failure does not mean the loss of something. Failure occurs only if the loss of that thing takes our enthusiasm, our courage, our zest for life, our faith, our conviction, and our happiness from us; that is loss indeed.

—Ernest Holmes in "Succeess or Failure
Is Up to You!," *Science of Mind*

Faith

616. People would feel a lot less sensitive about failure if they remembered it just doesn't matter, except as a guidepost for onself. Success is a bright sun that obscures and makes ridiculously unimportant all the little shadowy flecks of failure.

Faith

617. Faith is knowing there is an ocean because you have seen a brook.

—Dr. William Arthur Ward, Texas
Wesleyan College, Fort Worth

618. Faith does not create, it reveals. . . . Faith is to the soul what the telescope is to the astronomer or the microscope is to the scientist. These instruments reveal but do not create.

—C. Edwin Brown

619. After all, faith is not belief in spite of evidence, but life in scorn of consequence—a courageous trust in the great purpose of all things and pressing forward to finish the work in sight, whatever the prize may be.

—Kirsopp Lake

Falsehood—Falsehoods

620. Probably the best way to kill a falsehood is to let it lie.

621. No man is a successful liar unless someone believes him.

622. To tell a falsehood is like the cut of a sabre; for though the wound may heal, the scar of it will remain.

—Saadi

Fame

623. Lasting reputations are of slow growth; the man who wakes up famous some morning is very apt to go to bed some night and sleep it off.

—Josh Billings

624. Fame is a shuttlecock. If it be struck only at one end of the room, it will soon fall to the ground. To keep it up it must be struck at both ends.

—Dr. Samuel Johnson

625. Of present fame think little and of future less; the praises that we receive after we are buried, like the posies that are strewn over our grave may be gratifying to the living, but they are nothing to the dead: the dead are gone either to a place where they hear them not or where, if they do, they will despise them.

—Charles C. Colton

Familiarity

626. Familiarity in one's superiors causes bitterness, for it may not be returned.

—Friedrich Wilhelm Nietzsche

Family—Family life

627. History teaches us that there is no substitute for the family, if we are to have a society that stands for human beings at their best.

—Ray Lyman Wilbur

628. Every person needs someone to love him—someone to share in the pleasure of his achievements—someone to encourage him in the face of unusual difficulties—someone to brace him against temptation—someone to appreciate his efforts and his sacrifices—someone to give him an example of confidence and courage—someone to give him sympathy and help in sickness or in sorrow—someone to help him understand that material success is only desirable and not essential—someone to guide him toward the moral standards which give it meaning. That is why the family is so important in our social structure, for it is within the family that one is most likely to find the fulfillment of all these needs.

Fanaticism

629. That can never be reasoned down which was never reasoned up.

—Fisher Ames

630. The blind fanaticism of one foolish honest man may cause more evil than the united efforts of twenty rogues.

—Friedrich Melchior von Grimm

Farm—Farmer—Farming

631. Trade increases the wealth and glory of a country; but its real strength and stamina are to be looked for among the cultivators of the land.

—Lord Chatham

632. A farmer is both Faith and Fatalist—he must have faith to continually meet the challenges of his capacities amid an ever-present possibility that an Act of God (a late spring, an early frost, tornado, flood, drought) can bring his business to a standstill. You can reduce his acreage but you can't restrain his ambition.

633. A farmer is a paradox—he is an overalled executive with his home his office, a scientist using fertilizer attachments; a purchasing agent in an old straw hat; a personnel director with grease under his fingernails; a dietitian with a passion for alfalfa, aminos and antibiotics; a production expert faced with a surplus, and a manager battling a price-cost squeeze.

—Doris T. West

Farsightedness

634. Man is, spiritually, a long-sighted creature, and some of his most grievous errors are due to his failure to recognize that fact. He sees most clearly at a distance; a too-near look at a multiplicity of details confuses him. He must get away from that which he would judge in order to see it in its true perspective. The charm of summer is perceived on a winter's day.

Fate

635. Fate is something you believe in when things are not going well. When they are, you forget it.

—AUBREY MENEN

636. Fate is the friend of the good, the guide of the wise, the tyrant of the foolish, the enemy of the bad.

—W. R. ALGER

637. When once you get accustomed to the idea that you may be dead in a day, or in an hour, or in a minute, and when you are clear as to your future, your mood is relieved from constant depression. Involuntarily you become kind and helpful to those about you, you do not get vexed over trifles, you are ready to make all kinds of sacrifices.

—ANONYMOUS, AUGUST, 1917
IN *The Atlantic Year Book*

Fatherhood

638. Called *padre* in Spanish, *père* in French, *otets* in Japanese, Dad in different parts of the world has roles that differ even more from his many names. In the United States, a new father struts around handing out cigars. But among the Ainus of Japan and in many African and South American tribes, the father takes to his bed right after the baby is born and stays there for a period ranging from a few days to a month! The mother, in contrast, returns to her housekeeping as soon as possible. Why? Because it's believed that the newborn child is affected by whatever its father does. If he worked, hunted, chopped down trees or rowed during the first days of its life, the baby might be dangerously weakened by all that strenuous exercise! So Dad follows the safest course—and does nothing.

Father—Son

639. Let every father remember that one day his son will follow his example instead of his advice.

640. There must always be a struggle between a father and a son, while one aims at power and the other at independence.

—Dr. Samuel Johnson

Fault—Faults

641. Better a diamond with a flaw than a pebble without one.

—Chinese proverb

642. Nature didn't make us perfect, so she did the next best thing. She made us blind to our faults.

643. He who exhibits no faults is a fool or a hypocrite, whom we should mistrust. There are faults so intimately connected with fine qualities that they indicate them, and we do well not to correct them.

—Joseph Joubert

Fear—Fears

644. Fear is faithlessness.

—George Macdonald

645. Fear, rightly used, is the father of courage.

646. Fear is not an invincible force; it is only a challenge to courage.

647. The secret of overcoming fear is not so much the denial of fear, which is like whistling in the dark, but rather the strong and positive building of a faith which makes fear impossible.

648. Everyone is afraid. But the difference between a man and a coward is: A man knows he is afraid. Faces his fear. Prays to God to give him strength to conquer that fear. A coward is afraid to face his fear and is without faith in himself or his God.

649. To be ambitious for wealth, and yet always expecting to be poor; to be always doubting your ability to get what you long for, is like trying to reach east by traveling west. . . . No matter how hard you work for success, if your thought is saturated with the fear of failure, it will kill your efforts, neutralize your endeavors and make success impossible.

—ATTRIBUTED TO KING BAUDOUIN

Firmness

650. When firmness is sufficient, rashness is unnecessary.

—NAPOLEON I

Fishing

651. There are two reasons for the proverbial persistence of anglers. The first is that the fish are biting; the second is that they are not. Either is a sufficient justification for fishing a little longer.

—FRED STREEVER

652. Fishing is a chance to wash one's soul with pure air, with the ripple of the stream and the shimmer of the sun on the blue waters. It brings meekness and inspiration from the glory and wonder of nature, and charity toward tackle-makers. It brings mockery of profits; the quieting of hate and lift of the spirit. And it brings rejoicing that you do not have to decide a darned thing until next week. . . . An Assyrian tablet of 2000 B.C. says:

> The Gods Do Not Subtract
> From the Allotted Span of Men's Lives
> The Hours Spent in Fishing.

—FROM A SPEECH BY HERBERT HOOVER

Flag, United States

653. Although Old Glory has changed somewhat from the Betsy Ross original with the addition of more and more states until now 50 stars appear in the blue field, little else has changed concerning the flag. If anything, the flag is more important today than ever in history, but not just because it is the symbol of one of the greatest advocates of democracy. It represents, today, more states, more dead and more living than ever before in its history. It has survived war after war, domestic and foreign, as the standard of equal rights and freedoms. It has earned its place in history, but to keep it flying, countless men have had to die fighting for it.

654. *Tribute to the Flag*

Your flag and my flag and how it flies today
In your land and my land and half the world away.
Rose red and blood red its stripes forever gleam
Snow white and soul white, our good forefather's dream.
Sky blue and true blue with stars that shine aright.
A gloried guidon through the day
A shelter through the night.
Your flag and my flag and
Oh! how much it holds,
Your land and my land secure within its folds.
Your heart and my heart beat quicker at the sight,
Sunkissed, wind tossed, the red, the blue, the white;
The one flag, the great flag, the flag for me and you
Glorifies all else besides, the red, the white, the blue.

—WILLIAM NESBIT

655. *Old Glory*

I love each shining star because
　　It tells a wondrous story;
I love each stripe no whit the less,
　　Nor shall as I grow hoary!
I love its field of azure blue,
　　Wherein each star does twinkle;
I love its red and snowy white,
　　And every fold and wrinkle!
I love to see it float on high
　　Above each tower and steeple;
I love to doff my hat to it—
　　The flag of a free people.

I love Old Glory more each day,
    The banner of our nation;
The grandest country in the world,
    The best of God's creation.

        —ALONZO NEWTON BENN

656.   *Significance of Salute to Flag*

    When we salute the Flag we are not just doing a trivial, conventional act. We are giving outward testimony of our nationality. We are not making just a common-place gesture. We are giving visible expression of our love for our country, of which there is no greater or finer in the world. We are not just saluting a beautiful symbol. We are showing our respect for the ideals and traditions, the institutions and principles of which the Flag is the visible token.

    When one who knows that the Flag really symbolizes, salutes it, he sees not only a colorful display of red, white and blue, with clustering stars and waving stripes, but in his mind's eye he sees America, a great and mighty nation, created, united and preserved by the efforts and sacrifices of brave and loyal men and women to whom the ideals and honor of this wonderful country have been dearer than life itself.

    It is, inded, an honor and a privilege to pay tribute to the banner of such a country.

657.   *Our Flag*

Our Flag, the Red, the White, the Blue,
    Waves proudly over land and sea,
The banner of the tried and true,
    A hope for those who would be free.

The Red for courage to be strong,
    To face each day without a fear,
To stand for truth and right the wrong,
    To know that God is always near.

The White for purity of life,
    For love to lend a helping hand,
For peace to end all bitter strife,
    For hope to have a better land.

Flattery

The Blue for loyalty to right,
    For friends who never turn away,
To look above for guiding light,
    As on we go along our way.

God's stars to guide the whole way through
    With love quite free from bitter hates.
Our Flag, the Red, the White, the Blue
    The Emblem of United States.

—LESLIE E. DUNKIN

Flattery

658. Men who tolerate flattery will never accept criticism.

—DAGOBERT D. RUNES

659. The last thing people want is flattery—also the first.

660. We sometimes imagine we hate flattery, but we only hate the way we are flattered.

—FRANCOIS DE LA ROCHEFOUCAULD

Flower—Flowers

661. Where flowers degenerate man cannot live.

—NAPOLEON I

662. The flower in the vase still smiles, but no longer laughs.

—MALCOLM DE CHAZAL

663. Flowers and fruits are always fine presents,—flowers, because they are a proud assertion that a ray of beauty outvalues all the utilities of the world.

—RALPH WALDO EMERSON

106

Food

664.   One-third of the food you eat keeps you alive and the other two-thirds keeps the doctors alive.

665.   The average American reaching the age of 70 has consumed during his lifetime 150 head of cattle, 225 lambs, 26 sheep, 310 swine, 2400 chickens, 26 acres of grain and 50 acres of fruits, vegetables and potatoes.

Fool—Fools—Folly

666.   A fool is surer of everything than a wise man is of anything.

667.   Fools are not those who know little but rather those who know too much of what just isn't so.

Forgetting—Forgetfulness

668.   To want to forget something is to think of it.
—FRENCH PROVERB

669.   Forgiveness is a decision no longer to see the evil; forgetfulness is understanding it as a part of a chain of woe.
—DAGOBERT D. RUNES

670.   No man ever learns to forget himself by a conscious act of forgetting. He does it by doing things for other people, which absorb his thoughts until they become fixed, as by instinct, on something outside of himself.
—ARTHUR T. HADLEY

Forgiveness

671.   The public seldom forgive twice.
—JOHANN KASPAR LAVATER

107

672. A wrong forgotten is a wrong set right.

673. They who forgive most shall be most forgiven.
—Phillip James Bailey

674. It is easier to forgive an enemy than a friend.
—Madame Deluzy

675. Many forgive injuries, but none ever forgave contempt.

676. The highest charity is charity toward the uncharitable.
—John S. Buckminster

677. Beware of the man who does not return your blow; he neither forgives you nor allows you to forgive yourself.
—George Bernard Shaw

678. It is necessary to repent for years in order to efface a fault in the eyes of men; a single tear suffices with God.
—Francois de Chateaubriand

679. We should forgive freely, but forget rarely. I will not be revenged, and this I owe to my enemy; but I will remember, and this I owe to myself.
—Charles C. Colton

680. A more glorious victory cannot be gained over another man than this, that when the injury began on his part, the kindness should begin on ours.
—John Tillotson

681. "I can forgive, but I cannot forget," is only another way of saying, "I will not forgive." A forgiveness ought to be like a cancelled note, torn in two and burned up, so that it can never be shown against the man.

—HENRY WARD BEECHER

682.   Forgiving does not come easy. There is nothing in our human natures that makes us want to forgive. And one reason it is so hard for us to forgive is that there is at least one thing that's even harder for us than forgiving—that's confessing our own shortcomings and asking to be forgiven.

683.   Sir Eardley Wilmot was asked by a friend in public office who felt that he had been wronged by a fellow official: "Don't you think it would be manly to resent this offense?"

"Yes," replied Sir Eardley, "It would doubtless be manly to resent it, but it would be godlike to forgive."

Fortitude

684.   If Columbus had turned back, no one would have blamed him. But who would have remembered him?

685.   We should possess fortitude even in adversity, for all is not lost by a single adverse cast of fortune; he who is prepossessed with the assurance of overcoming, at least overcomes the fear of failure; whereas, he who is apprehensive of losing, loses in reality all hopes of subduing.

—HENRY VENN

686.   Don't give up hoping when the ship goes down,
Grab a spar or something—just refuse to drown.
Don't think you are dying just because you're hit,
Smile in face of danger and hang on to your grit.
Folks die too easy—they sort of fade away;
Make a little error and give up in dismay.
Kind of man that's needed is the man of ready wit,
To laugh at pain and trouble and keep up his grit.

—LOUIS E. THAYER

Fortune

687. Fortune does not change men; it only unmasks them.
—Marie Jeanne Riccoboni

688. We rise to fortune by successive steps; we descend by only one.
—Leckinska Stanislaus

689. The bad fortune of the good turns their faces up to heaven; and the good fortune of the bad bows their heads down to the earth.
—Saadi

Frankness

690. The man who says what he thinks is courageous and friendless.

691. Impertinence is one thing, frankness another.
—F. H. Converse

Freedom

692. Freedom was never won by people who were satisfied just to survive.

693. In the final choice a soldier's pack is not so heavy a burden as a prisoner's chains.
—Dwight D. Eisenhower

694. We feel free when we escape—even if it be but from the frying pan into the fire.
—Eric Hoffer

695. A man's worst difficulties begin when he is able to do as he likes.
—Thomas H. Huxley

696.   People hardly ever make use of the freedom they have, for example, freedom of thought; instead they demand freedom of speech as a compensation.

—Sören Kierkegaard

697.   The price of freedom is always, sooner or later, resolute action —often in the face of alternatives that are easier, more immediately profitable.

—William S. Paley

698.   "Freedom is only good as a means," wrote Herman Melville, author of *Moby Dick*. It is what we do with freedom that makes it worth having and worth fighting to defend.

699.   He who thinks with his own head is a free man. He who struggles for what he believes to be right it a free man. Even if you live in the freest country in the world and you are lazy, callous, apathetic, irresolute, you are not free but a slave.

—Ignazio Silone

700.   So long as the people do not care to exercise their freedom, those who wish to tyrannize will do so; for tyrants are active and ardent, and will devote themselves in the name of any number of gods, religious and otherwise, to put shackles upon sleeping men.

—Voltairine de Cleyre

701.   Freedom is a right. But it is a right to be gained only by working for it, by making sacrifices to keep it. Freedom is enforced by the morals of a people. Freedom is tolerance and intelligence. It is ravaged by bigotry and corruption and ignorance. Freedom is justice. It is, in essence, equal opportunity. It is dignity and it is honesty. In a sense, it is life. For so much as life is deprived of freedom, so much is it robbed of its meaning and enjoyment. Without freedom, we wither and degenerate.

702.   *Freedom is Not Negotiable*
    Freedom cannot be put in a bottle, or on a stick like a popsicle, or sliced, or weighed out in pounds. You cannot reduce it to print,

or compress it, or define it, or spray it, or explode it. It is teasingly remote in one way, but deeply personal and prescient and immanent in another.

Freedom is a gift of God to all men, everywhere, for all time. You can try to sell it or exchange it for security. But what you get in the deal is slavery, or slow death. The other word is security.

You can try to buy it. But you cannot really buy it, no matter how much security you think you are willing to throw into the scales, for FREEDOM IS NOT NEGOTIABLE!

You have it, that is, whether you like it or not, whether you appreciate it or do not use it. You got it when you were born. You will have it until you die. And no man or state or dictator, no matter how tyrannical, can take it away from you.

The Declaration of Independence states with crystal clarity that all men "are endowed by their Creator with certain unalienable rights." Here is the precise and exact meaning of the word "unalienable": *freedom cannot be taken away*—ever!

We may not appreciate freedom enough to exercise it. We may not practice it. We may ignore it. We may pass laws or insensibly allow our representatives to pass laws to limit, obscure, or circumvent freedom. But with or without us freedom remains, set by the hand of God, fixed in eternity.

We can stand up tall and live up to it or we can supinely lie low and let it go by without us.

And freedom will surely go by without us if that is the way we want it.

—Donald Haynes, *Liberty*, 1963

Freedom of Speech. See Speech, Freedom of

Friendship

703. No man lacks friends who is one.

704. The corpse of friendship is not worth embalming.
—William Hazlitt

705.   Friendship ends where deception begins.

706.   The secret of friendship is to make first impressions last.
—ARNOLD H. GLASOW

707.   The ideal of friendship is to feel as one while remaining two.
—ANNE SOPHIE SWETCHINE

708.   He who is true to one friend thus proves himself worthy of many.

709.   The friends you make in prosperity are those you lose in adversity.

710.   Use friendship as a drawing account if you wish, but don't forget the deposits.

711.   The difficulty is not so great to die for a friend as to find a friend worth dying for.
—HENRY HOME

712.   Wheat does not come without chaff. If you want your friend, accept all that goes with him.

713.   An absent friend gives us friendly company when we are well assured of his happiness.
—JOHANN WOLFGANG VON GOETHE

714.   One reason why friendships are so transient, is because we so often mistake a companion for a friend.
—HENRY W. SHAW

715. In life it is difficult to say who do you the most mischief—enemies with the worst intentions or friends with the best.

—EDWARD GEORGE BULWER-LYTTON

716. To let friendship die away by negligence and silence, is certainly not wise. It is voluntarily to throw away one of the greatest comforts of this weary pilgrimage.

DR. SAMUEL JOHNSON

717. There is no cement in this world, whatever there may be in the next, strong enough to mend a broken friendship. If it was brittle when whole what must it be when mended?

—RICHARD HENRY STODDARD

718. Be courteous to all, but intimate with few, and let those few be well tried before you give them your confidence. True friendship is a plant of slow growth, and must undergo and withstand the shocks of adversity before it is entitled to the appellation.

—GEORGE WASHINGTON

719. Too many *acts* of friendship, particularly those excessive ones we call acts of self-sacrifice, may endanger the relationship. One should not have to be overgrateful to a friend. The sense of obligation and the sense of guilt are neighbors. Perfect friends owe each other nothing but themselves.

—CLIFTON FADIMAN

720. Friendship implies loyalty, esteem, cordiality, sympathy, affection, readiness to aid, to help, to stick, to fight for, if need be. The real friend is he or she who can share all our sorrows and double all our joys. Radiate friendship and it will return sevenfold.

—B. C. FORBES

721. This is one reason why the making of new friends is so much easier in youth than later on. Friendship comes to youth seemingly without any conditions, and without any fears. There is no past to look back at, with much regret and some sorrow. We never look behind us, *till we miss something*. Youth is satisfied with the joy of present possession. To the young friendship comes as the glory of spring, a very miracle of beauty, a mystery of birth; to the old it has the bloom of autumn, beautiful still, but with the beauty of decay. To the young it is chiefly hope; to the old it is mostly memory. The man who is conscious that he has lost the best of his days, the best of his powers, the best of his friends, naturally lives a good deal in the past.

—Hugh Black

Future, The. See also Past—Present—Future

722. Tomorrow belongs to those who don't wait for it.

723. When all else is lost, the future still remains.
—Christian Nevell Bovee

724. If there was no future life, our souls would not thirst for it.
—Jean Paul Richter

725. Real generosity toward the future consists in giving all to what is present.

—Albert Camus

726. Cease to think what the future has in store, but take as a gift whatever the day brings forth.

—Horace

Gambling

727. The gambling known as business looks with severe disfavor upon the business known as gambling.

728.   All gaming, since it implies a desire to profit at the expense of another, involves a breach of the tenth commandment.

—RICHARD WHATELY

729.   Gambling promises the poor what property performs for the rich; that is why the bishops dare not denounce it fundamentally.

—GEORGE BERNARD SHAW

730.   The history of gambling is extremely ancient. There is hardly a known society in the present or past where gambling, in some form, has not taken place. Recorded evidence going back as far as 321 B.C., for example, reveals that in India there were special officials who supervised various forms of gambling in which the populace engaged and from which, it might be added, public revenues were derived. As part of religious ritual and recreation in the past, among primitive as well as civilized peoples, games of chance are to be found sharing many common characteristics.

—DR. HERBERT A. BLOCH

Garden—Gardens—Gardening

731.   Gardening has many advantages. Among them is it's ability to keep one down to earth.

732.   One of the nicest things about gardening is that if you put it off long enough it eventually is too late.

Generosity

733.   Generosity will always be a more pleasant memory than stinginess.

734.   Men resemble the gods in nothing so much as in doing good to their fellow creatures.

—CICERO

735. When you give, take to yourself no credit for generosity unless you deny yourself something in order that you may give.

—HENRY TAYLOR

736. What is called generosity is usually only the vanity of giving; we enjoy the vanity more than the thing given.

—FRANCOIS DE LA ROCHEFOUCAULD

Genius

737. A man who is a genius and doesn't know it probably isn't.

—STANISLAUS J. LEC

738. Genius is more than having a high IQ: it is doing something worthwhile with it.

Gentleman—Gentlemen

739. To be born a gentleman is an accident. To die one is an achievement.

740. A cunning person seeks for opportunities to deceive; a gentleman shuns them. A cunning person triumphs in deceiving; a gentleman is humiliated by his success.

—JOHN RUSKIN

741. The true gentlemen is the man whose conduct proceeds from goodwill and an acute sense of propriety, and whose self-control is equal to all emergencies; who does not make the poor man conscious of his poverty, the obscure man of his obscurity, or any man of his inferiority or deformity; who is himself humbled if necessity compel him to humble another; who does not flatter wealth, cringe before power, or boast of his own possessions or achievements; who speaks with frankness, but always with sincerity and sympathy, and whose deed follows his word; who thinks of the rights and feelings of others rather than of his own; who appears well in any company and who is at home what he seems to be abroad—a man with whom honor is sacred.

Genuineness

742. Honest vulgarity is far preferable to phony sophistication.
—BRIAN O'DOHERTY

743. The shortest and surest way to live with honor in the world is to be in reality what we appear to be.
—SOCRATES

Gift—Gifts

744. The greatest gift is the art of giving.

745. The nice thing about a gift of money for Christmas is that it's so easily exchanged.
—ARNOLD H. GLASOW

746. The greatest grace of a gift, perhaps, is that it anticipates and admits of no return.
—HENRY WADSWORTH LONGFELLOW

747. The ideal gift should be in keeping with the relationship between the giver and the receiver.
—CHARLES L. LAPP

748. Who gives a good book gives more than cloth, paper, and ink ... more than leather, parchment, and words. He reveals a foreword of his thoughts, a dedication of his friendship, a page of his presence, a chapter of himself, and an index of his love.
—DR. WILLIAM ARTHUR WARD, TAXES
WESLEYAN COLLEGE, FORT WORTH

749. The essence of giving is sharing. The more we retreat from this concept the less giving means to us. The first Christmas offerings, whether they derived from shepherd or kind, represented a sharing of the donor's own treasures. There is no gift more personal than the gift of something you love yourself.

Giving

750.   Who gives to me teaches me to give.

—OLD PROVERB

751.   One must be poor to know the luxury of giving.

—GEORGE ELIOT

752.   Too many friends of the church are close friends.

753.   He who gives too much belittles the recipient.

754.   That comes too late that comes for the asking.

—SENECA

755.   When it comes to giving, some people stop at nothing.

756.   First relieve the needy, then question them if you must.

—RULES OF THE BENEDICTINES

757.   He is no fool who gives what he cannot keep to gain what he cannot lose.

758.   Liberality consists less in giving profusely than in giving judiciously.

—JEAN DE LA BRUYERE

759. The poorest can give as much as the richest if he will give all he can.

760. In this world, it is not what we take up, but what we give up, that makes us rich.

—Henry Ward Beecher

761. He's the kind of man who gives until it hurts but he's also very sensitive to pain.

762. Posthumous charities are the very essence of selfishness when bequeathed by those who, when alive, would part with nothing.

—Charles C. Colton

763. Give freely to him that deserveth well and asketh nothing; and that is a way of giving to thyself.

—Thomas Fuller

764. Do not respect men merely for their riches, but rather for their philanthropy. We do not value the sun for its height, but for its use.

765. He gives not best who gives most, but he gives most who gives best. If then I cannot give bountifully, yet I will give freely; and what I want in my hand, supply by my heart. He gives well who gives willingly.

—Arthur Warwick

766. If you find pleasure in giving, so do others. You have only to stop and think how you feel when your giving is rebuffed or looked upon with suspicion, or when someone is slow to enter into the spirit of it, to realize how important it is to accept quickly and to acknowledge graciously the thoughtfulness of others toward you.

—David Dunn

767. Anyone who hasn't learned the joy of giving when he or she hasn't super-abundance, is little likely to part with anything no matter how his or her bank account may expand.

—B. C. FORBES

768.   The root of all unhappiness is the desire to take; the root of all suffering, all sorrow, is the desire to take; but the root of all joy, happiness and true progress is the desire to give. Those who give must give with hands untied by the fear of growing poorer themselves; for the soul that gives becomes like a powerful and strongly magnetized orb, exposed to the light from a thousand stars, and in reflecting light receives but more.

769.   Some men give so that you are angry every time you ask them to contribute. They give so that their gold and silver shoot you like a bullet. Other persons give with such beauty that you remember it as long as you live; and you say, "It is a pleasure to go to such men." There are some men who give as springs do: whether you go to them or not, they are always full; and your part is merely to put your dish under the ever-flowing stream. Others give just as a pump does where the well is dry, and the pump leaks.

—HENRY WARD BEECHER

Goal—Goals

770.   He shot at a sparrow
    And spoiled a good arrow.

—FROM THE CHINESE

771.   It is one of the sad facts of our world that the man who announces a minor goal and reaches it is held in greater esteem than the man who attempts the spectacular and fails.

—HASKEL FRANKEL

772.   Everything has its price—we get what we pay for in this world. If I settle for a cheap suit instead of a custom-tailored one, it won't cost me so much, but then neither will it wear as well. This is just as true when we set our goals in life. What are we willing to settle for? If we set our sights high, it will cost more in effort and time than if we

God

are content with less. The important thing is to know what we want and then go about getting it. Without a goal we don't even know how much effort we need to expend. There's no sense even buying a ticket, much less running to catch the train, until we know where we want to go.

—Don Hall

God

773.   The finger of God never leaves identical fingerprints.
—Stanislaus J. Lec

774.   All I have seen teaches me to trust the Creator for all I have not seen.
—Ralph Waldo Emerson

775.   The very impossibility in which I find myself to prove that God is not discovers to me His existence.
—Jean de La Bruyère

776.   God offers to every mind its choice between truth and repose. Take which you please—you can never have both.
—Ralph Waldo Emerson

God-Man

777.   To neglect God is to oppose Him; to oppose God is to perish.
—Dr. William Arthur Ward, Texas Wesleyan College, Fort Worth

778.   Of all the creatures God ever made, man is the only one that ever asks "WHY?"

779.   Do not blame God for the harvest when you yourself do the sowing.

780. Man is responsible to God for becoming what God has made possible for him to become.

781. More people ask the Lord to lighten their burdens than ask Him to strengthen their backs.

782. The hardest thing any man can do is to fall down on the ice when it's slippery, and get up and praise the Lord.

—Josh Billings

783. Anybody who ignores the church is like a person who builds a house without windows and then blames God because he has to live in the dark.

784. Once a man in India asked a holy man, "How can I find God?" Again and again he asked the question.

Finally the holy man said: "Let's go to the River Ganges." At the river the holy man seized him by the neck, plunged him under the water, and held him under till he nearly drowned. When the man had his breath back enough to speak, the holy man asked what he wished for most when he thought he was drowning.

"Air, of course, only air!"

"Exactly," replied the holy man, "and when you want God as much as you then wanted air, you'll find Him, but not before."

785. One day St. Augustine, the great church father, was walking along the seashore in quiet meditation. His thoughts were centered on the doctrine of the Holy Trinity. How could God be three—and yet be one?

While wrestling with this baffling thought, his attention was suddenly drawn to a little girl playing in the sand. Back and forth she went, carrying a shovel full of water from the receding waves to a little hole that she had dug.

"What are you doing, little girl?" he asked. Without hesitation, and with an air of childlike confidence, she replied: "Oh, I'm going to empty the sea into this little hole I've dug."

Golden Rule

The wise theologian smiled and resumed his walk. But as he strolled along the shore, he said to himself: "I am trying to do exactly what that little girl is doing—trying to crowd the infinite God into this finite mind of mine."

—Herman W. Gockel

Golden Rule

786. Do to others as you say you do.

—Dagobert D. Runes

787. Practicing the Golden Rule is not a sacrifice; it's an investment.

788. The Golden Rule is of little value unless you realize that you must make the first move.

Golf

789. Some men play golf religiously—every Sunday.

790. If you break 100, watch your golf. If you break 80, watch your business.

—Walter Winchell

791. Golf is deceptively simple and endlessly complicated. A child can play it well, and a grown man can never master it. . . . It is almost a science, yet it is a puzzle without an answer. It is gratifying and tantalizing, precise and unpredictable; it requires complete concentration and total relaxation. It satisfies the soul and frustrates the intellect. It is at the same time rewarding and maddening—and it is without doubt the greatest game mankind has ever invented.

—Arnold Palmer

Goodness

792. No amount of good deeds can make us good persons. We must be good before we can do good.

—REV. CHESTER A. PENNINGTON

793. He that does good to another man does also good to himself, not only in the consequences, but in the very act of doing it, for the consciousness of well-doing is an ample reward.

—SENECA

794. He is good that does good to others. If he suffers for the good he does, he is better still; and if he suffers from them to whom he did good, he is arrived to that height of goodness that nothing but an increase of his sufferings can add to it; if it proves his death, his virtue is at its summit,—it is heroism complete.

—JEAN DE LA BRUYÈRE

Gossip

795. Gossip is like a balloon, it grows bigger with every puff.

796. A conceited person has at least one good point—he doesn't talk about other people.

797. Gossips are social vultures who flutter to the cliffs of respectability when disturbed while feeding at carrion in the alleys of depravity.

—DOUGLAS MEADOR

Government

798. Govern a great nation as you would cook a small fish. Don't overdo it.

—LAO-TZU

Gratitude

799. There is nothing the federal government can give you without taking it away from you first.

—Dr. Edward R. Annis

800. Society is well governed when the people obey the magistrates, and the magistrates the laws.

—Solon

801. Government should restrain men from injuring one another but leave them otherwise free to follow their own pursuits of industry and employment.

—Thomas Jefferson

802. The preamble to the United States Constitution talks about guaranteeing to promote the general welfare—not to provide it.

803. The surest way of governing, both in a private family and a kingdom, is for a husband and a prince sometimes to drop their prerogative.

—Edwin Holt Hughes

804. The great principle . . . is that the majority must govern, from which there can be no appeal but the sword. That majority ought to govern wisely, equitably, moderately, and constitutionally; but govern it must.

—Henry Clay

805. There are no necessary evils in government. Its evils exist only in its abuses. If it would confine itself to equal protection, and, as heaven does its rain, shower its favors alike on the high and on the low, the rich and the poor, it would be an unqualified blessing.

—Andrew Jackson

Gratitude

806. The man who forgets to be thankful has fallen asleep in life.

—Robert Louis Stevenson

807.   He who receives a benefit with gratitude repays the first installment on his debt.

—SENECA

808.   An unthankful man is like a pig under a tree eating acorns, never looking up to see from whence they come.

809.   Gratitude is a duty which ought to be paid, but which none have a right to expect.

—JEAN JACQUES ROUSSEAU

810.   Gratitude takes three forms: a feeling in the heart, an expression in words and a giving in return.

811.   There is a selfishness even in gratitude, when it is too profuse: to be over-thankful for one favor is in effect to lay out for another.

—RICHARD CUMBERLAND

Greatness

812.   He who is truly great has one consuming desire—to remain small.

813.   Greatness alone is not enough, or the cow would out-run the hare.

—GERMAN PROVERB

814.   If you cannot do great things yourself, remember that you may do small things in a great way.

815.   The beginning of greatness is to be little, the increase of greatness is to be less, and the perfection of greatness is to be nothing.

—DWIGHT LYMAN MOODY

816. When the oak is felled the whole forest echoes with its fall, but a hundred acorns are sown in silence by an unnoticed breeze.

—Thomas Carlyle

817. It is always a sign of poverty of mind when men are ever aiming to appear great; for they who are really great never seem to know it.

—Richard Cecil

818. The great men of earth are the shadowy men, who, having lived and died, now live again and forever through their undying thoughts. Thus living, though their footfalls are heard no more, their voices are louder than the thunder, and unceasing as the flow of tides or air.

—Henry Ward Beecher

819. I believe the first test of a truly great man is his humility. I do not mean, by humility, doubt of his own power, or hesitation in speaking of his opinions; but a right understanding of the relation between what *he* can do and say, and the rest of the world's saying and doings.

—John Ruskin

820. Truly great persons are more interested in controlling themselves than in controlling others. If monuments are put up to honor persons less worthy than themselves, they do not mind, for humility is one of their traits. It is probable that Einstein, acclaimed as the greatest scientist of his time, was more humble than most of the students at the university where he taught. Greatness is modest; it avoids publicity.

—Clinton E. Bernard

Greed

821. Who wants the last drop out of the can gets the lid on his nose.

—Old proverb

822. A beggar chanced to meet Fortune one day. Touched by his pleadings she agreed to fill his sack with gold coins from her horn of plenty.

She set only one condition—any gold falling to the ground should turn into dust.

The begger eagerly watched the golden stream pour into his sack. He held the mouth of the sack open wide so that not a single coin could escape its yawning mouth. When his sack was quite full, and surely contained more than enough gold to satisfy his needs for the rest of his life, Fortune asked, "Is that enough?"

The greedy beggar shook his head. He reminded her that she had promised to fill his sack. He insisted that Fortune keep on pouring for he was sure his sack would hold a few more coins. So Fortune continued to pour, and then without warning the sack burst. All the gold fell through to the ground, making only a small pile of dust.

Greeting—Greetings

823. A famous story of French history recounts that Voltaire, a notorious infidel, was standing beside a friend one day on the streets of Paris where there passed by a religious procession carrying a crucifix. Voltaire lifted his hat. His friend noticing this unexpected gesture said: "What is this? Are you reconciled to God?" "No," said Voltaire with sharp irony. "We salute, but we do not speak."

—Rev. Richard R. Potter

824. When people of various nations greet each other, here are their usual greetings: How do you do?—*American.* How do you carry yourself?—*French.* How do you stand?—*Italian.* How do you find yourself?—*German.* How do you fare?—*Dutch.* How can you?—*Swedish.* How do you perspire?—*Egyptian.* How is your stomach? or, Have you eaten your rice?—*Chinese.* How do you have yourself?—*Polish.* How do you live on?—*Russian.* May thy shadow never be less!—*Persian.*

And they all mean about the same!

Grief

825. Grief is a species of idleness.

—Dr. Samuel Johnson

Guidance

826. One can bear grief, but it takes two to be glad.

—ELBERT HUBBARD

Guidance

827. A fallen lighthouse is more dangerous than a reef.

828. A young fellow, who was going somewhere with his minister, explained to him that he disliked having to obey. He said,, "A fellow hates to have a 'shall' and 'shall not' flung at him every minute. It's so arbitrary."

The minister didn't reply. Shortly they came to a sign pointing the way to the place they wished to reach. The minister ignored the sign. The young man exclaimed, "We're going the wrong way! You missed the sign back there." The minister calmly replied, "I saw the sign all right, but I thought this looked the better road, and I hate to be told to go this way and that by an arbitrary old sign post." The young man laughed, but he got the point, as they turned around to go in the direction pointed out by that "arbitrary sign post."

—VIVIAN D. GUNDERSON

Gullibility

829. More persons are humbugged by believing in nothing than by believing too much.

—P. T. BARNUM

830. Gullibility is the key to all adventures. The greenhorn is the ultimate victor in everything; it is he that gets the most out of life.

—G. K. CHESTERTON

Habit—Habits

831. Habit is either the best of servants, or the worst of masters.

—DELOS EMMONS

832.   Habit is hard to overcome. If you take off the first letter, it does not change "a bit." If you take off another, you still have a "bit" left. If you take off still another, the whole of "it" remains. If you take off another it is wholly used up. All of which goes to show that if you want to get rid of habit you must throw it off altogether.

Happiness

833.   You can't pursue happiness and catch it. Happiness comes upon you unawares while you are helping others.

834.   Happiness may be thought, sought, or caught, but for certain, it cannot be bought.

835.   If we cannot live so as to be happy, let us at least live so as to deserve happiness.
—JOHANN GOTTLIEB FICHTE

836.   Never miss an opportunity to make others happy—even if you have to leave them alone to do it.

837.   We have no more right to consume happiness without producing it than to consume wealth without producing it.
—GEORGE BERNARD SHAW

838.   Happiness in this world, when it comes, comes incidentally. Make it the object of pursuit, and it leads to a wild-goose chase, and is never attained.
—NATHANIEL HAWTHORNE

839.   Happiness is like a butterfly—pursue either and they will evade you. Make yourself busy, and each will come and sit on your shoulder when you aren't looking.

Happiness

840. The man who makes everything that leads to happiness depend upon himself, and not upon other men, has adopted the very best plan for living happily. This is the man of moderation, the man of manly character and of wisdom.

—PLATO

841. I have heard people say, "If I only had this or that, I could be happy." But those who search for happiness will never find it, because happiness is not a goal, it is a by-product. The way to happiness is not from without but from within.

—RABBI IRVING J. BLOCK

842. The happiness of life is made up of minute fractions—the little soon-forgotten charities of a kiss or smile, a kind look, a heartfelt compliment, and the countless infinitesimals of pleasurable and genial feeling.

—SAMUEL T. COLERIDGE

843. There is no duty we so much underrate as the duty of being happy. By being happy, we sow anonymous benefits upon the world, which remain unknown even to ourselves, or when they are disclosed, surprise nobody so much as the benefactor.

—ROBERT LOUIS STEVENSON

844. If we want to be happy ourselves, we should aim to add to the happiness of others. Happiness is one thing that is wholly unselfish. We do not gain it by taking it away from someone else. We gain it for ourselves by giving it to others. It is "bread upon the waters" returned one-hundred fold.

845. The little girl came downstairs one morning exuberant as only a child seems to be in the early hours of the day. She rushed into the kitchen and noticed that her mother was a bit glum for some reason. "Mommy," she said, "aren't you happy?" "Why, certainly I'm happy," the mother replied, reassuringly. "Well," said the little girl, "you certainly haven't told your face yet."

—REV. EMIL D. MCADAMS

846.　The biggest thrill, the moment of great happiness, is something that is a long time abuilding. It comes of making up your mind about just what is important and pursuing your own sense of values independently of social pressures and of mores with which you don't agree. Happiness is to be free of the attrition of doubt. To be happy you have to be tough.

—Dr. Murdock Head

847.　There is happiness in being free from envy, hatred and fear; there is happiness in loving and helping others; there is happiness in doing the work one loves, with all one's might; there is happiness in gaining knowledge and imparting it to others; there is happiness in becoming a channel for forces that can regenerate and uplift humanity. There are many roads to happiness, and every seeker after it must choose the one best suited to his humor and gait.

848.　Not all of us can be an Edison, or a Florence Nightingale, or a Henry Ford, a Salk, a Churchill or Madame Curie. Each of them contributed much and each achieved a measure of happiness in the doing. We lesser men and women can do likewise—on a smaller scale, but no less importantly to ourselves and for others.

　　　　The very fundamental of happiness is that its possession comes from the fullest realization of self in terms of achievement—and most often on behalf of others.

849.　Happiness I have discovered is nearly always a rebound from hard work. It is one of the follies of men to imagine that they can enjoy mere thought, or emotion, or sentiment! As well try to eat beauty! For happiness must be tricked. She loves to see men at work. She loves sweet weariness, self-sacrifice. She will be found not in palaces, but lurking in cornfields and factories and hovering over littered desks. She crowns the unconscious head of the busy child. If you look up suddenly from hard work you will see her, but if you look too long she fades sorrowfully away.

—David Grayson

850.　Benjamin Franklin, with his sagacity and wit, was a man who thoroughly enjoyed trimming hecklers down to size. During the early days of the American Republic, he spoke many times on that great document, the Constitution of the United States.

After one such stirring speech an uncouth fellow rose and boldly walked a few paces toward the platform. "Aw, them words don't mean nothin' a-tall!" he shouted at Franklin. "Where's all that happiness you say it guarantees us?"

Franklin smiled benevolently at the questioner, and quickly, blandly, Old Ben replied, "My friend, the Constitution only guarantees the American people the right to *pursue* happiness. You have to *catch* it yourself!"

851.   There are two ways of being happy,—we may either diminish our wants or augment our means, —either will do, the result is the same; and it is for each man to decide for himself, and do that which happens to be the easiest. If you are idle or sick or poor, however hard it may be to diminish your wants, it will be harder to augment your means. If you are active and prosperous, or young, or in good health, it may be easier for you to augment your means than to diminish your wants. But if you are wise, you will do both at the same time, young or old, rich or poor, sick or well; and if you are very wise, you will do both in such a way as to augment the general happiness of society

—Benjamin Franklin

Harm—Harmfulness

852.   A hurtful act is the transference to others of the degredation which we bear in ourselves.

—Simone Weil

853.   The number of people who can do us good is very small; but almost anyone can do us harm.

—Baltasar Gracián

Haste

854.   Hurry is the visible form of worry.

855.   Many hurry to catch up; few hurry to get ahead.

856.   A man of sense may be in haste, but can never be in a hurry.
—Lord Chesterfield

857.   Striking while the iron is hot is all right, but don't strike while the head is hot.

858.   We are in such haste to be doing, to be writing, to be gathering gear, to make our voice audible a moment in the derisive silence of eternity, that we forget that one thing, of which these are but the parts—namely, to live.
—Robert Louis Stevenson

859.   The story is told of a motorcycle driver who, on a wintry night, reversed his jacket so that the bitter winds would not come through the gaps between the buttons. The jacket was somewhat uncomfortable back-to-front, but it served the purpose. As he sped along the road, he skidded on an icy spot and the poor fellow crashed into a tree. When the ambulance arrived, the first-aid men pushed through the crowd and asked a man who was standing over the victim what happened. He replied that the motorcycle rider seemed to be in pretty good shape after the crash, but by the time they got his head straightened out he was dead. So it goes when people get excited and take quick action to provide a remedy for a problem without clearly understanding what the problem is.
—John A. Howard

860.   A pompous Bishop of Oxford was once stopped on a London street by a ragged urchin.

"Well, my little man, and what can I do for you?" inquired the churchman.

"The time o' day, please, your lordship."

With considerable difficulty, the portly bishop extracted his timepiece.

"It is exactly half past five, my lad."

Hatred

"Well," said the boy, setting his feet for a good start, "at 'alf past six you go to 'ell!"—and he was off like a flash and around the corner. The bishop, flushed and furious, his watch dangling from its chain, floundered wildly after him. But as he rounded the corner he ran plumb into the outstretched arms of the venerable Bishop of London.

"Oxford, Oxford," remonstrated that surprised dignitary, "why this unseemly haste?"

Puffing, blowing, spluttering, the outraged bishop gasped out:

"That young ragamuffin—I told him it was half past five—he—er—told me to go to hell at half past six."

"Yes, yes," said the Bishop of London with the suspicion of a twinkle in his kindly old eyes, "but why such haste? You've got almost an hour."

Hatred

861. Small men hate; great men pity.

862. One does not hate so long as one despises.
—Friedrich Wilhelm Nietzsche

863. Hate no one,—hate their vices, not themselves.
—John G. Brainard

864. Mourning the loss of someone is happiness compared with having to live with someone we hate.
—Jean de La Bruyère

865. We fear something before we hate it; a child who fears noises becomes a man who hates noise.
—Cyril Connolly

866. Impotent hatred is the most horrible of all emotions; one should hate nobody whom one cannot destroy.
—Johann Wolfgang von Goethe

867. If you are constantly "hating," the cause lies within yourself. If you fill your heart with love of your fellow-mortals and are possessed of a consuming desire to be of service in the world, you will have little room left in you for "hating" this, that and the next thing and person.
—B. C. FORBES

868. The disease of hate is a disease to which people have not yet become immune. It is a disease of the human mind which people, by and large, have not yet learned to control. To understand it and to keep it from spreading and from destroying our integration and peace, we must attack it in much the same way we would attack a disease of the body.
—DOROTHY W. BARUCH

869. Hitherto, although we have been told on Sundays to love our neighbor, we have been told on weekdays to hate him, and there are six times as many weekdays as Sundays. Hitherto, the harm that we could do to our neighbor by hating him was limited by our incompetence, but in the new world upon which we are entering there will be no such limit, and the indulgence of hatred can lead only to disaster.
—BERTRAND RUSSELL

Health

870. In early times sick people were put in prison in order to drive out the evil spirits believed responsible for their illness.

Health, Mental. See Mental health

Heaven

871. An old country preacher once explained that man's election to Heaven is a tie vote the day he is born. The Lord voted for him and Satan voted against him. Man himself then breaks the tie; for he votes with the Lord, or with Satan, by the kind of life he leads.

Helpfulness

872. How incomparably excellent is the glory of heaven, where no changes shall be, where shall be wonderful advancement, but without injustice; abundance of glory, but without envy; infinite wealth, but without woe; admirable beauty and felicity, but without vanity or infirmity.

—ROBERT BOLTON

Helpfulness

873. You can lend a friend a hand without losing either hand or friend.

874. Live and let live is not enough; live and help live is not too much.

—ORIN E. MADISON

875. Quite often the outstretched hand is not seeking financial help but only the handclasp of understanding and encouragement.

876.   A little kindness every day
While we're at work or at our play!
  A little smile, a little song,
  A word of cheer when things go wrong.
To help a brother on his way!

It's such a little thing to do,
Yet means so much to me and you!
  Let's not forget that little smile,
  That little kindness all the while,
Which gives us joy and courage, too!

A little kindness . . . 'twas the Plan
To help us all since Time began!
  The only heaven that we can know
  Along life's pathway as we go,
Is love bestowed by man to man!

—ANONYMOUS

Hero—Heroes—Heroism

877. Worship your heroes from afar; contact withers them.
—MADAME SUZANNE NECKER

878. Of two heroes, he who esteems his rivals the most is the greater.
—LAURENT A DE BEAUMELLE

879. Many a man gets credit for being a hero who didn't realize he was in danger until it was too late to run.

Historian—Historians

880. An historian is a prophet in reverse.
—FRIEDRICH SCHLEGEL

881. The first qualification for an historian is to have no ability to invent.
—STENDHAL (MARIE HENRI BEYLE)

History

882. The uncertainty of history is chiefly to be ascribed to the partiality of historians.
—JOHN HINTON

883. Life must be lived forwards, but can only be understood backwards.
—SÖREN KIERKEGAARD

884. There is nothing new in the world except the history you don't know.
—HARRY S. TRUMAN

885. Learning history is easy; learning its lessons seems almost impossible.

—Nicolas Bentley

886. If we knew history better, our expectation would be less and our consolations more.

—Will Durant

887. The real history of a nation is not so much what the big shots have done as what its plain people have experienced.

—Wheeler McMillen

888. Not to know what has been transacted in former times is to continue always a child. If no use is made of the labors of past ages, the world must remain always in the infancy of knowledge.

—Cicero

889. History is certainly not bound to repeat itself, and it actually fails to repeat itself more often than not. At the same time, history is also *not* bound not to repeat itself; and since it may repeat itself, our past experience is always worth bringing to bear when we are peering into the future.

—Arnold J. Toynbee

890. The past is intelligible to us only in the light of the present; and we can fully understand the present only in the light of the past. To enable man to understand the society of the past and to increase his mastery over the society of the present is the dual function of history.

—Edward Hallett Carr

891. History is the cumulative memory of mankind, and without it neither individuals nor nations can fully understand the present or seriously plan for the future. History shows us how much we owe to the past sacrifices of others. It kindles in us a quiet pride in the accomplishments of our forebears, and makes us determined to put the future in debt to us. This resolve is that true patriotism, without which no nation or people can survive.

—Stewart L. Udall

892.   Although he was a man of action, rather than words, Henry Ford, American industrialist, born July 30, 1863, made his share of terse, epigramatic observations. He is recalled, however, for one brief, thoughtless sentence, spoken in a moment of pique and exasperation. It was on a hot July day in 1919. Mr. Ford was on the witness stand at Mt. Clemens, Michigan, during the course of his libel suit against the *Chicago Tribune*. Reminded by defense counsel that a certain event was a matter of historic record, the motor man exploded:

"History is the bunk."

Hobby—Hobbies

893.   A hobby, no matter what it is as long as it is enjoyed, provides an escape for pent-up energy. Unlike the work done for a living, the work done on a hobby can be suspended at will and resumed in the same fashion. Working on a hobby is a matter of choice, not necessity. When weariness or even the wrong mood descends on the hobbyist, he can simply stop. But a hobby offers even more in that, instead of being just one man whose efforts are just a part of the end product or service, the hobbyist can claim that he and only he made something.

Home—Homes

894.   A happy home is more than a roof over your head—it's a foundation under your feet.

—Arnold H. Glasow

895.   It isn't the bigness of the house, it is the bigness of the hearts in the house that make it a happy home.

896.   Home is the only place where you can go out and in. There are places you can go into, and places you can go out of, but the one place, if you do but find it, where you may go out and in both, is home.

—GEORGE MACDONALD

897. If liberty is the touchstone of our society, the American home must be its exemplification. Here we learn the great virtues of today's world; the recession of prejudice and poverty and disease; the nurturing of the spiritual; the expressions of the creative; and the intelligent use of the wonders and the brilliance of the sciences.

—MRS. DEXTER OTIS ARNOLD

898. Our homes are not merely refuges from the storms and vicissitudes of life, where we find rest and renewal. They are also places where young lives are bent, molded and trained. A house may be built with materials of brick, stone, wood and plaster, but a true home is built with faith in God, love, unselfishness, consideration, patience, prayer, praise and work.

—L. NELSON BELL

899. An artist who wanted to paint the most beautiful picture in the world, asked a pastor, "What is the most beautiful thing in the world?" Faith," answered the pastor. "You can feel it in every church, find it at every altar."

The artist asked a young bride the same question. "Love," she replied. "Love builds poverty into riches; sweetens tears; makes much of little. Without it there is no beauty."

A weary soldier said: "Peace is the most beautiful thing in the world. War is the most ugly. Wherever you find peace, you find beauty."

"Faith, Love and Peace! How can I paint them?" thought the artist. Entering his door he saw Faith in the eyes of his children and Love in the eyes of his wife. And there in his home was the Peace that Love and Faith had built. So he painted the picture of the "Most Beautiful Thing in the World." And, when he had finished, he called it "Home."

Honesty. See also **Integrity**

900. The world is so corrupt that a reputation for honesty is acquired by not doing wrong.

—DUC FRANCOIS GASTON DE LÉVIS

901. Socrates, being asked the way to honest fame, said: "Study to be what you wish to seem."

—JOHN BATE

902. It is folly to suppose that there is one code of honesty or ethics for business and another for private life. Honesty is required of all of us at all times if we are to live decently with ourselves.

903. The first step toward greatness is to be honest, says the proverb; but the proverb fails to state the case strong enough. Honesty is not only "the first step toward greatness,"—it is greatness itself.

—CHRISTIAN NEVELL BOVEE

Hope—Hopefulness

904. To travel hopefully is a better thing than to arrive.

—ROBERT LOUIS STEVENSON

905. You can't live on hope, nor can you live without it.

906. Hope is the best part of our riches. What sufficeth it that we have the wealth of the Indies in our pockets, if we have not the hope of heaven in our souls?

—CHRISTIAN NEVELL BOVEE

Host-Guest—Hosts-Guests

907. Visits always give pleasure—if not the arrival, the departure.

—PORTUGUESE PROVERB

908. A hotel isn't like a home, but it's better than being a house guest.

—WILLIAM FEATHER

Human nature

909. Part of human nature resents change, loves equilibrium, while another part welcomes novelty, loves the excitement of disequilibrium. There is no formula for the resolution of this tug-of-war, but it is obvious that absolute surrender to either of them invites disaster.

—J. BARTLET BREBNER

910. People may change their minds as often as their coats, and new sets of rules of conduct may be written every week, but the fact remains that human nature has not changed and does not change, that inherent human beliefs stay the same; the fundamental rules of human conduct continue to hold.

—LAMMOT DU PONT

Humility

911. The flower of sweetest smell is shy and lowly.

—WILLIAM WORDSWORTH

912. Be wise; soar not too high to fall, but stoop to rise.

—PHILIP MASSINGER

913. If a man makes himself a worm he must not complain when he is trodden on.

—IMMANUEL KANT

914. The person with true humility never has to be shown his place; he is always in it.

915. If you are right, take the humble side—you will help the other fellow. If you are wrong, take the humble side—and you will help yourself.

—R. L. ERWIN

916. To be humble to superiors is duty; to equals, is courtesy; to inferiors, is nobleness; and to all, safety; it being a virtue that, for all her lowliness, commandeth those souls it stoops to.

—THOMAS MOORE

144

917.   William Allen White, onetime dean of newspapermen in America, was awarded an honorary degree by Columbia University. At the commencement, a quiet, unassuming man stood next to him in the colorful academic procession. Mr. White turned to this man and said in a friendly manner: "We ought to know each other. I'm a small-town editor from Emporia, Kansas. My name is White." The man replied: "I'm a small-town doctor from Rochester, Minnesota, and my name is Mayo."

918.   Charles F. Kettering was a good example of a man who, though world famous, remained "poor in spirit" all his life. One of the greatest scientific researchers this country has ever known, Kettering kept alive the will to know more by recognizing what he called "his ignorance." When he was graduated from college, he did not frame and mount his diploma. Instead he tore it up. He never wanted to be aware of his lacks, deficiencies and "wants" so that he could learn more.

Humor

919.   A joke isn't old if you haven't heard it.

920.   A philosopher makes something out of nothing—a humorist makes nothing out of everything.

—Arnold H. Glasow

921.   Humor is one of the democratic experiences of mankind. Whatever may be our differences—differences of age, education, experience, religion, politics—the moment we laugh together in appreciating a joke, we are, for that golden moment, united and equal.

—Marius Risley

922.   There is a disappointed expectation at the heart of every joke you laugh at. A joke is a trick played on your mind by the person who tells it. . . . He starts your mind off in the direction of an anticipated meaning, and just before you get there he yanks you back—or maybe lands you in some other meaning miles away. That's what you enjoy in a joke.

—Max Eastman

Humor, Sense of

923. A man without mirth is like a wagon without springs. He is jolted disagreeably by every pebble in the road.

—Henry Ward Beecher

924. A sense of humor is possessed by people who have the ability to be objective about themselves and about life in general. They see life steadily and see it whole. They are the rare folk who realize we must never take ourselves too seriously.

—Aaron N. Meckel

Husband-Wife

925. An archaeologist is the best husband any woman can have: the older she gets, the more interested he is in her.

926. A man's wife may not be the only woman he ever loved, but she's the only woman who ever made him prove it.

927. "My wife and I get along perfectly," boasted a man of the world. "I never find her in, and she never finds me out."

Hypocrisy

928. Hypocrisy lies not in what you say to a person but in what you think of him.

—Frank Rooney

929. There is some virtue in almost every vice except hypocrisy; and even that, while it is a mockery of virtue, is at the same time a compliment to it.

—William Hazlitt

Idea—Ideas

930. Don't entertain ideas—put them to work.

931. The man with a new idea is a crank until the idea succeeds.

—Mark Twain

Ideal—Ideals

932. A large portion of human beings live not so much in themselves as in what they desire to be. They create what is called an ideal character, in an ideal form, whose perfections compensate in some degree for the imperfections of their own.

—Edwin Percy Whipple

933. Keep your ideals high enough to inspire you, but low enough to encourage you.

934. The idealist is incorrigible—if he is turned out of his heaven, he makes an ideal of his hell.

—Friedrich Wilhelm Nietzsche

935. Ideals are like stars—we can see them but we cannot touch them. Destroy a man's idealism and you destroy his civilization.

—Byron B. Gentry

Identification

936. Whenever two people meet there are really six people present. There is each man as he sees himself, each man as the other person sees him, and each man as he really is.

—William James

937. This story is about heaven and how St. Peter keeps a pretty close watch on who knocks at the door. One day a fellow shows up and says his name is Picasso and St. Peter makes him prove it by drawing a picture. Next day Leopold Stokowski arrives and St. Peter requires him to conduct a symphony.

Then Harry Truman arrives and demands admittance and St. Peter explains the procedure.

"You've got to prove who you are," he says. "Even Picasso and Stokowski had to do that."

"Who the hell are Picasso and Stokowski?" says Truman

"Okay," says St. Peter. "You're Harry Truman."

—Jack Guinn

Idiosyncrasy—Idiosyncrasies

938. James Fenimore Cooper could not write unless he was chewing gumdrops, of which he consumed vast quantities as he developed his famous novels.

Robert Browning was unable to sit still when writing, and holes were worn in the carpet at his desk as the result of the constant shuffling of his feet.

Edgar Allan Poe always took his cat to bed with him; the writer was said to be very vain of the small size and shapeliness of his feet.

It is recorded of Thackeray that, every time he passed the house in which he wrote *Vanity Fair,* he lifted his hat; and Hawthorne always washed his hands before sitting down to read a letter from his wife.

A peculiarity of the younger Dumas was that, every time he published a novel, he went out and bought a painting to celebrate the occasion.

Oliver Wendell Holmes was given to carrying a potato in one pocket and a horse chestnut in the other, in the belief that these kept rheumatism away.

Peculiarities of dress in certain authors are remarkable. For instance, Disraeli wore corsets; Dickens had a weakness for flashy jewelry; and Tolstoy liked French perfumes.

Francis Bacon was so fond of fine clothes that he spent his odd time in trying to design new styles and fashions. When he could not persuade anyone to wear them, he got what satisfaction he could by hiring men to don his grotesque creations and thus promenade the streets.

The ruling passion of Peter the Great was to ride about in a wheelbarrow, and many of his state visits to cities and towns over which he ruled were made in this fashion, the monarch being wheeled along in his homely conveyance, pushed by a perspiring manservant.

—ADAPTED FROM CONTACT FROM ELLIS

Idleness

939. As pride is sometimes hid under humility, idleness is often covered by turbulence and hurry.

—DR. SAMUEL JOHONSON

940. The idle man does not know what it is to enjoy rest. Hard work, moreover, not only tends to give us rest for the body, but, what is more important, peace in the mind.

—SIR JOHN LUBBOCK

941. Laziness grows on people; it begins in cobwebs, and ends in iron chains. The more business a man has to do, the more he is able to accomplish; for he learns to economize his time.

—SIR MATTHEW HALE

Ignorance

942. A wise man in the company of those who are ignorant has been compared by the sages to a beautiful girl in the company of blind men.

—SAADI

Imagination

943. The power of imagination makes us infinite.

—JOHN MUIR

944. The artist is driven to submit himself in humility to the discipline of Objective Vision. But the inner vision is not cast out. It remains the organ by which outer vision is controlled, and it takes on structure as the latter is absorbed within it. The interaction is Imagination.

—JOHN DEWEY

149

Imitation

945. Man consists of body, mind, and imagination. His body is faulty, his mind untrustworthy, but his imagination has made him remarkable. In some centuries, his imagination has made life on this planet an intense practice of all the lovelier energies.

—John Masefield

946. Although British Prime Minister Benjamin Disraeli was not widely traveled, he possessed a vivid imagination which compensated for his lack.

One night he was present when a famous explorer was recounting his experiences. The latter was amazed at Disraeli's knowledge of the distant places to which he referred.

"I have traveled extensively and have seen more than I can remember," said the explorer, "but where did you glean your information? Have you traveled a great deal?"

"No, I have traveled very little," said Disraeli, "but I can remember more than I have seen."

Imitation

947. It is better to work badly in one's own style than in that of others. And besides, the more beautiful the model is, the more ridiculous the imitation becomes.

—Georges Bizet

948. To be as good as our fathers, we must be better. Imitation is not discipleship. When someone sent a cracked plate to China to have a set made, every piece in the new set had a crack in it.

—Wendell Phillips

Immortality

949. To destroy the ideas of immortality of the soul, is to add death to death.

—Mme. Adele de Souza

950.   There is only one way to get ready for immortality, and that is to love this life and live it as bravely and faithfully and cheerfully as we can.

—HENRY VAN DYKE

951.   We are born for a higher destiny than that of earth; there is a realm where the rainbow never fades, where the stars will be spread before us like islands that slumber on the ocean, and where the beings that pass before us like shadows will stay in our presence forever.

—EDWARD GEORGE BULWER-LYTTON

952.   Immortality is the complement of mortality, as water becomes steam, and steam becomes power, and power becomes heat, and heat becomes light. The conclusion that life beyond is the conservation of energy of life here may be as scientific as that great natural law for material things.

—WILFRED GRENFELL

953.   A man is immortal for as long as he is remembered, and he is remembered longest for what he gives to the world rather than what he takes from it, for what he creates rather than for what he hoards, and for the way he uses power rather than the power itself. An inveterate playboy is likely to be consigned to oblivion, but a poor man who makes a contribution to mankind will be remembered forever—immortal, successful.

—DR. MORRIS FISHBEIN

Impartiality

954.   I can promise to be sincere, but not to be impartial.

—JOHANN WOLFGANG VON GOETHE

955.   There are only two ways to be quite unprejudiced and impartial. One is to be completely ignorant. The other is to be completely indifferent. Bias and prejudice are attitudes to be kept in hand, not attitudes to be avoided.

—CHARLES P. CURTIS

Imperfection—Imperfections

956. Why is there seldom enough time to do a job right, but always enough time to do it over?

957. All things are literally better, lovelier and more beloved for the imperfections which have been divinely appointed, that the law of human life may be Effort, and the law of human judgment, Mercy.

—JOHN RUSKIN

Impossible, The

958. Folks who claim it can't be done are a dime a doesn't.

959. Few things are impossible in themselves. It is not so much means, as perseverance, that is wanting to bring them to a successful conclusion.

—FRANCOIS DE LA ROCHEFOUCAULD

Inaction

960. Words without actions are the assassins of idealism.

—HERBERT HOOVER

961. To know what is right and not to do it is the worst cowardice.

—CONFUCIUS

962. If you want to get somewhere, you can get behind and push; or you can get ahead and pull; but you can't sit in the middle and do nothing.

963.   What ails America is not the deterioration of "our concept of beauty and decency and morality," but that millions of us are being rendered superfluous and are robbed of our sense of worth and usefulness.... Inaction is the only poison that can corrupt and deprave us.

—Eric Hoffer

Incompleteness

964.   There is nothing so fatal to character as half-finished tasks.

—David Lloyd George

965.   Doing things by halves is worthless. It may be the other half that counts.

Incomprehensibility

966.   The minds of men are full of shadows and reflections of things they cannot grasp.

—Robert M. Hutchins

967.   It is by their ability to die for something incomprehensible to the vast majority that a handful of men have succeeded, over the centuries, in winning the respect of the world.

—Jean Anouilh

Indecision

968.   Indecision in daily living is like a short circuit in a powerful battery; the longer the delay in making repairs, the greater the drain on the power supply.

969.   I wish to preach not the doctrine of ignoble ease but the doctrine of the strenuous life.

Far better it is to dare mighty things, to win glorious triumphs, even though checkered by failure, than to take rank with those poor spirits who neither enjoy much nor suffer much because they live in the gray twilight that knows not victory nor defeat.

—THEODORE ROOSEVELT

970. A mistake is a detour, but that doesn't mean we'll never get back on the main road! The path of progress is pebbled with mistakes someone turns into stepping stones to success. The most important decision a person can make is to resolve not to let the fear of failure prevent him from making a decision. Even failure has its sunny side: It makes us more appreciative of success.

—EVELYN ZEMKE

971. Two boys were skating on an ice floe, when one of them noticed that it was moving slowly away from the shore. With a warning shout he swam in, and, after a desperate struggle, escaped to safety. The other hesitated, watching the widening distance between him and safety as the ice caught the sweep of the tide. With a wild cry he, too, sprang in—but he never reached the shore. One moment of indecision had cost him his life.

Independence

972. Only a strong tree can stand alone.

973. Our dependence outweighs our independence, for we are independent only in our desire, while we are dependent on our health, on nature, on society, on everything in us and outside us.

—HENRI FRÉDÉRIC AMIEL

Inferiority complex

974. An inferiority complex could be a blessing if the right people had it.

154

975. . . . inferiority complex is the origin of . . . museum-making. It was the motive of the Hellenistic tyrants when they collected Greek statues of the good period. . . . When the Renaissance princes collected ancient statues with such passion . . . was it not because they were ashamed of the legacy of the preceding age and had caught from Rome the feeling of an aesthetic inferiority of the present as against the past?

—Germain Bazin

Inflation

976. Today a penny saved isn't worth the money.

977. Money saved for a rainy day buys a much smaller umbrella than it used to.

978. A dollar may not do as much for you as it used to, but you don't do as much for a dollar, either.

979. The best proof that appearances are deceiving is the fact that the dollar looks just the same as it did ten years ago.

Innocence

980. The want of punishment is no proof of innocence.

981. I hear much of people's calling out to punish the guilty, but very few are concerned to clear the innocent.

—Daniel Defoe

Inquisitiveness

982. No man really becomes a fool until he stops asking questions.

—Charles P. Steinmetz

Insurance, Life

983. Every man ought to be inquisitive through every hour of his great adventure down to the day when he shall no longer cast a shadow in the sun. For if he dies without a question in his heart, what excuse is there for his continuance.

—FRANK MOORE COLBY

Insurance, Life

984. With life insurance a man can make his will before he makes his money.

985. Life insurance is not a new liability added—it is rather a new asset created.

986. Life insurance puts the strength of men standing together against the frailty of men standing alone.

987. Life insurance does not mean that men are sentimental about death, but that they are sensible about life.

988. Life insurance guarantees to a man's family when he is dead the very things for which he works to provide them while he lives.

989. Life insurance is the oldest and safest mode of making certain provisions for one's family. It is a strange anomaly that men should be careful to insure their homes, their ships, their merchandise and yet neglect to insure their lives, surely the most important of all to their families and more subject to loss.

—BENJAMIN FRANKLIN

Integrity. See also Honesty

990. The best way to climb high is to remain on the level.

991. The individual who aims deliberately at convincing others that he possesses integrity is foredoomed to failure, because the very attempt to convey such an impression is an almost certain indication that he is in doubt either as to the validity of his own code of ethics or as to his ability to live up to it.

—Robert Tannenbaum, Irving R. Wecshler and Fred Massarik, *Leadership and Organization: A Behavioral Science Approach* (McGraw-Hill)

Intellectuality

992. Bertrand Russell's sharp rejoinder when asked if he considered himself an intellectual: "I have never called myself an intellectual, and nobody has ever dared to call me one in my presence. I think an intellectual may be defined as a person who pretends to have more intellect than he has, and I hope that this definition does not fit me."

—Claude Bissell

993. The association of cleverness with intellectual capacity in the popular mind is false. There is really no connection at all between them. The clever man may be intellectually powerful; and the intellectual may be clever, or he may not. But there is no more reason why a clever man should be an intellectual (or vice versa) than that he should be a fat man, or a baldheaded one. The two are simply not related.

—John O'London

Intention—Intentions

994. The smallest good deed is better than the grandest good intention.

—Gaspard Dughet

995. To be always intending to live a new life, but never to find time to set about it: this is as if a man should put off eating and drinking, and sleeping, from one day and night to another, till he is starved and destroyed.

—JOHN TILLOTSON

Interdependence

996. God has made no one absolute. The rich depend on the poor, as well as the poor on the rich. The world is but a mere magnificent building; all the stones are gradually cemented together. There is no one subsists by himself alone.

—OWEN FELTHAM

997. How beautifully is it ordered, that as many thousands work for one, so must every individual bring his labor to make the whole! The highest is not to despise the lowest, nor the lowest to envy the highest; each must live in all and by all. Who will not work, neither shall he eat. So God has ordered that men, being in need of each other, should learn to love each other, and bear each other's burdens.

—GEORGE AUGUSTUS SALA

Intervention

998. Necessity is the mother of intervention.

999. Those who in Quarrels interpose,
Must often wipe a bloody Nose.

—BENJAMIN FRANKLIN

Invention—Inventions

1000. The greatest invention of the 19th century was the invention of the method of invention.

—ALFRED NORTH WHITEHEAD

1001. Thomas A. Edison, the great inventor, was talking one day with the governor of North Carolina, and the governor complimented him on his inventive genius.

"I am not a great inventor," said Edison. "But you have

over a thousand patents to your credit, haven't you?" queried the governor. "Yes, but about the only invention I can really claim as absolutely original is the phonograph," was the reply. "I guess I'm an awfully good sponge. I absorb ideas from every source I can, and put them to practical use. Then I improve them until they become of some value. The ideas which I use are mostly the ideas of other people who don't develop them themselves."

1002.   Elias Howe spent nearly all his money in experiments before he discovered where the eye of the needle of a sewing-machine should be located. He might have failed altogether if he had not dreamed he was making a sewing-machine for a savage king in a strange country. He dreamed the king gave him twenty-four hours to complete the machine and make it sew, otherwise he was to be put to death. Howe worked and puzzled, and finally gave it up. Then he thought they were leading him to the place where he was to be executed. He noticed that the warriors carried spears which were pierced near the head. Instantly, the inventor saw the solution of the difficulty, and while he was asking for time he awoke. It was four o'clock in the morning. He jumped out of bed, ran to his workshop, and before nine he had modeled a needle with the eye at the point.

Investment—Investments

1003.   In investing money, the amount of interest you want should depend on whether you want to eat well or sleep well.

—J. K. Morley

1004.   A miser buried his gold in a hole in a field and each night went to count and gloat over it. A servant discovered the hoard and absconded with it. The rich miser screamed in despair! Suggested a friend: "You really haven't lost a thing. The money wasn't doing you or anybody else any good. You still have the hole left. Why don't you pretend the gold is still there and go and look at the hole every night?"

Jealousy

1005.   Jealousy, the jaundice of the soul.

—John Dryden

Joint effort

1006. Plain women are always jealous of their husbands; beautiful women never are. They are always so occupied with being jealous of other people's husbands.

—Oscar Wilde

Joint effort

1007. Coming together is a beginning; keeping together is progress; working together is success.

—Henry Ford

Journalism

1008. For those who govern, the first thing required is indifference to newspapers.

—Louis Adolphe Thiers

1009. A journalist is a grumbler, a censurer, a giver of advice, a regent of sovereigns, a tutor of nations. Four honest newspapers are more to be feared than a thousand bayonets.

—Napoleon I

Judge—Judges

1010. A popular judge is a deformed thing, and plaudits are fitter for players than for magistrates.

—Francis Bacon

1011. *A salty old judge's advice to an ambitious young lawyer:* "To be a good judge, you must have inestimable good judgment, a sense of fair play and a darn good bladder."

1012. When a lawyer asked Chief Justice John Marshall's personal advice because he had "reached the acme of judicial distinction," Marshall interrupted: "Let me tell you what that means, young man. The acme of judicial distinction means the ability to look a lawyer straight in the eyes for two hours and not hear a damned word he says."

—ALBERT J. BEVERIDGE, *The Life of*
John Marshall (HOUGHTON MIFFLIN)

Jury—Jurors

1013.   *The Juror's Creed*

I am a JUROR.

I am a seeker after truth.

I must listen carefully and with concentration to all of the evidence.

I must heed and follow the instructions of the Court.

I must respectfully and attentively follow the arguments of the lawyers, dispassionately seeking to find and follow the silver thread of truth through their conflicting assertions.

I must lay aside all bias and prejudice.

I must be led by my intelligence and not by my emotions.

I must respect the opinions of my fellow jurors, as they must respect mine, and in a spirit of tolerance and understanding must endeavor to bring the deliberations of the whole jury to agreement upon a verdict; . . . but

I must never assent to a verdict which violates the instructions of the Court or which finds as a fact that which, under the evidence and in my conscience, I believe to be untrue.

In fine, I must apply the Golden Rule by putting myself impartially in the place of the plaintiff and of the defendant, remembering that although I am a juror today passing upon the rights of others, tomorrow I may be a litigant whose rights other jurors shall pass upon.

My verdict must do justice, for what is just is "true and righteous altogether"; and when my term of jury service is ended, I must leave it with my citizenship unsullied and my conscience clear.

—JOHN H. FLANIGAN

Justice

1014.   Mercy to the criminal may be cruelty to the people.

—ARABIAN NIGHTS

Juvenile delinquency

1015.   Justice is the great interest of man on earth. It is the ligament which holds civilized beings and civilized nations together.

—Daniel Webster

1016.   The robe of justice will not be defiled
Where laws are strict, but magistrates are mild.

—From the Chinese

Juvenile delinquency

1017.   We could blame some of our troubles on the safety razor. It made the razor strop obsolete.

1018.   Juvenile delinquency was unheard of in the good old days because the problem was thrashed out in the woodshed.

1019.   Not only in the United States, but in all countries that are industrialized, there has been a sharp increase in delinquency since World War II. Most countries have special names for these delinquents. In our country they are *Hoods,* in England *Teddy Boys,* in Germany they are called *Halbstarke,* in France *Blousons Noirs,* in Australia and New Zealand *Bodgies,* in Japan *Mambo Boys,* in Russia and Poland *Hooligans,* in Italy *Vitelloni,* and in South Africa the whites are *Ducktails,* the colored are *Skollies,* and the native Africans are *Tsotsies.*

—Robert J. Havighurst

Kindness

1020.   Kindness isn't sacrifice so much as it is being considerate for the feelings of others, sharing happiness, the unselfish thought, the spontaneous and friendly act, forgetfulness of our own present interests.

—Carl Holmes

1021.   Kindness is one of the great secrets of life. It is the power that has transported the feted leader from the crowded streets of mediocrity to renown. It is the music that rises above the grinding agony of hatred, selfishness and jealousy; the sunlight that spreads impartial glory. Kindness is without capacity for criticism.

—Douglas Meador

Knowledge

1022. The key to knowledge is to discover and discard.

1023. Only when we know little do we know anything; doubt grows with knowledge.

—Johann Wolfgang von Goethe

1024. When a man's knowledge is not in order, the more of it he has the greater will be his confusion.

—Herbert Spencer

1025. Knowledge humbles the great man, astonishes the common man, and puffs up the little man.

—Frank E. Butterworth

1026. The world does not pay for what a person knows. It pays for what a person does with what he knows.

—Laurence Lee

1027. Knowledge is the only instrument of production that is not subject to the law of diminishing returns.

1028. It ain't the things we don't know that cause us so much trouble—it's the things we do know that ain't so.

1029. Never try and find out anything, or try to learn anything, till you have found the not knowing it to be a nuisance to you for some time.

Labor Day

Then you will remember it, but not otherwise.

—SAMUEL BUTLER

1030. It is the glorious prerogative of the empire of knowledge that what it gains it never loses. On the contrary, it increases by the multiple of its own power: all its ends become means; all its attainments help to new conquests.

—DANIEL WEBSTER

1031. It is supposed that all knowledge is at the bottom of a well, or the far end of a telescope. . . . As a matter of fact, an intelligent person, looking out of his eyes and hearkening in his ears, with a smile on his face all the time, will get more true education that many another in a life of heroic vigils.

—ROBERT LOUIS STEVENSON

Labor Day

1032. Men who drive their own cars to work every day find it a bit tiring to walk in a Labor Day parade.

1033. We salute the American laboring man on his special day. Our whole economic system depends on the industriousness and reliability of the "laboring man." He is one source of our national pride and strength. But who is our laboring man? We pay our respects to everyone who works, to all working Americans. Our hope for the future lies in the work of all— labor, management, doctors, teachers, housewives, and even children—boys who are up before dawn delivering newspapers, girls with their after-school chores. We salute all Americans who are doing their jobs well.

—ARTHUR H. MOTLEY

1034. Back in 1882, a young New York carpenter, Peter J. Mc-Guire, had an idea. He felt that the working people of America deserved a note of thanks and that a day should be set aside to honor them.

Before a meeting of the Central Labor Union of New York, he made the proposal that the first Monday in September be chosen as the date for the holiday. The idea was enthusiastically acclaimed and put into operation, and on September 5, 1882, in New York City, labor had its day!

Until 1884, Labor Day was a local event in New York, but in October of that year Chicago came into the picture. At the fourth annual convention of the American Federation of Labor held there, the following resolution was proposed and adopted:

Resolved, that the first Monday in September of each year be set apart as a laborer's national holiday, and that we recommend its observance by all wage workers, irrespective of sex, calling or nationality."

During the next few years, labor set out to make the holiday legal. The first state to enact legislation was Oregon, in 1887. By 1894, when Congressional action was taken to make it a national holiday, 23 states were celebrating Labor Day. President Grover Cleveland signed the bill on June 26, 1894. It was official—a national holiday.

1035. Labor Day is not just for those who work with their hands. Perhaps that was its original conception when inaugurated back in 1882, but workers have moved a long way since then. Today it should properly be for all who work, and that takes in a high percentage of adult America.

Coming on a Monday and contributing to a long weekend, Labor Day is more frequently treated as an opportunity for a last fling at summer recreation than as a day for parades and speeches, although in some industial areas those still play an important part.

Perhaps it is the shame of prosperity that workers do make Labor Day more of a holiday for pleasure than a day of dedication to the needs and aims of Labor. For the fact is that there are problems still unsolved which require a great deal of study and thought.

Only those who have been unemployed for a long period of time in depressed areas around the country can fully appreciate what a privilege it is to be able to work. Unwanted idleness is the curse—not the necessity to earn one's living by the sweat of one's brow.

While Labor Day will always be a happy holiday for most of the workers of America, it should also be a day when the rank and file as well as the leaders give sober thought to some of Labor's problems. How can jobs be provided for people everywhere who want the opportunity to do useful work to earn their living? That perhaps is the biggest problem of all, one that will require a great deal of study and a great deal of statesmanship to solve. On Labor Day we should think some about it.

Language

1036. Some people use language to express thought, some to conceal thought and others instead of thought.

1037. It is almost impossible to state what one in fact believes, because it is almost impossible to hold a belief and to define it at the same time.

—CHARLES WILLIAMS

1038. The highest compliment ever paid me came from a GI in the Pacific who wrote that he had read an entire story of mine without having to look up a single word in the dictionary.

—W. SOMERSET MAUGHAM

1039. The native Hawaiian language has no word for "weather." Nature reduced the hazards of Hawaii's weather. The struggle was missing and the natives found the weather problem not worth wasting words upon.

—STANLEY YANKUS

1040. Confucius once was asked what he would do first if he were to administer a country.

"It would certainly be to correct language," he replied.

His listeners were surprised. "Why?" they asked.

The master's answer: "If language is not correct, then what is said is not what is meant; if what is said is not meant, then what ought to be done remains undone; if this remains undone, morals and arts will deteriorate; if morals and arts deteriorate, justice will go astray; if justice goes astray, the people will stand about in helpless confusion. Hence there must be no arbitrariness in what is said. This matters above everything."

1041. An Indian went to see a doctor because he did not seem to have the vim and vigor to which he was accustomed. The doctor could not find anything very much wrong when he examined the Indian and concluded that his stomach might be a little upset.

"Go on home," advised the doctor, "and be careful what you eat. I would say don't eat anything until you get an appetite."

As requested by the doctor, the Indian came back a week later.

"How do you feel now," the doctor asked.

"Fine," replied the Indian. "I wait one day; appetite no come. I wait two days; appetite no come. I wait three days; still appetite no come. By then I get so hungry I eat anyway."

1042.   Of the four major languages, English is the most difficult to learn. Here's why::

"We'll begin with the box, the plural of which is boxes; but the plural of ox is oxen, not oxes.

One fowl is a goose, and two are called geese; but the plural of mouse is never meese.

You may find a lone mouse, or a whole nest of mice but the plural of house is houses, not hice.

If the plural of man is men, why shouldn't the plural of pan be pen?

If I speak of a foot and you show me two feet, or give you a boot, would a pair be called beet?

If one is a tooth and a whole set are teeth, why shouldn't the plural of booth be beeth?

Then, the masculine pronouns are he, his and him; but imagine the feminine as she, shis, and shim!"

—Gretchen Robinson

1043.   Mario Pei, Professor of Romance Philology, Columbia University:

The bulk of our spoken language is made up of one-syllable words; ten commonly used words account for 25 percent of our conversation, and 100 high-frequency words for as much as 75 percent of all small talk. Yet individuality is expressed by uncommon words, and one is as definitely identified by his language as by his fingerprints. We should strive for the special words that will best express our true selves and above all avoid parrot-like repetition of ready-coined words and slogans.

—Review of Wendell Johnson's
Your Most Enchanted Listener
(Harper) in *New York Times Book Review*

Laughter

1044. The freedom of any society varies proportionately with the volume of its laughter.

—Zero Mostel

1045. Laughter is full of optimistic vitamins. It provides oxygen for the soul. It massages the body. It has a cleansing power for the mind. It upgrades morale. It is greatly needed whenever we face dark moments in our lives.

1046. Men show their character in nothing more clearly than in what they think laughable. Laughter is a surface indicator of strength and stability—a just balance of all the faculties of man—the ultimate safeguard against tension and fear—a safety valve to keep sane and relaxed.

—Eugene P. Bertin

Law—Laws

1047. If you have ten thousand regulations you destroy all respect for the law.

—Winston Churchill

1048. No individual has the right to determine what law shall be obeyed and what law shall be enforced.

—Herbert Hoover

1049. Laws cannot make people do good acts; but at least they can prevent them from performing evil ones.

—Arthur Meyer

1050. There are more than two million laws of one kind or another in force in the United States. If a man could familiarize himself with them at the rate of ten each day, he could qualify as a law-abiding citizen in 6,000 years.

1051. In reality, the man who defies or flouts the law is like the proverbial fool who saws away the plank on which he sits, and a disrespect or disregard for law is always the first sign of a disintegrating society. Respect for law is the most fundamental of all social virtues, for the alternative to the rule of law is that of violence and anarchy.

—Arthur Bryant

1052. Law is a great teacher. It does not represent that minimum of morality necessary to hold the community together. It stands rather for such moral truth as the community has discovered that can and should be supported by the authority of the community. The conception of law as coercion, or the command of the sovereign, or the expression of power, or what the courts will do leads to the conclusion that every effort should be made to avoid law and that it is proper to do anything that nobody can compel you to abstain from doing.

—Robert M. Hutchins

Law enforcement

1053. There will be less need for law enforcement when every man lives up to the laws he expects others to obey.

1054. The individual police officer today is, above all, a citizen who has been selected to devote his full time to the enforcement of law. Law enforcement as such is the responsibility of every citizen. The police are the citizen's vehicle for full-time enforcement. They must depend on citizen cooperation and support in order to perform effectively. This is true in any society unalterably opposed to despotism.

Lawyer—Lawyers. See also **Legal profession**

1055. A lawyer without some knowledge of history or literature is a mechanic, a mere working mason; if he possesses some knowledge of these, he may venture to call himself an architect.

—Sir Walter Scott

Leadership

1056. If I were to give you an orange, I'd simply say, "I give you this orange." But when the transaction is entrusted to a lawyer he puts down, "I hereby give and convey to you all and singular, my estate and interests, rights, title, claim and advantages of and in said orange, together with all its rind, juice, pulp, and pits and all rights and advantages with full power to bite, cut, and otherwise eat the same, or give the same away with and without the rind, skin, juice, pulp, or pits, anything herein-before or herein after or in any other deed, or deeds, instruments of whatever nature or kind whatsoever to the contrary in anywise not withstanding."

Then another smart lawyer comes along and takes the orange away from you.

—GERALD F. LIEBERMAN

Leadership

1057. The test of leadership is a refusal to panic.

1058. Great leaders, like diamonds, are products of pressure.

1059. Leadership is the ability to let others have *your* way.

1060. A real leader faces the music even when he doesn't like the tune.

—ARNOLD H. GLASOW

1061. You can't lead anyone else any further than you have gone yourself.

1062. Being elected to office does not make a man a leader, but it obligates him to become one.

—WILLIAM LOERKE

1063. Leadership appears to be the art of getting others to want to do something you are convinced should be done.

—VANCE PACKARD

170

1064. The vitality and force of leadership in a democracy spring from the people's making demands upon that leadership in response to the facts known to them. Without facts, there are no demands. Without demands, there is no leadership.

—FRANK STANTON in *Journalism—Half-Slave and Half-Free*

1065. Leadership is usually thought of as resulting from natural endowments and traits of personality. These may be helpful but they are incidental. The real qualities of leadership are to be found in those who are willing to suffer for the sake of objectives great enough to demand their wholehearted allegiance.

—MARK W. LEE

1066. The definition of leadership in modern times has developed far beyond the concept of authoritarianism or giver of directions. A leader in today's modern society evokes the action from his group—he does not order or demand it. He has faith in people. He believes in them, trusts them, and thus draws out the best in them which will bring the best for the group concerned.

—AGNES M. KINNEY

Learning

1067. Learning is not wisdom any more than cloth is clothes.

1068. We learn gratitude from the ungrateful, generosity from the greedy and courtesy from the ill-mannered.

—ARNOLD H. GLASOW

1069. Learning is the heart of life—the mystical power that turns a word into a sign, a look into a smile, a house into a home, and a people into a civilization.

—EUGENE P. BERTIN

Legal profession. See also **Lawyer—Lawyers**

1070. Such professions as the soldier and the lawyer . . . give ample opportunity for crimes but not much for mere illusions. If you have composed a bad opera you may persuade yourself that it is a good one; if you have carved a bad statue you can think yourself better than Michelangelo. But if you have lost a battle you cannot believe you have won it; if your client is hanged you cannot pretend that you have got him off.

—Lord Chesterfield

1071. If a man has no great acquisitiveness but wants to live comfortably, have children, educate them and make some provision for his widow; has no definite artistic or literary flair; is not facile in mathematics or things scientific but has an interest in the intellectual, and perhaps particularly in argument, analysis and logical presentation, orally or in writing; wants to be free to take a position on public questions and to play a part in the affairs of the community in which he lives and, perhaps above all, has confidence in his physical and mental ability to work hard enough and do enough good work to survive in keen competition—then the law seems to offer him the best chance for happiness.

—Harrison Tweed at dedication
of new University of Chicago
Law School Building, October 8, 1959

Legislation

1072. Bad laws are the worst sort of tyranny.

—Edmund Burke

1073. The way of the world is to make laws, but follow customs.

—Michel E. de Montaigne

Leisure

1074. Leisure is most enjoyable when there is plenty of hard work both before and after it.

1075. Idleness and the incapacity for leisure correspond with one another; leisure is the contrary of both. Leisure is only possible to a man who is at one with himself and also at one with the world. These are the presuppositions of leisure, for leisure is an affirmation. Idleness, on the other hand, is rooted in the omission of these two affirmations.

—John Piper

Liberty

1076. Liberty is a natural right only for those who are willing to bear its natural responsibility.

—WHEELER McMILLEN, *Possums, Politicians and People*

1077. True liberty consists not merely in being free *from* something, but also in being free *for* something.

—DR. RALPH W. SOCKMAN

1078. The Spirit of Liberty is the spirit which is not too sure that it is right; the Spirit of Liberty is the spirit which seeks to understand the minds of other men and women; the Spirit of Liberty remembers that not even a sparrow falls to earth unheeded; the Spirit of Liberty is the spirit of Him, who nearly 2000 years ago, taught mankind that lesson it has never learned, but has never quite forgotten: That there may be a kingdom where the least shall be heard and considered side by side with the greatest.

—LEARNED HAND

Library—Libraries

1079. Knowledge is power and libraries are its filling station.

1080. A librarian is a shepherd. He acquires books; he comes to know them; then tends, lends, and mends them.

—HARRY C. BAUER

1081. The library stands as the only ameliorating force amidst science, government and industry that can tie down the growing fund of knowledge. All these giants go off in their own directions. The library is the one force that can bring them together and coordinate the efforts of each institution and organization so that all may benefit.

—EMERSON GREENAWAY

1082. No one person can live long enough, or under circumstances varied enough, to experience personally all the successes and failures

Life

which develop wisdom. That is why we need and have books and libraries. Through them everyone has an opportunity to share in the wisdom developed from the experiences of many different persons under the widest variety of circumstances.

Life

1083.   Life is not so much a cup to be drained, as a measure to be filled.

1084.   Learn as if you were to live forever; live as if you were to die tomorrow.

1085.   Life is never fair ... And perhaps it is a good thing for most of us that it is not.
—Oscar Wilde

1086.   Our two chief problems are the high cost of living and the cheapness of human life.

1087.   Life is not complex. We are complex. Life is simple and the simple thing is the right thing.
Oscar Wilde

1088.   We have too many people who live without working, and we have altogether too many who work without living.
—Charles R. Brown

1089.   Live each day as though it were your first. Refuse to identify yourself with the failures of yesterday.

1090.   The purpose of life is not to be happy—but to *matter*, to be productive, to be useful, to have it make some difference that you lived at all.
—Leo Rosten in *The Free Mind*

1091. We are here just for a spell and then pass on. So get a few laughs and do the best you can. Live your life so that whenever you lose, you are ahead.

—WILL ROGERS

1092. Life is easier to take than you'd think; all that is necessary is to accept the impossible, do without the indispensable and bear the intolerable.

—KATHLEEN NORRIS

1093. While there is no certainty to life, yet to live well one must plan as if there were. When the unexpected happens, whether for good or ill, the big test is the ability to adjust to the change.

1094. The object of living is work, experience, happiness. There is joy in work. All that money can do is buy us someone else's work in exchange for our own. There is no happiness except in the realization that we have accomplished something.

—HENRY FORD

1095. Life is currently described in one of four ways: as a journey, as a battle, as a pilgrimage, and as a race. Select your own metaphor, but the finishing necessity is all the same. For if life is a journey, it must be completed. If life is a battle, it must be finished. If life is a pilgrimage, it must be concluded. And if life is a race, it must be won.

—DR. J. RICHARD SNEED

1096. Life is a bank; we open an account at the moment of our birth. The bank is scrupulously just; it pays us interest on all our savings, but it knows no false generosity. It never sends us a false statement; it never permits us to overdraw our account.

1097. Stated in the simplest terms, science is but a sense of curiosity about life, religion is a sense of reverence for life, literature is a sense of wonder at life, art is a taste for life, while philosophy is an attitude toward life, based on a greater or lesser, but always limited, comprehension of the universe as far as we happen to know it.

—LIN YUTANG

1098. Our life is not a book with old age its last chapter. Rather it is a series of short stories—each with its own adventures and consummations. Struggle and rest are phases of our lives at every stage. One kind of struggle is always ending, perhaps, but another is beginning; the same is true of intellectual and spiritual growth, of practical and artistic achievement.

—GEORGE LAWTON

1099. Why you are born and why you are living depend entirely on what you are getting out of this world and what you are giving to it. I cannot prove that this is a balance of mathematical perfection, but my own observation of life leads me to the conclusion that there is a very real relationship, both quantitatively and qualitatively, between what you contribute and what you get out of this world.

—OSCAR HAMMERSTEIN II

1100. Life is like a road—a road that is always going around corners. When we are young, we expect to find something new and delightful around every turn.

But the road gets harder as we get farther along, and there are often rocks in the path, and unpleasant surprises meet us when we turn corners.

And it isn't always easy to be kind and honest, and keep a cheerful face. Lines come, and wrinkles. But if the lines come from being sorry for others, and the wrinkles from laughing at ourselves, then they are kind lines and happy wrinkles, and there is no need of trying to hide them with paint and powder.

1101. We win half the battle when we make up our minds to take the world as we find it, including the thorns. The world is made up of things which are not perfect and of people who are not motivated by the highest ideals. Only frustration haunts those who think there is some quick way to change all this. To make material conditions better for all people is a long, hard struggle; and to make people better is an even longer one. When we recognize this and try to live constructive, purposeful lives ourselves, we are contributing our small share toward the improvement we all want.

—Orison S. Marden

Life insurance. See **Insurance, Life**

Listening

1102.   Nobody ever listened himself out of a job.

—Calvin Coolidge

1103.   To listen well is a great accomplishment. No one shows his ignorance quicker than the man who persists in talking without saying anything. If you have something to say—say it. If you have nothing to say—listen.

—George Matthew Adams

Literature

1104.   In literature, as in conduct, you can never hope to do exactly right. All you can do is to make as sure as possible.

—Robert Louis Stevenson

1105.   The most influential books, and the truest in their influence, are works of fiction. They do not pin the reader to a dogma, which he must afterwards discover to be inexact; they do not teach him a lesson, which he must afterwards unlearn. They repeat, they rearrange, they clarify the lessons of life; they disengage us from ourselves, they constrain us to the acquaintance of others; and they show us the web of experience, not as we can see it for ourselves, but with a singular change—that monstrous, consuming ego of ours being, for the nonce, struck out.

—Robert Louis Stevenson

Litigation

1106. "Mine" and "Thine" is the source of most lawsuits.

—OLD PROVERB

1107. Litigants in a lawsuit are like two men ducking their heads in a bucket and daring each other to remain longer under water.

1108. Discourage litigation. Persuade your neighbor to compromise whenever you can. As a peacemaker the lawyer has a superior opportunity of being a good man. There will still be business enough.

—ABRAHAM LINCOLN

Little things

1109. The least movement is of importance to all nature. The entire ocean is affected by a pebble.

—BLAISE PASCAL

1110. A speck cuts the value of a diamond in half—a race horse that can run a mile a few seconds faster than any other is worth twice as much. That little extra all through life proves to be the greatest value.

—JOHN D. HESS

1111. Sometimes when I consider what tremendous consequences come from little things—a chance word, a tap on the shoulder, or a penny dropped on a newsstand—I am tempted to think, there are no little things.

—BRUCE BARTON

1112. One of the things all of us need to learn in this rushing age is to enjoy the little things more. Most big things are made out of a combination of little things, so naturally, if we enjoy the part intensely, we cannot help enjoying the whole.

—THOMAS DREIER

Living, High cost of

1113. Two can live as cheaply as one when the two are Mom and Pop and the one is a daughter in college.

1114. These days every time one is about to make both ends meet, something breaks in the middle.

1115. The one thing that keeps many people from going into the stock market is the super market.

Loneliness

1116. People are often lonely because they build walls instead of bridges.

1117. Loneliness is a universal experience and it comes to all of us. We all need something in the bank for these times. Specialists in aging tell us that an interest other than one's self that can be pursued throughout life, wherever one is, is one of the greatest protections against unhappiness in old age.

—ANTHONY DEL VECCHIO

1118. Loneliness generally means movement away from people. If the direction can be changed and the lonely one begin to perform some service in behalf of others who are needy, he soon finds his own ache relieved even in the act of relieving the ache others have.

—GORDON JACKSON

1119. Loneliness is a state of mind. If men will not use their minds for thinking, nature steps in and fills the vacuum with that woeful feeling we call loneliness. It is a poor bargain, as many have discovered to their great benefit. Forced back upon their own resources, faced by the prospect of a long spell of the blues, they have in a kind of desperation started thinking along some sensible and and profitable line. Thereupon their loneliness has vanished like the morning mist.

1120. It is not the absence or presence of other human beings which produces loneliness or curses it. It is the emptiness or fullness of the mind which makes the difference. Some people find their most lonesome moments in the hurry and confusion of the market place, or the chatter of a social gathering, and their richest, finest experience in the remoteness of the hill or mountain top or the seclusion of the woods with the nearest human being miles away. It is such as these who do not know how to be lonely when alone.

Longevity

1121. Life, if well used, is long enough.

—Seneca

1122. But that is the object of long living, that man should cease to care about life.

—Robert Louis Stevenson

1123. The real reason women live longer than men is that they know how to accept illness with equanimity, whereas a man fights illness and makes himself worse by refusing to come to terms with his health. To women, illness is a fact; to men, a threat.

Long-windedness

1124. One of the most important ingredients in a recipe for speechmaking is plenty of shortening.

1125. Sleep...has been compared to death and it has also been called the great restorer.... It is also the audience reaction which tells the wise speaker when to stop.

—Dr. William W. Bauer

1126. When General B. F. Butler was in Congress, he rose in his place and insinuated that the member who was occupying the floor was transgressing the limit of debate. "Why, General," said the member in respectful tones, "you divided your time with me." "I know I did," rejoined the general, "but I did not divide eternity with you."

—JOHN DE MORGAN

Loss—Losses

1127. Prefer a loss to a dishonest gain. The one brings pain at the moment, the other for all time to come.

1128. Loss, every loss the mind of man can conceive of, creates a vacuum into which will come (if allowed) something new and fresh and beautiful, something unforeseen—and the greatest of these is love. . . . Loss, by itself, is not tragic. What is tragic is the failure to grasp the opportunity which loss presents.

—From ROBERT FROST's *'Directive'*
and the Spiritual Journey,
Copyright 1963 by Robert K.
Greenleaf. Privately printed.

Love

1129. There is no remedy for love but to love more.

—HENRY DAVID THOREAU

1130. It is not the perfect but the imperfect who have need of love.

—OSCAR WILDE

1131. The crucial test of love is to be able to give without counting the cost.

1132. Like the measles, love is most dangerous when it comes late in life.

—LORD BYRON

1133. Love is the history of a woman's life, but only an episode in a man's.

—Madame de Staël

1134. Love does not consist in gazing at each other, but in looking outward together in the same direction.

—Antoine de Saint-Exupéry

1135. Someone has written that love makes people believe in immortality because there seems not to be room enough in life for so great a tenderness.

—Robert Louis Stevenson

1136. Love is the by-product of our capacity to give what is deepest within ourselves and to receive what is deepest within another person, whether that person be of our own sex or the other.

—Lloyd J. Averill

1137. If you wish to witness the greatest of all miracles—the operation in your own life of the great law that governs human nature—just use the formula of *love*. This formula is the most effective means of attaining perfect tranquility—the basis of health, happiness and longevity.

—Walter M. Germain

1138. It is difficult to define love. All that we can say of it is, that in the soul it is a passion for reigning; in minds it is a sympathy; and in the body it is nothing but a latent and delicate desire to possess the loved object, after a good deal of mystery.

—Francois de La Rochefoucauld

1139. Love is of two kinds, the selective earthly love, which is given to what is delightful, beautiful or good, and the impartial heavenly love, which is given to all indifferently. The earthly love is balanced by an opposing hatred: to friends are opposed foes; to saints, sinners; to God, the Devil. But the heavenly love does not demand that its object shall be delightful, beautiful or good. . . . It is merely compassion for it does not merely wish to relieve misfortune, but find joy in what it loves . . . it is contemplative as well as active . . . and it is a kind of love to which there is no opposing hatred.

—BERTRAND RUSSELL

Loyalty

1140. Our main reliance for security from domestic subversion lies in the willing, informed and participating loyalty of American citizens. Loyalty is many faceted, but at its core is voluntary personal identification with other persons in a living community whose traditions are understood and believed, whose present purposes are shared and promoted and whose objectives inspire the cooperation of all.

1141. Asked the secret of the success of the greatest industrial and commercial business organization of the nineteenth century, its founder, John D. Rockefeller, told me: "We gathered together round one table the ablest brains we could find in the country and we hid nothing from one another. We each gave the business our undivided attention and loyalty." Without loyalty nothing can be accomplished in any sphere. The person who renders loyal service in a humble capacity will be chosen for higher responsibilities, just as the Biblical servant who multiplied the one pound given him by his master was made ruler over ten cities, whereas the servant who did not put his pound to use lost that which he had.

—B. C. FORBES

Luck

1142. Luck is always against the man who depends on it.

1143. *Friday is Not Unlucky*
Friday, February 22, 1732, George Washington was born.
Bismarck, Gladstone, and Disraeli were born on Friday.
Friday, March 25, 1609, the Hudson river was discovered.

183

Machine age

Friday, June 30, 1461, Louis XI, humbled the French nobles.

Friday, June 13, 1492, Columbus discovered the continent of America.

Friday, December 22, 1620, the Pilgrims made the final landing at Plymouth Rock.

Friday, June 13, 1785, General Winfield Scott was born in Dinwiddie County, Virginia.

Friday, June 10, 1834, Spurgeon, the celebrated English preacher, was born.

Friday, November 20, 1721, the first Masonic lodge was organized in North America.

Thomas Sutton, who saved England from the Spanish Armada, was born on Friday.

Friday, January 12, 1433, Charles the Bold, of Burgundy, was born, the richest sovereign of Europe.

Friday, November 28, 1814, the first newspaper ever printed by steam, the London *Times*, was printed.

Friday, June 12, 1802, Alexander von Humboldt, in climbing Chimborazo, reached an altitude of 19,200 feet.

Friday, September 7, 1465, Menéndez founded St. Augustine, the oldest town in the United States by more than forty years.

Friday, April 8, 1646, the first known newspaper advertisement was published in *The Imperial Intelligencer*, in England.

Friday, May 14, 1586, Gabriel Fahrenheit, usually regarded as the inventor of the common mercurial thermometer, was born.

Fiday, March 5, 1496, Henry VIII of England, gave to John Cabot his commission, which led to the discovery of North America. This is the first American state paper in England.

Friday, July 7, 1776, the motion was made in congress by John Adams, and seconded by Richard Henry Lee, that the United States colonies were, and of right ought to be, free and independent.

Friday, March 20, 1738, Pope Clement XII, promulgated his bull of excommunication against the Freemasons. Ever since the allocution excommunicating indiscriminately all Freemasons the order has received an immense impetus in Italy, France and Spain.

Machine age

1144.   Without doubt machines will be able to determine the means and avenues to goals, but men will continue to set the goals themselves.

For what machine can ever apply the considerations of compassion and justice which, as man's enlightenment spreads and his awareness of brotherhood awakens, will enter ever more often into the decisions that affect his future in the world...in the universe?"

—Lewis L. Strauss

Malice

1145. Malice will always find bad motives for good actions.

—Thomas Jefferson: Letter to James Madison, 1810

Man—Men

1146. Men are cruel, but Man is kind.

—Rabindranath Tagore

1147. Man is a book telling the world about its Author.

1148. Man does not live by bread alone, but by beauty and harmony, truth and goodness, work and recreation, affection and friendship, aspiration and worship.

Man—Woman—Men—Women

1149. A woman's chief asset is man's imagination.

1150. It is because of men that women dislike one another.

—Jean de La Bruyère

1151. When men have a way with women it's seldom their own.

1152. A man will tell you where to go—a woman will lead you there.

185

Management

1153. One thing men can't understand about women is how women understand so much about men.

1154. The difference between a man and a woman is a man looks forward and a woman remembers.

1155. Without a woman man is lost; without a man woman is lost. Together many are still miles apart.

B. P. SPONG

1156. There are more men than women in mental hospitals, which just goes to show who's driving who crazy.

1157. Every man needs two women in his life—a secretary to take everything down, and a wife to pick everything up.

1158. A man keeps another's secret better than he does his own. A woman, on the other hand, keeps her own better than another's.

—JEAN DE LA BRUYÈRE

1159. It is all right for men to preach the dominance of the male over the female as long as they don't try to practice what they preach.

Management

1160. Management is the ability to get things done through others.

1161. Good management consists in showing average people how to do the work of superior people.

—JOHN D. ROCKEFELLER

1162. It is easy for an executive to do other people's work. When he does he's neglecting his own job—managing.

Manners

1163. Good manners are thoughts filled with kindness and refinement, and then translated into behavior.

1164. The great secret, Eliza, is not having bad manners or good manners or any other particular sort of manners, but having the same manners for all human souls; in short, behaving as if you were in Heaven, where there are no third-class carriages, and one soul is as good as another.
—GEORGE BERNARD SHAW

Marriage

1165. The only thing perfect mates come in is shoes and gloves.

1166. Marriage is three parts love and seven parts forgiveness of sins.
—LANGDON MITCHELL

1167. One should not marry to find happiness, but to share happiness.

1168. A marriage is happy when the couple are as deeply in love as they are in debt.

1169. It is not marriage that fails; it is people that fail. All that marriage does is to show people up.
—HARRY EMERSON FOSDICK

1170. Those contempating marriage will do well to remember that in "wedding" the "we" comes before the "I".

1171. A certain divorce judge gave this advice to newly married couples: "A good marriage is like a good handshake—there's no upper hand."

Married life

1172. A man taking a wife, is either adding another mile-stone toward his eventual success, or another millstone toward his ultimate defeat.

1173. It is a mistake for a taciturn, serious-minded woman to marry a jovial man, but not for a serious-minded man to marry a light-hearted woman.

—Johann Wolfgang von Goethe

1174. Small men marry to add a pretty woman to their intimate possessions. Great men marry in order to found a home in partnership with a woman who is or whom they can help to become a homemaker.

—Jenny Lee

1175. If Americans can be divorced for "incompatibility," I cannot conceive why they are not all divorced. I have known many happy marriages, but never a compatible one. The whole aim of marriage is to fight through and survive the instant when incompatibility becomes unquestionable.

—G. K. Chesterton

1176. Marriage is one long conversation, chequered by disputes. The disputes are valueless; they but ingrain the difference; the heroic heart of woman prompting her at once to nail her colors to the mast.

But in the intervals, almost unconsciously and with no desire to shine, the whole material of life is turned over and over, ideas are struck out and shared, the two persons more and more adapt their notions one to suit the other, and in process of time, without sound of trumpet, they conduct each other into new worlds of thought.

—Rovert Louis Stevenson

Married life

1177. A man is in general better pleased when he has a good dinner on his table than when his wife talks Greek.

—Dr. Samuel Johnson

1178. The sum which two married people owe to one another defies calculation. It is an infinite debt, which can only be discharged through all eternity.

—JOHANN WOLFGANG VON GOETHE

Maturity

1179. To live with fear and not be afraid is the final test of maturity.

—EDWARD WEEKS

1180. One indication of personal maturity is a man's readiness to accept other people as they are, and not to allow himself to be irritated or offended by them.

—ALVIN H. GOESER

1181. The process of growing up is largely unlearning psychological subservience to authority and replacing it with rational acceptance of authority.

—DON ROBINSON

1182. This is maturity: To be able to stick with a job until it is finished; to be able to bear an injustice without wanting to get even; to be able to carry money without spending it; and to do one's duty without being supervised.

Medical profession

1183. Whenever a doctor can do no good, he must be kept from doing harm.

—HIPPOCRATES

1184. Medicine is the only profession that labors incessantly to destroy the reason for its existence.

—JAMES BRYCE

Meeting—Meetings

1185. The trouble with so many club meetings: They open at 7:30 sharp and close at ten o'clock dull.

Memorial Day

1186. In a larger sense this day is not a memorial to war. It is a memorial to lives bruised and broken by war, lives animated and sustained by a living sense of social responsibility and a generous willingness to spend and be spent in a common cause.

—GLENN FRANK

1187. Memorial Day is not a time for mourning, but a day for remembering and honoring the valiant dead who have fought the good fight and passed on before us to the quiet calm of "green pastures."

In 1868, General John A. Logan, Commander-in-Chief of the Grand Army of the Republic, issued an order setting aside May 30th in the United States for the purpose of strewing flowers on the graves of the soldiers, and for such exercises as local posts might direct. It became commonly known as "Decoration Day."

Previous to this, however, the observance had already been adopted in honor of the men in gray of the Southern states, so credit for this beautiful courtesy belongs to women of the South. Owing to the earlier appearance of flowers in the South, they had set dates previous to May 30th.

—JOHN RANDOLPH STIDMAN

Mental health

1188. Anguish of mind has driven thousands to suicide; anguish of body, none. This proves that the health of the mind is of far more consequence to our happiness than the health of the body, although both are deserving of much more than either of them receives.

—CHARLES C. COLTON

1189. Let us define mental health as the adjustment of human beings to the world and to each other with a maximum of effectiveness and happiness, not just efficiency, or just contentment—or the grace of obeying the rules of the game cheerfully. It is all of them together. It is the ability to maintain an even tongue, an alert intelligence, socially considerate behavior, and a happy disposition.

—Dr. Karl Menninger (1930)

Mind, Change of

1190. Changing your mind is sometimes better than changing your job.

1191. It shows a mature mind to be able to say, "Last year I thought thus and so, but now I've changed my mind," or "I know I was wrong, and I admit it." Why hold on to something that no longer means anything? It's much better to be able to adapt at the right moment. "The bamboo which bends is stronger than the oak which resists."

—Brooke Astor

Mind, Peace of

1192. If you are robbed, remind yourself that your peace of mind is of more value and importance than the thing which has been stolen from you.

—Epictetus

Misfortune—Misfortunes

1193. There are no misfortunes, only ill health and death. Everything else is just events.

—Jean Monnet

1194. Mishaps are like knives, that either serve us or cut us, as we grasp them by the blade or handle.

—James Russell Lowell

Mistake—Mistakes

1195. All some of us learn from our mistakes is to blame them on others.

191

Modern age

1196. It is the highest form of self-respect to admit mistakes, and make amends for them.

1197. Let's learn from the mistakes of others. We can't live long enough to make them all ourselves.

1198. A man must be big enough to admit his mistakes, smart enough to profit from them, and strong enough to correct them.

1199. Ten mistakes to avoid: Remorse over yesterday's failure. Anxiety over today's problem. Worry over tomorrow's uncertainty. Waste of the moment's opportunity. Procrastination with one's present duty. Resentment of another's success. Criticism of a neighbor's imperfection. Impatience with youth's immaturity. Skepticism of our nation's future. Unbelief in God's providence.

Modern age

1200. Because his wife is of such a delicate nature, a man avoids using certain . . . words all through his married life, and then one day he picks up a best-seller she is reading and finds five of the words in the first chapter.

—WILLIAM FEATHER

Modesty

1201. Teach thy tongue to say, "I do not know."

—*The Talmud*

1202. Modesty is a jewel, but one may wear too much jewelry.

Money

1203. There are not three ways of getting money: there are but two: to earn and steal.

—ROBERT LOUIS STEVENSON

1204. If you want to know what God thinks about money, take a look at some of the people he gives it to.

1205. The value of money is that with it we can tell any man to go to the devil. It is the sixth sense which enables you to enjoy the other five.

—W. Somerset Maugham

1206. There is one pleasure which money can buy that is a continuous satisfaction. The man with money can grow nostalgic for the days when he was poor. It is a subtle vice; it combines arrogance with humility.

—Aubrey Menen

1207. Money will buy a bed, but not sleep; books, but not brains; food, but not appetite; finery, but not beauty; a house, but not a home; medicine, but not health; luxuries, but not culture; amusements, but not happiness; religion, but not salvation.

1208. Money is the most important thing in the world. It represents health, strength, honor, generosity, and beauty as conspicously as the want of it represents illness, weakness, disgrace, meanness and ugliness. Not the least of its virtues is that it destroys base people as certainly as it fortifies and dignifies noble people.

—George Bernard Shaw

1209. We often make the mistake of believing that money is wealth. Of course it is only the symbol of work done, services rendered, value received. It is not meant to be used as power over others, not to be hoarded, stolen, or squandered. It is stamped *In God We Trust,* but many have mentally inserted an "L" in the word God, making it read "In Gold We Trust." Our personal standard has sometimes been the Gold Standard; a much finer one is the Golden Rule.

—Edgar White Burrill

1210. Henry Ford was accustomed to spending millions in his automobile business, but he spent practically nothing for his own personal use.

In the morning, when he went to work, he never took money with him. Knowing this, his secretary would have an envelope containing $200 waiting for him when he arrived at his office. Ford would put it in his pocket and then forget all about it.

At night, when he emptied his pockets before going to bed, he would come upon the envelope, still unopened, and toss it into a drawer.

After his death, several drawers filled with these envelopes were found.

Monument—Monuments

1211. The marble keeps merely a cold and sad memory of a man who would else be forgotten. No man who needs a monument ever ought to have one.

—Nathaniel Hawthorne

Moral power

1212. We are told that there are two kinds of people in the world; the good and the bad. The good decide which is which.

1213. Economic and military power can be developed under the spur of laws and appropriations. But moral power does not derive from any act of Congress. It depends on the relations of a people to their God. It is the churches to which we must look to develop the resources for the great moral offensive that is required to make human rights secure, and to win a just and lasting peace.

—John Foster Dulles

Motherhood

1214. Mighty is the force of motherhood. It transforms all things by its vital heat; it turns timidity into fierce courage and dreadless defiance into tremulous submission; it turns thoughtlessness into foresight and yet stills all anxiety into calm content; it makes selfishness become self-denial and gives even to hard vanity the glance of admiring love.

—George Eliot

1215. Some years ago a mother was carrying her baby over the hills of South Wales. But she never reached her destination alive. A blizzard overtook her and a search party later found her frozen beneath the snow.

The searchers were surprised that she did not have outer garments on but soon discovered why. She had wrapped them around her baby. When they unwrapped the child they found baby David Lloyd George alive and well.

David Lloyd George grew up to become the prime minister of Great Britain during World War I and one of England's great statesmen. The vital contribution which he made to humanity was possible because his mother had given her life to save him.

—B. Charles Hostetter

Mourning

1216. They truly mourn who mourn without a witness.

—Lord Byron

1217. Excess of grief for the deceased is madness; for it is an injury to the living, and the dead know it not.

—Xenophon

Music

1218. Music is only useful if it is good music, whether light or serious. Unless it provides one with some vital experience which no other art can convey, it is not only useless but a nuisance.

—Constance Lambert

1219. Music is queer. Its power seems unrelated to the other affections of man, so that a person who is elsewhere perfectly commonplace may have for it an extreme and delicate sensitiveness.

—W. Somerset Maugham

1220. Music is both an art and a discipline. It is an art of tone which inspires men to lofty heights of thinking, feeling, and aspiration.

Music appreciation

It is a discipline which demands rigorous learning and practice from anyone who would understand it and perform it. There is both the art and a craft.

—ALICE M. SNYDER

1221. One evening Sir Arthur Sullivan, the famous English musician, and a friend were to visit at a home which was one of a row of houses that were similar in outward appearance. They had forgotten the number of the house and were therefore uncertain which one to approach, although both had been there before. Sir Arthur walked up to one house and scraped his foot on the footscraper. He shook his head, repeated the performance at the second house, and then went up to the third house. When he scraped his foot there his face lighted up. "This is the place," he said, "the scraper gives off E flat." His view of even such a commonplace matter as a footscraper was musical.

Music appreciation

1222. When Toscanini, the great musical director, made his debut in New York, he made an unusual request. He asked that the programs be printed upon silk so that the beauty of his music would not be lost in the rustle of paper.

1223. When a very throaty tenor finished his song in a talent contest, there was only a smattering of applause, but one man in the audience kept repeating to himself in a scarcely audible voice, "Extraordinary! Wonderful! Unbelievable!"

"Pardon me, sir," said a puzzled man sitting in the next seat to him. "I know a little something about music and take my word for it that fellow cannot sing. I don't see how you can sit there and say his voice was extraordinary and wonderful."

"Not his voice," explained the first man, "but his nerve—his colossal nerve."

Name—Names

1224. Painted on the many yachts moored in a Florida port are the usual romantic names—Sea Sprite, Moonbeam, Wanderer, etc. However, the one that catches everyone's eye is a small, neat craft named simply: $18,500.

1225. It is estimated that more than half the people of the civilized world have names originating in the *Bible*. There are 3,017 men referred to by name in the Holy Book, while only 181 women are mentioned by name.

1226. It may be surprising to some to learn that Jones is not the most popular family name in the United States. In frequency of occurrence, Smith leads as the predominant family name, followed by Johnson, Brown, Williams, Jones, Miller, Davis, Anderson, Wilson and Moore.

1227. A name is made up of little things, the host of little things you do during the course of your days. It is made up of being pleasant and smiling to whomever you talk. It is made up of little promises kept to the letter. It is made up of efficiency in your business. It is made up of faithfulness, loyalty, honesty. In short, a name is the blueprint of the thing we call character.

Nationalism

1228. It is peculiar that national zealots are not even natives of the countries they allegedly wish to glorify: Alexander was not a Greek, Napoleon not a Frenchman, Hitler not a German, and Stalin not a Russian.

—Dagobert D. Runes

1229. Nationalism is a state of mind in which we give our paramount political loyalty to one fraction of the human race—to the particular tribe of which we happen to be tribesmen. In so far as we are captured by this ideology, we hold that the highest political good for us is our own nation's sovereign independence; that our nation has a moral right to exercise its sovereignty according to what it believes to be its own national interests, whatever consequences this may entail for the foreign majority of the human race; and that our duty, as citizens of our country, is to support our country, right or wrong.

—Arnold J. Toynbee

Nationality

1230. There is a great difference between nationality and race. Nationality is the miracle of political independence. Race is the principle of physical analogy.

—BENJAMIN DISRAELI

1231. A man was filling in a government form. "Nationality—you're French, aren't you?" said the official. "No, English. Both my father and mother are English." "But you were born in France?" "What's that got to do with it? If your dog had puppies in a stable, you wouldn't call them horses."

Nature

1232. A thing in Nature becomes much lovelier if it reminds us of a thing in Art, but a thing in Art gains no real beauty through reminding us of a thing in Nature.

—OSCAR WILDE

1233. Men have learned that there is only one source of their knowledge, which is nature, however much they may differ in their interpretation of nature's facts.

—LOUIS AGASSIZ

Necessity—Necessities

1234. Necessity poisons wounds which it cannot heal.

—LUC DE CLAPIERS VAUVENARGUES

1235. We do not need more national development, we need more spiritual development. We do not need more intellectual power. We do not need more knowledge, we need more character. We do not need more law, we need more religion. We do not need more of the things that are seen, we need more of the things that are unseen.

—CALVIN COOLIDGE

1236. Some years back, when Bruce Barton earned his living largely with his pen, he gave a talk before an evening class in writing. During the question period which followed, one of the students boldly asked, "Mr. Barton, where do you get the inspiration for your magazine articles?" The whole class awaited the answer eagerly. Now they would learn the writer's secret source of inspiration.

"Well," said Mr. Barton, "picture me sitting at breakfast in the morning. As I sip my coffee, my wife across the table glances down at the floor and observes, 'Bruce, we really need a new dining room rug. This one is wearing through.' Right there and then I have the inspiration to write another article."

The students were much disappointed in this answer, little realizing that they had been let in on the great secret of inspiration in nearly every field of human activity—*necessity.*

Negative approach

1237. When upon a trial a man calls witnesses to his character, and those witnesses only say, that they never heard, nor do not know anything ill of him, it intimates at best a neutral and insignificant character.

—Lord Chesterfield

1238. A man will please more on the whole by negative qualities than by positive; by never offending, than by giving a great deal of delight. In the first place, men hate more steadily than they love; and if I have said something to hurt a man once, I shall not get the better of this by saying many things to please him.

Negro—Negroes

1239. The Negro in his original native state was an honest race; it was slavery that unmanned him in this respect.

—Booker T. Washington

1240. Let the young colored man feel that he can be not only a waiter in hotels but part proprietor, that on Pullman cars he can be not only porter but conductor, and he will go forward.

—Booker T. Washington

1241. It takes one hundred per cent of Caucasian blood to make a white American. The minute it is proven that a man possesses one one-hundredth part of Negro blood in his veins, it makes him a black man. He falls to our side; we claim him. The ninety-nine per cent of white blood counts for nothing when weighed against one per cent of Negro blood.

—Booker T. Washington

1242. It has been said that the whites will absorb the blacks, and thus settle the "Negro Problem." Still another proposition is to put the colored people in a part of the country entirely by themselves. This would require the building of a wall to keep the blacks in, and another wall to keep the whites out. The only way to settle the question is to treat the Negro as you would treat any other man; treat him as a brother and a citizen, and there will be no further talk about the much vexed "Negro Problem."

—Booker T. Washington

Neighbor—Neighbors

1243. We make our friends; we make our enemies; but God makes our next-door neighbor.

—G. K. Chesterton

1244. All social life, stability, progress, depend upon each man's confidence in his neighbor, a reliance upon him to do his duty.

—A. Lawrence Lowell

Neutrality

1245. There are neutral men but they usually lack intelligence. Intelligent, thinking people may have views. They will be strong views or weak views. But if they do not have views, it means they lack intelligence.

—Jawaharlal Nehru

New Year

1246. About the best resolution you can make for this year is to have resolution. No man can fight his way to the top and stay at the top without exercising the fullest measure of grit, courage, determination, resolution. Every man who gets anywhere does so because he first firmly resolves to progress in the world and then has enough stick-to-itiveness to transform his resolution into a reality. Sometimes I feel that if a person has enough resolution, he has almost all that is necessary to the attaining of a reasonable measure of success. Without resolution, no man can win any worthwhile place among his fellowmen. At the beginning of this New Year, therefore, resolve to have resolution.

—B. C. FORBES

1247. During the year ahead there may be many things which you have resolved you will do, but there are also some things which it might be wise to remember not to do. For example:

Don't attempt to set up your own standards of right and wrong. Try to conform to the standards which mankind has recognized through the centuries.

Don't try to impose your ideas of what is enjoyable on others. Have your own fun your way with those whose tastes are similar, but recognize that what you enjoy may be a bore to someone else.

Don't expect even your closest friends to agree with you on everything. Opinions in the world will always be diverse, never uniform.

Don't fail to appreciate the value of experience. No matter how much you think you know, strange things often happen to ideas when put into practice.

Don't fail to differentiate between the important and the trivial. Always yield on the things which make no great difference one way or the other.

Don't fail to work for perfection in what you do yourself. You may not attain it, but the effort always produces better results than otherwise.

Don't worry yourself and others over things which you can neither control nor remedy. There will always be many unpleasant facts you must live with.

Don't fail to offer help to anyone who needs it when it is within your power to do so. It is the finest exercise you can give your own soul.

Nonconformity

Don't fail to make allowances for the weakness of others. Always remember those words of Christian humility and understanding, "There but for the grace of God, go I."

Don't fail to realize that some day someone may be able to do what seems utterly impossible to you today.

And in your relations with others, don't be too hasty in judging from outside appearances. Wait until you know something of the man within.

—*Nuggets*

Nonconformity

1248. Take the course opposite to custom and you will almost always do well.

1249. If you think you're a nonconformist, would you wear tan shoes with a tuxedo or black hose with a white evening gown?

1250. We try to be like others, to conform, so that we will be accepted. But only to the degree that one is different has he anything to offer. Every contribution is an evidence of difference, of uniqueness.

—Don Robinson

1251. Robot executives who cling to this—is—the—way—it's—always—been—done conformity are not only stifling their own careers but are precipitating a case of hardening of the arteries throughout U.S. industry. Playing safe causes a great loss of creativity and subsequent waste of ideas that are never tried out for fear of rocking the boat.

—Louis Wolfson

Novelty

1252. Every new idea has something of the pain and peril of childbirth about it.

—Samuel Butler

1253. I am a great admirer of my own stuff while it's new, but after a while I'm not gone on it—like the true maternal instinct that kicks off an offspring as soon as it can go on its own legs.

—D. H. LAWRENCE

Observation—Observations

1254. He alone is an acute observer, who can observe minutely without being observed.

—JOHANN KASPAR LAVATER

1255. By observation men take their first apprehension of things; for no man can have a fixed judgment unless he is a close observer.

—JAMES ELLIS

Obstacle—Obstacles

1256. Without obstacles how can we gauge our powers?

1257. The brook would lose its song if we removed the rocks.

1258. No one ever would have crossed the ocean if he could have gotten off the ship in the storm.

—CHARLES F. KETTERING

1259. It is the feeling of exerting effort that exhilarates us, as a grasshopper is exhilarated by jumping. A hard job, full of impediments, is thus more satisfying than an easy job.

—H. L. MENCKEN

Old age

1260. The evening of life brings with it its lamps.

—JOSEPH JOUBERT

1261.   After the age of eighty, all contemporaries are friends.

—MME. DE DINO

1262.   For my own part, I had rather be old only a short time than be old before I really am so.

—CICERO

1263.   Old age is like everything else. To make a success of it you've got to start young.

1264.   Each departed friend is a magnet that attracts us to the next world, and the old man lives among graves.

—JEAN PAUL RICHTER

1265.   We are happier in many ways when we are old than when we were young. The young sow wild oats. The old grow sage.

—WINSTON CHURCHILL

1266.   William Gladstone, premier of England at 83, was asked: "Mr. Gladstone, how old is old?" He replied, "We are always as young as our impulses to discover new experiences."

1267.   Age and youth look upon life from the opposite ends of the telescope; it is exceedingly long,—it is exceedingly short.

—HENRY WARD BEECHER

1268.   Old age gives you a chance to change your mind. . . . One is bound to look at people and events in a new perspective and to learn some tolerance and patience. . . . One can't cover as much ground, can't hear as many sounds, can't read the fine print. But the inner world expands.

—BISHOP HERBERT WELCH

1269.   A wise old lady of eighty tells her friends, as they reach sixty: "You have spent sixty years in preparation for life, and you will now begin to live. At sixty you have learned what is worthwhile. You have conquered the worst forms of foolishness, you have reached a balanced period of life, knowing good from evil; what is precious, what is worthless. Danger is past, the mind is peaceful, evil is forgiven, the affections are strong, envy is weak. It is the happy age."

Omission—Omissions

1270. When it shall be found that much is omitted, let it not be forgotten that much likewise is performed.

—Dr. Samuel Johnson

1271.   *Omissions*

It is not so much the things I do
    That causes me regret;
It's the little things I leave undone,
    The things that I forget.

It's words I fail to utter,
    The songs I fail to sing,
The letters I forget to write,
    That may great comfort bring.

It's the little acts of kindness,
    The joy I fail to give,
The smiles I fail to scatter
    As day by day I live.

It's the sick I fail to visit,
    Flowers I fail to send;
It's the hand I fail to offer
    Unto a fallen friend.

It's not so much the things I do
    That cause me regret;
It's the little things I leave undone,
    The things that I forget.

—Alice L. Whitson

Open-mindedness

1272. He who knows only his own side of the case knows little of that.

—JOHN STUART MILL

1273. He that is not open to conviction is not qualified for discussion.

—RICHARD WHATELY

1274. Until man places on tolerance and open-mindedness a value equal to the value that he places on material possessions, he will continue to be stranded on an island surrounded by his own prejudices, ideas, preconceived opinions, and knowledge that is limited by the horizon of his own ignorance.

—CECIL A. POOLE

Opportunity—Opportunities

1275. Necessity is the mother of "taking chances."

—MARK TWAIN

1276. The opportunity of a lifetime is seldom so labelled.

1277. What we call adversity God calls opportunity.

—DR. WILLIAM ARTHUR WARD, Texas
Wesleyan College, Fort Worth

1278. It's no good offering a reward for a lost opportunity.

1279. Opportunities are never lost. The other fellow takes those you miss.

1280. Between tomorrow's dreams and yesterday's regrets is today's opportunity.

1281. A wise man will make more opportunities than he finds.

—Francis Bacon

1282. Opportunity seems to have an uncanny habit of favoring those who have paid the price of years of preparation.

1283. The big opportunity you are always looking for may not be worth half as much as some of the little opportunities you overlook.

Oppression

1284. Give all the power to the many and they will oppress the few; give all the power to the few and they will oppress the many.

—James Madison

1285. Laws just or unjust may govern men's actions. Tyrannies may restrain or regulate their words. The machinery of propaganda may pack their minds with falsehoods and deny them truth for many generations of time. But the soul of man thus held in trance or frozen in a long night can be awakened by a spark coming from God knows where, and in a moment the whole structure of lies and oppression is on trial for its life.

—Winston Churchill

Optimism

1286. The darkest hour is onely sixty minutes long.

1287. It is not always possible to ignore the setbacks that hurt. There is no great virtue in being so naive as to doubt that justice can be unjust, that work can be futile, and luck partial. The true optimist does not deceive himself about all these things which the pessimist cannot let himself forget. But in spite of his willingness to recognize these facts, he has the faith to believe that they are only temporary, that a future is coming in which their influence will be negligible.

Optimism—Pessimism

1288. When the pessimist thinks he is taking a chance, the optimist is grasping an opportunity.

1289. An old Arab tale points up the difference between the optimist and the pessimist. A caliph brought a veiled girl into a room and asked the ten friends present what significance they attached to the veil.

The five optimists among them said he must be trying to protect a rare treasure and chided him for denying other men the pleasure of looking upon the girl's beautiful face.

The five pessimists said he must surely be ashamed of her face to conceal it behind a veil, and complimented his good taste in sparing men the annoyance of having to look at such an ugly girl.

Originality

1290. No one can be original by trying.

—W. Somerset Maugham

1291. Originality does not consist in saying what no one has ever said before, but in saying exactly what you think yourself.

—James Stephen

Outer space

1292. *Spaceism* is scrambled *Escapism.*

—Sir Robert Watson-Watt

1293. In space, one has the inescapable impression that here is a virgin area of the universe in which civilized man, for the first time, has the opportunity to learn and grow without the influence of ancient pressures. Like the mind of a child, it is yet untainted with acquired fears, hate, greed, or prejudice. In space, as yet, there is only one enemy—space itself. It is an environment hostile to all men and all nations, and one which will challenge all men's greatest abilities.

—John H. Glenn

Overconfidence

1294. Better be despised for too anxious apprehensions than ruined by too confident security.

—EDMUND BURKE

Overindulgence

1295. Use, do not abuse: neither abstinence nor excess ever renders man happy.

—VOLTAIRE

Overweight. See also **Diet—Dieting**

1296. If you want to spend your money and have something to show for it, try eating rich food.

1297. When a woman can't get into her last year's swim suit, it's pretty hard to convince her it didn't shrink.

Overwork

1298. Doctors doubt that hard work ever really killed anybody, but they have known cases where it seemed to scare them half to death.

1299. If you get up earlier in the morning than your neighbor, work harder and scheme more, stick closely to your job and stay up later planning how to get ahead of him while he is snoozing, not only will you leave more money behind you when you die, BUT you will leave a lot sooner.

Pain

1300. Those who do not feel pain seldom think that it is felt.

—DR. SAMUEL JOHNSON

209

Painting—Paintings

1301. The most painful part of our bodily pain is that which is bodiless, or immaterial, namely, our impatience, and the delusion that it will last forever.

—Jean Paul Richter

Painting—Paintings

1302. A room hung with pictures is a room hung with thoughts.

—Sir. Joshua Reynolds

1303. A picture is an intermediate something between a thought and a thing.

—Samuel T. Coleridge

1304. The painter who is content with the praise of the world in respect to what does not satisfy himself is not an artist, but an artisan; for though his reward be only praise, his pay is that of a mechanic.

—Washington Allston

1305. When Sir Winston Churchill showed a close friend a group of paintings he had recently completed, the friend asked him why he painted only landscapes and never portraits. Sir Winston replied with a smile, "Because a tree doesn't complain that I haven't done it justice."

Parent—Child

1306. Insanity is hereditary. You can get it from your children.

1307. The accent may be on youth, but the stress is still on the parents.

1308. The only thing more annoying than a precocious child is its mother.

—John W. Maxson, Jr.

1309. The most important thing a father can do for his children is to love their mother.

—REV. THEODORE HESBURGH

1310. When a father gives to his son, both laugh; when a son gives to his father, both cry.

—JEWISH PROVERB

1311. Setting a good example for your children takes all the fun out of middle age.

1312. When you feel like criticizing the younger generation, just remember who raised them.

1313. If you make children happy now, you will make them happy twenty years from now by the memory of it.

1314. We have been so anxious to give our children what we didn't have that we have neglected to give them what we did have.

1315. The child who drives his parents half crazy asking questions sends them the rest of the way when he grows up and thinks he knows all the answers.

1316. Sometimes parents who make everything too easy for their children do them more harm than good. They rob them of the satisfaction which only those know who have done something for themselves. The old-fashioned chores of another day may have interfered with some youthful pleasure, but they did contribute to strength and character.

1317. What do we owe our parents? No man can *owe* love; none can *owe* obedience. We owe, I think, chiefly pity; for we are the pledge of their dear and joyful union, we have been the solicitude of their days the anxiety of their nights, we have made them, though by no will of ours, to carry the burden of our sins, sorrows, and physical infirmities; and too many of us grow up at length to disappoint the purpose of their lives and require their care and piety which cruel pangs.

—ROBERT LOUIS STEVENSON

Partnership

1318. No man is ever quite so anxious to take in a partner as the man who has only himself to blame.

1319. Queen Elizabeth I of England once sent a merchant to a remote country on national business. "But, Madam," he said, "my business will suffer in my absence." She replied: "You look after my business, and I will look after yours." He accepted the royal partnership. Upon his return he found that he was a rich man.

Past, The

1320. Those who cannot remember the past are condemned to repeat it.

—GEORGE SANTAYANA

1321. There have been many men who left behind them that which hundreds of years have not worn out. The earth has Socrates and Plato to this day. The world is richer yet by Moses and the old Prophets than by the wisest statesmen. We are indebted to the past. We stand in the greatness of ages that are gone rather than in that of our own. But of how many of us shall it be said that, being dead, we yet speak?

—HENRY WARD BEECHER

Past—Present—Future

1322. The best way to look ahead is by looking back.

1323. If a tomorrow were never to come, it would not be worth living today.

1324. You can't get a firm grip on the present without letting go of the past.

1325. The only way we can pay our debt to the past is to put the future in debt to us.

1326. The present rests on the past, and neither nation nor man is wholly master of his destiny.

—ARTHUR BRYANT

1327. You can't change the past but you can ruin a perfectly good present by worrying about the future.

1328. May we have our feet planted deeply in the past, our minds keenly absorbed with the present and our vision directed unafraid toward the future.

—HARRY G. MENDELSON

1329. Despair of the future is often remorse for the past; for those who can look backward only with regret may have reason to look forward only with fear.

1330. We come to some understanding of ourselves and our particular situation only if we are able to see the significant activity of the past in terms of our own present. The trouble with those who turn their backs self-consciously on the past is less that they throw the baby out with the bath-water than that they are unaware that there was ever a baby in the bath at all.

—JOHN O'LONDON

Patience

1331. *"The Past is Prologue"* is the inscription on a plaque on the United States Archives building in Washington.

"What does that mean?" asked a visitor to the Capital City of the tour guide.

"In simple language, it means 'You ain't seen nothing yet,' " was the reply.

1332. It is necessary to look forward as well as backward, as some think it always necessary to regulate their conduct by things that have been done of old times; but that past which is so presumptuously brought forward as a precedent for the present, was itself founded on an alternation of some past that went before it.

—MADAME DE STAËL

1333. Finish each day and be done with it. You have done what you could. Some blunders and absurdities no doubt crept in; forget them as soon as you can. Tomorrow is a new day; begin it well and serenely, and with too high a spirit to be cumbered with your old nonsense. The day is all that is good and fair. It is too dear with its hopes and invitations to waste a moment on the yesterdays.

—RALPH WALDO EMERSON

1334. We all live in the past, because there is nothing else to live in. To live in the present is like proposing to sit on a pin. It is too minute, it is too slight a support, it is too uncomfortable a posture, and it is of necessity followed immediately by totally different experiences, analogous to those of jumping up with a yell. To live in the future is a contradiction in terms. The future is dead, in the perfectly definite sense that it is not alive.

—G. K. CHESTERTON

Patience

1335. Most things come a lot faster to those who won't wait.

1336. Patience is the support of weakness; impatience is the ruin of strength.

—CHARLES C. COLTON

1337. An admirer once asked pianist Ignace Paderewski: "Is it true that you still practice every day?"

"Yes," said the pianist. "At least eight hours a day."

"You must have a world of patience," said the other.

"I have no more patience than the next fellow," said Paderewski. "I just use mine."

Patriotism

1338. It is said that patriotism is the love of country. I think it is the love of the things about your country that you don't want to see lost, that you want to see perpetuated, and for which you're willing to sacrifice. Patriotism is something for our hearts, a faith, a dedication.

—GEN. DAVID M. SHOUP

1339. True patriotism does not require that we approve of everything men do, Americans or otherwise. It does not require that we approve everything that our own government does. Americans can admit their mistakes precisely because there is a standard which calls them to practice the highest kind of political and social morality—a morality that is based upon the fundamental idea that all men are created equal. Patriotism thus becomes love of our country guided by these ideals.

—PHILIP JOHNSON

1340. Patriotism isn't marching behind a band and puffing out your chest. Patriotism isn't a flash of fireworks one day of the year, and then submerging one's emotions the rest of the year. Patriotism isn't found in the whooping of the crowd or maudlin flag-waving. Patriotism is the sum of the three cardinal virtues: Faith, Hope, and Charity. Faith in the principles of our government; Hope in the future of our country; Charity toward all and malice toward none.

—KEYSTONE BUTLER

Peace

1341. After burying the hatchet, don't mark the spot.

1342.   Peace is to be desired unless it is purchased at the price of man's dignity.

—Douglas Meador

1343.   Peace is not the absence of conflict from life, but rather the ability to cope with it.

1344.   Peace was the first thing the Angels sang. Peace is the mark of the sons of God. Peace is the nurse of love. Peace is the mother of unity. Peace is the rest of blessed souls. Peace is the dwelling place for eternity.

—Leo the Great

Perfection

1345.   If you insist on perfection, make the first demand on yourself.

1346.   Give them the third best to go on with; the second best comes too late, the best never comes.

—Sir Robert Watson-Watt

1347.   A perfectionist is just as effective as an obstructionist in keeping something worthwhile from getting done.

1348.   Aristotle said that all creative people are dissatisfied because they are all looking for happiness in perfection and seeking for things that do not exist. This is one of the hopes of the world. There is no progress where people are satisfied. Discontent is perhaps the most potent challenge to improvement.

—Clarence Edwin Flynn

1349.   An Italian duke came upon a workman one day who seemed to be taking infinite care and pains in his work. He asked the laborer, "For what will the box you are making be used?"

"Flowers will be planted in it, sir."

Amused, the duke continued, "It will be filled with dirt. Why take such pains to make each joint and surface perfect?"

"I love perfect things," the man replied.

"Ah, wasted effort! No one will observe its perfection. A mere flower box does not require such perfection."

"But my spirit does," insisted the man. "Do you suppose that the Carpenter of Nazareth ever made anything less perfect than He could? ..."

Angrily, the duke replied, "Sacrilege! Your impudence deserves a flogging. What is your name?"

The reply came: "Michelangelo, sir."

—Rev. A. Purnell Bailey

Persecution

1350. The way of this world is to praise dead saints and persecute living ones.

—Rev. N. Howe

1351. Blessed are they which are persecuted for righteousness' sake, for theirs is the kingdom of heaven.

—*The Bible*

1352. The history of persecution is a history of endeavors to cheat nature, to make water run up hill, to twist a rope of sand. ... The martyr cannot be dishonored. Every lash inflicted is a tongue of flame; every prison a more illustrious abode; every burned book or house enlightens the world; every suppressed or expunged word reverberates through the earth from side to side. ... It is the whipper who is whipped and the tyrant who is undone.

—Ralph Waldo Emerson

Perseverance

1353. A very small river will carry a good deal of water to the sea—if it keeps running.

1354. All of the finest things we have today were discovered, fashioned, or conceived by those who kept constantly in sight the motto, "I may be wrong."

—HEYWOOD BROUN

1355. Believe if you can, and you can; believe if you will, and you will. See yourself achieving, and you will achieve. Never give up; giving up is like letting go of a life preserver when you are almost saved.

—GARDNER HUNTING

1356. There was once a man who had an idea that India rubber could be made useful. People laughed at him, but for eleven years he struggled with hardships to make his dream come true. He pawned his clothing and the family jewels to buy for his children. His neighbors called him insane. But he still insisted that India rubber could be made of practical use. The man was Charles Goodyear. Dreams do come true—if you make them.

—KATHERYN C. METZ

1357. F. W. Woolworth, founder of the five-and-dime chain, was once hired as a janitor for fifty cents a day by a retail store owner who didn't think Woolworth had enough business sense to wait on customers.

When Zane Grey was still an unknown trying to sell his book manuscripts, a publisher told him he had no ability for writing fiction; and Louisa May Alcott, author of *Little Women* and other famed works, was a tomboy marked by her fellow townspeople as a girl who would never amount to much. A publisher once told her to give up the idea of writing.

The first time George Gershwin ever played the piano on the stage, he was laughed out of the theater by both the audience and his fellow actors.

Albert Einstein's teachers classified him as a dunce, and even his parents thought him backward.

And when Thomas A. Edison was in school, he was always at the foot of his class because he couldn't remember his three R's. His teachers called him stupid, and doctors predicted that he would have serious brain trouble.

Persuasion

1358. People are generally better persuaded by the reasons which they have themselves discovered than by those which have come into the mind of others.

—Blaise Pascal

1359. Persuasion, kind, unassuming persuasion, should be adopted to influence the conduct of men. The opposite course would be a reversal of human nature, which is God's decree and can never be reversed.

—Abraham Lincoln

Physical exercise. See Exercise, Physical

Physiognomy

1360. Be it ever so homely, there's no face like your own.

1361. The thoughts we think, the acts we perform, the motives we follow shape our faces. Everyone carries his life in his face. Ruskin says that there are four enemies of a beautiful face: pride, sensuality, cruelty, and fear. Pride brings a cynical smile and an unpardonably dull expression.

1362. Nature has written a letter of credit on some faces which is honored wherever presented. You cannot help trusting them; their very presence gives confidence. There is a "promise to pay" in their faces which you prefer to another's endorsement. Character is credit.

—William Makepeace Thackeray

1363. No person with a very short nose has ever, so it is said, made a profound impression on the world. Civilization has always had to push its way against formidable obstacles. The Roman nose is a moral battering-ram to beat down these walls. Napoleon possessed a Roman nose, but Wellington's was larger.

Pioneering

A long nose is supposed to signify a shrewd and determined personality, and a thick one that the owner is blunt and outspoken. Nostrils are important too. Persons with wide nostrils are thoughtful and possess creative genius. Among those who possessed this characteristic were Shakespeare and Dr. Johnson.

—PAUL BROCK

Pioneering

1364. Too many of us know the short cuts, and too few know or care where the path leads. Too few of us dare to leave the path, because the path is always the easy way, the way most people go. But there is no path to the future, no path to greatness, no path to progress. No path to outer space or to inner satisfaction.

—CHARLES H. BROWER

Plagiarism

1365. It wasn't luck that made the house organ editor a success. It was shear work.

—HARRY J. HIGDON

1366. Honest thinkers are always stealing from each other. Our minds are full of waifs and estrays which we think are our own. Innocent plagiarism turns up everywhere.

—DR. OLIVER WENDELL HOLMES

1367. If we steal thoughts from the moderns, it will be cried down as plagiarism; if from the ancients, it will be cried up as erudition. But in this respect every author is a Spartan, being more ashamed of the discovery than of the depredation.

—CHARLES C. COLTON

Plan—Plans—Planning

1368. When schemes are laid in advance, it is surprising how often the circumstances fit in with them.

—SIR WILLIAM OSLER

1369. It is wise to keep in mind always that what you plan for the future will one day be your past.

1370. It is actually true that a man can accomplish twice as much with less energy if he plans. It is the very essence of efficiency to do this.
—Herbert N. Casson

Poet—Poets—Poetry

1371. Modern poets put a great deal of water in their ink.
—Johann Wolfgang von Goethe

1372. A poet is the translator of the silent language of nature to the world.
—Rufus W. Griswold

1373. A poet, or creator, is therefore a person who puts things together, not as a watchmaker steel, or a shoemaker leather, but who puts life into them.
—John Ruskin

1374. No man was ever yet a great poet, without being at the same time a profound philosopher. For poetry is the blossom and the fragrancy of all human knowledge, human thoughts, human passions, emotions, language.
—Samuel T. Coleridge

Point of view

1375. We see things not as they are, but as we are.
—Henry Major Tomlinson

1376. Walking is a pleasure only when you can afford to ride if you want to.

Politeness

1377. When we say God gives us our relatives but we choose our friends, we must never forget that we are the relatives God gave to someone.

1378. It is said that Edison tried more than 200 different substances in attempting to find a filament for his incandescent bulb. Someone once said to him, "You have failed more than 200 times; why don't you give up?" His answer was, "Not at all. I have discovered more than 200 things that will not work. I will soon find one that will."

—W. E. Phifer

1379. To hold the same views at forty as we held at twenty is to have been stupefied for a score of years, and take rank, not as a prophet, but as an unteachable brat, well birched and none the wiser. It is as if a ship captain should sail to India from the Port of London; and having brought a chart of the Thames on deck at his first setting out, should obstinately use no other for the whole voyage.

—Robert Louis Stevenson

Politeness

1380. When two goats met on a bridge which was too narrow to allow either to pass or return, the goat which lay down that the other might walk over it was a finer gentleman than Lord Chesterfield.

—Richard Cecil

1381. A man who had read that courtesy pays and the world would run more smoothly if everyone were friendly and polite decided to put the theory into practice. In a few weeks he noticed that many of his friends and neighbors were beginning to avoid him. Cornering one of them, he asked him pointblank what the trouble was. "Well, Ed," he replied, "you suddenly got so doggone polite, people are afraid you are trying to get them involved in something."

Politician—Politicians

1382. Few politicians climb high enough to be above suspicion.

1383.   Politicians with an itch for office often make rash promises.

1384.   Since a politician never believes what he says, he's always astonished when others do.

—CHARLES DE GAULLE

1385.   Politicians and wives agree on one thing—if you postpone payment until some time in the future, it's not really spending.

—BILL VAUGHAN

1386.   A bishop once advised a politician to go out into the rain and lift his head heavenward. "It will bring a revelation to you," the old bishop promised.

Next day the politician reported: "I followed your advice and no revelation came. The water poured down my neck and I felt like a fool."

"Well," said the bishop, "isn't that quite a revelation for the first try?"

Politics

1387.   Practical politics consists in ignoring facts.

—HENRY BROOKS ADAMS

1388.   An Englishman merely stands for election; an American runs.

1389.   The world of politics is always twenty years behind the world of thought.

—JOHN JAY CHAPMAN

1390.   The toughest part of politics is to satisfy the voter without giving him what he wants.

—DAN BENNETT

223

Popularity

1391. Judge a candidate more by what he is for than by what he is against.

1392. The man of mediocre ability wouldn't be so successful in politics if he had some competition from well-trained minds.
—Joseph V. McKee

1393. Politics has always been a rough game, but there are certain rules . . . and the first of these is to utter no falsehood that can be refuted easily.
—Charles Michelson

1394. Whatever happens politically, too many of us are apt to put the blame on the politicians. . . . We talk a lot about "they." But what we should be talking about is "we." . . . Political action is something you help create—by action or inaction—no matter where you live in this country.
—Arthur H. Motley

1395. Politics, like any other human endeavor, is based upon the give-and-take of human relationships. It is easy to criticize a politician who has yielded a little as being craven and spineless until you, as an informed citizen, realize that his opponent was also forced to yield an equal amount and that between them progress was made.
—Gale McGee

Popularity

1396. The secret of popularity is mediocrity.

1397. The secret of popularity is always to remember what to forget.

1398. One way to be popular is to listen closely to a lot of things we already know.

224

1399. Popularity is a crime from the moment it is sought; it is only a virtue where men have it whether they will or not.

—GEORGE SAVILE (Marquis of Halifax)

Poverty

1400. He who knows how to be poor knows everything.

—JULES MICHELET

1401. Poverty is seldom a reflection on man's honesty, but extended over a lifetime, it may cast a shadow on his industry.

—DOUGLAS MEADOR

1402. I am glad I was born poor. Poverty gives one so much more than riches—the priceless gift of real ambition.

—SOPHIA LOREN

Power

1403. Power does not corrupt men; fools however, if they get into a position of power, corrupt power.

—GEORGE BERNARD SHAW

1404. Where love rules, there is no will to power; and where power predominates, there love is lacking. The one is the shadow of the other.

—CARL JUNG

1405. The genius of the American (political) system is that it limits all power—including the power of the majority. Absolute power, whether in a king, a President, a legislative majority, a popular majority is alien to the American idea.

—WALTER LIPPMANN

Praise

1406. If you would make men praiseworthy, praise them.

1407.   Modesty is the only sure bait when you angle for praise.
—Lord Chesterfield

1408.   He who praises you for what you lack wishes to take from you what you have.
—Juan Manuel

1409.   I could say nice things about him for hours, but I'd rather tell the truth.

1410.   Great tranquility of heart is his who cares for neither praise nor blame.

1411.   The praises of others may be of use in teaching us not what we are, but what we ought to be.
—Augustus Hare

1412.   The trouble with many of us is that we would rather be ruined by praise than saved by criticism.

1413.   Honest praise will oil the machinery of life and make it run smoothly. The praise must be honest; otherwise it will degenerate into flattery, lose its value, and even become a liability.
—Clinton E. Bernard

1414.   Undeserved praise causes more pangs of conscience later than undeserved blame, but probably only for this reason, that our powers of judgment are more completely exposed by being overpraised than by being unjustly underestimated.
—Friederich Wilhelm Nietzsche

1415.   There is an old Jewish legend about the origin of praise. After God created mankind, says the legend, He asked the angels what they thought of the world He had made. "Only one thing is lacking," they said. "It is the sound of praise to the Creator." So, the story continues, "God created music, the voice of birds, the whispering wind, the murmuring ocean, and planted melody in the hearts of men."

Prayer—Prayers

1416. Prayer is not a monologue, but a dialogue.

1417. A lot of kneeling keeps you in good standing with God.

1418. Prayer does not change God, but changes him who prays.
—Sören Kierkegaard

1419. Pray to your conscience for guidance and not to the Lord for deliverance.
—Dagobert D. Runes

1420. Prayer is the prelude to peace, the prologue to power, the preface to purpose, and the pathway to perfection.
—Dr. William Arthur Ward,
Texas Wesleyan College, Fort Worth

1421. Do not pray for easy living, pray to be stronger men! Do not pray for tasks equal to your powers, pray for powers equal to your tasks!

1422. Forbidding prayers in school won't hurt the nation half as much as forgetting prayers at home.

1423. A person's most fervent prayers are not said when he is on his knees, but when he is flat on his back.

1424. A generous prayer is never presented in vain; the petition may be refused, but the petitioner is always, I believe, rewarded by some gracious visitation.

—ROBERT LOUIS STEVENSON

1425. Prayer is like an emergency candle, always within easy reach, requiring no outside machinery to keep it in order, only needing the match of faith and courage to light it.

1426. Charles Steinmetz, the great scientist, was once asked which field for future research offered the greatest promise.

"Prayer," he replied instantly. "Find out about prayer!"

—WILLIAM R. PARKER

1427. Spoken prayers are not the most effective kind, because then the mind is busy with speech. Mental prayer is best. God is not impressed by what you say aloud to Him if you are thinking of something else.

—PARAMAHANSA YOGANANDA

1428. God chooses to speak with us. But we expect either to do all the talking ourselves or to be told by God what to do with no participation in conversation with Him. In either instance, it would be like weaving cloth without both the warp and the woof; it would be impossible whichever one you have.

1429. Prayer is not a substitute for work; it is a desperate effort to work further and to be efficient beyond the range of one's powers. It is not the lazy who are most inclined to prayer; those pray most who care most, and who, having worked hard, find it intolerable to be defeated.

—GEORGE SANTAYANA

1430. Amid the confusion of my day, give me the calmness of the everlasting hills. Teach me the art of taking minute vacations, of slowing down to look at a flower, to chat with a friend, to pet a dog, to read from a good book. Remind me to look upward at the towering oak, and to know that it grew tall and strong because it grew slowly and well.

—ANONYMOUS

Prejudice

1431.   Water and oil are more compatible than Christianity and prejudice.

—DR. WILLIAM ARTHUR WARD,
Texas Wesleyan College, Fort Worth

1432.   Sometimes we are converted in our passions but not in our pocketbooks. We are decent but we are stingy. Sometimes we are converted in our religious sentiments but not in politics. We are pious in our prayers but vote our prejudices.

—DR. RALPH W. SOCKMAN

Preparation

1433.   Joy is the child of service; friendship is the heir of concern; improvement is the son of discontent; achievement is the progency of effort; and success is the offspring of preparation.

1434.   A fussy traveler was finding much trouble in placing her belongings. She put bundles first on the seat, then on the floor. She opened and closed windows, adjusted shades and fidgeted about like a nervous hen. When her husband protested, she said, "I want to get fixed so I can see the scenery comfortably." But he shook his head. "Susan, we ain't goin' far, and the scenery will be all over before you get fixed to enjoy it." Many people go through life "getting fixed to enjoy it"—while life passes and is gone.

—ROBERT E. LUCCOCK

Preparedness

1435.   Be peaceful yet prepared, for harm is quick.
A sheep will bite a man without a stick.

—FROM THE CHINESE

1436.   We can't cross a bridge until we come to it; but I always like to lay down a pontoon ahead of time.

—BERNARD BARUCH

1437.   No one should make such thorough preparation for the rainy days that he can't enjoy today's sunshine.

Presidency, U. S.

1438.   *The Story of Eleven Poor Boys*

John Adams, second President of the United States, was the son of a grocer of very moderate means. The only start he had was a good education.

Andrew Jackson was born in a log hut in North Carolina, and was reared in the beautiful pine woods for which the state is famous.

James K. Polk spent the earlier years of his life helping to dig a living out of a new farm in North Carolina. He was afterward a clerk in a country store.

Millard Fillmore was the son of a New York farmer, and his home was a humble one. He learned the business of a clothier.

James Buchanan was born in a small town in the Allegheny Mountains. His father cut the logs and built the house in what was then a wilderness.

Abraham Lincoln was the son of a wretchedly poor farmer in Kentucky, and lived in a log cabin until he was twenty-one years old.

Andrew Johnson was apprenticed to a tailor at the age of ten years by his widowed mother. He was never able to attend school, and picked up all the education he ever had.

Ulysses S. Grant lived the life of a village boy, in a plain house on the banks of the Ohio River, until he was seventeen years of age.

James A. Garfield was born in a log cabin. He worked on the farm until he was strong enough to use carpenter's tools, when he learned the trade. He afterward worked on a canal.

Grover Cleveland's father was a Presbyterian minister with a small salary and a large family. The boys had to earn their living.

William McKinley's early home was plain and comfortable and his father was able to keep him at school.

1439.   *Where U.S. Presidents Are Buried*
Arlington National Cemetery is the burial place of only two Presidents—John F. Kennedy and William Howard Taft. Places where the Presidents are buried:

George Washington, 1732-1799, Mount Vernon, Virginia family vault.

John Adams, 1735-1826, Quincy, Massachusetts, First Unitarian Church.

Thomas Jefferson, 1743-1826, Charlottesville, Virginia.

James Madison, 1751-1836, Montpelier, Virginia, family plot.

James Monroe, 1758-1831, Richmond, Virginia, Hollywood cemetery.

John Quincy Adams, 1767-1848, Quincy, Massachusetts, First Unitarian Church.

Andrew Jackson, 1767-1845, Hermitage, Nashville, Tennessee.

Martin Van Buren, 1782-1862, Kinderhook, New York, Kinderhook cemetery.

William Henry Harrison, 1773-1841, North Bend, Ohio, William Henry Harrison Memorial State Park.

John Tyler, 1790-1862, Richmond, Virginia, Hollywood cemetery.

James Knox Polk, 1795-1849, Nashville, Tennessee, State Capitol grounds.

Zachary Taylor, 1784-1850, Springfield, Kentucky.

Millard Fillmore, 1800-1874, Buffalo, New York, Forest Lawn cemetery.

Franklin Pierce, 1804-1869, Concord, New Hampshire, Old North cemetery.

James Buchanan, 1791-1868, Lancaster, Pennsylvania, Woodward Hill cemetery.

Abraham Lincoln, 1809-1865, Springfield, Illinois, Oak Ridge cemetery.

Andrew Johnson, 1808-1875, Greeneville, Tennessee, Andrew Johnson National Cemetery.

Ulysses S. Grant, 1822-1885, New York, Grant's tomb.

Rutherford B. Hayes, 1822-1893, Fremont, Ohio, Spiegel Grove State Park.

James A. Garfield, 1831-1881, Cleveland, Ohio, Lake View cemetery.

> *Chester A. Arthur,* 1830-1886, Albany, New York, rural cemetery.
>
> *Grover Cleveland,* 1837-1908, Princeton, New Jersey.
>
> *Benjamin Harrison,* 1833-1901, Indianapolis, Indiana, Crown Hill cemetery.
>
> *William McKinley,* 1843-1901, Canton, Ohio, adjacent to Westlawn cemetery.
>
> *Theodore Roosevelt,* 1858-1919, Oyster Bay, Long Island, Young's Memorial cemetery.
>
> *William Howard Taft,* 1857-1930, Arlington National Cemetery.
>
> *Woodrow Wilson,* 1856-1924, Washington National Cathedral.
>
> *Warren Harding,* 1865-1923, Marion, Ohio, Hillside cemetery.
>
> *Calvin Coolidge,* 1872-1933, Plymouth, Vermont, Hillside cemetery.
>
> *Franklin Delano Roosevelt,* 1882-1945, Hyde Park, New York, family plot.
>
> *John Fitzgerald Kennedy,* 1917-1963, Arlington National cemetery.

Press, Freedom of the

1440. The pen is mightier than the sword only when there is freedom to use the pen.

1441. Despotism can no more exist in a nation until the liberty of the press be destroyed than the night can happen before the sun is set.
—Charles C. Colton

Principle—Principles

1442. When you say that you agree to a thing in principle, you mean that you have not the slightest intention of carrying it out in practice.
—Prince Otto von Bismarck

1443. When Henry Clay was called upon to define his position on the subject of slavery, he read his argument to his close friend Colonel Preston.

"I quite agree with you in your views, Mr. Clay," said the latter, "but I think the expression of your opinions will injure your prospects for the presidency in my part of the country."

"Am I right, sir?" said Mr. Clay.

"I think you are, sir," replied Preston.

"Then, sir," said Clay with stern pride, "I shall say every word of it and compromise nothing. I would rather be right than be President!"

—*"If Elected, I Promise ...",*
by John F. Parker (Doubleday)

Printer—Printers—Printing

1444. Of all inventions, of all discoveries in science and art ... of all the great results in the wonderful progress of mechanical energy and skill ... the printer is the only product of civilization necessary to the existence of free men.

—Charles Dickens

Problem—Problems

1445. Never resent problems on your job. Experience comes from learning what to do when something goes wrong.

1446. Social problems can no longer be solved by class warfare any more than international problems can be solved by wars between nations. Warfare is negative and will sooner or later lead to destruction, while good will and cooperation are positive and supply the only safe basis for building a better future.

—William Lyon Phelps

Procrastination

1447. Procrastination is the art of keeping up with yesterday.

—Don Marquis

233

Professional fees

1448. What we put off until tomorrow is too often what should have been done yesterday.

1449. The trouble with some people is that they keep putting off until tomorrow the things they've already put off until today.

1450. Time is the essence of life. Tomorrow is now. Don't procrastinate any longer by putting off today what you should have done yesterday, last week, last month, last year or the years before or during your more youthful years. Those men and women filling top positions today didn't reach their goals between today or yesterday but they set their sights high, chose wisely during their youthful years and followed the best advice. Tomorrow is now. Begin today.

—GEORGE WESLEY BLOUNT

1451. Every person has a backlog of things he is going to do when he has "more time." Those two words are the most deceptive cheats in life. They seem to assure us that someday we will have more time. And nothing is further from the truth, say those who are living in their sunset years.

Few people ever find the time to go back and pick up the things they put off enjoying until some future date. Tastes change and the physical capacity to do things changes. The wise thing is to find "more time" by selective use of the hours and minutes of today to enjoy the things that appeal to you now.

—*Nuggets,* January 1963

Professional fees

1452. "Doctor, what did you operate for?" asked the friend of a surgeon.

"Five hundred dollars."

"No, I mean what did the patient have?"

"Four hundred fifty dollars."

Profit—Profits

1453. You were born into the world with nothing. Everything that happens to you after that is sheer profit.

1454. One of the biggest jobs before us is to scrub the dirt off the word "profit" and re-acquaint the American public with the difference between "making a profit" and "profiteering."

—RAY R. EPPERT

Progress

1455. Progress comes from making people sit up when they want to sit down.

1456. Progress consists of preserving and cherishing as well as changing and improving.

—ERIC SEVAREID

1457. Progress always involves risks. You can't steal second base and keep your foot on first too.

1458. However long and hard the climb to the top may be, the bottom is only one misstep away.

1459. Progress and success cannot always be measured by immediate results. Some projects take longer.... Others merely lay the groundwork for future accomplishments.

—EDWIN S. ROWSE, JR.

Proof

1460. It takes a lot of things to prove you are smart, but only one thing to prove you are ignorant.

—DON HEROLD

1461. In looking for the facts to prove we are right, too often we overlook the facts that prove we could be wrong.

Propinquity

1462. An old farmer had returned home after a visit to the city. The local reporter asked him for an observation. The old fellow replied: "It seems that the closer people live together, the farther friends are apart."

Prosperity

1463. The American nation has observed that the mathematics of prosperity consist not in division but in multiplication.

F. A. SZARVASY

Proverb—Proverbs

1464. A proverb is the wisdom of years crystallized in the wit of a moment.

1465. Proverbs are salt pits from which you may extract salt, and sprinkle it where you will.

—CICERO

Public service

1466. I have the consolation of having added nothing to my private fortune during my public service, and of retiring with hands as clean as they are empty.

—THOMAS JEFFERSON: *Letter to Count Diodati*, 1807. From *A New Dictionary of Quotations on Historical Principles from Ancient and Modern Sources*, by H. L. MENCKEN (Knopf)

1467. As soon as public service ceases to be the chief business of the citizens, and they would rather serve with their money than with their persons, the state is not far from its fall.

—JEAN JACQUES ROUSSEAU

236

Public speaking

1468. Some speakers electrify audiences; others simply gas them.

1469. Many a speaker exhausts his audience before he exhausts his subject.

1470. Many men rise to the occasion, but few know when to sit down.

—J. FIELDS

1471. Don't pop off like a firecracker. It is good to always bear in mind what one of them looks like after the noise is over.

1472. When a speaker is too profound those who hoped to be enlightened end up being confused.

1473. The good speaker, like the good cook, becomes famous for the flavor of his product—and the secret is all in the seasoning.

—E. A. PATCHEN

1474. While a great speech can never move mountains, it can move people to the mountains and stir them to begin their necessary tasks.

—RICHARD M. HUNT

1475. The memorial chapel had been rebuilt and a luncheon was following the dedication. The local builder got up to speak.

"Ladies and gentlemen, dear friends," he began, his face very red. "I am a good deal better fitted for the scaffold than for public speaking!" Then he realized what he had said and sat down, amid roars of laughter.

1476. There is widespread misunderstanding of this thing called "public speaking." We usually think of it as an art, like singing, dancing, or painting. Nothing is further from the truth. Public speaking is not an exhibition. True, in the days of elocution it was so considered, but that approach has long been outmoded. A good speaker is simply a man expressing himself effectively. Speaking is not something to be done according to all sorts of rules and techniques. It is simply the natural expression of the individual.

—Eric Butterworth

1477. Henry Ward Beecher had a genius for bringing the most somnolent audience to life. One July morning he rode into a West Virginia town which was widely known in lecture circles as "Death Valley"—for the reason that any speaker unfortunate enough to have an engagement to lecture there wilted and curled up when he faced the town's stupid and indifferent audience.

Beecher was duly warned. That afternoon, when he was being introduced, half the audience was already dozing. Beecher rose from his chair and, wiping his brow with a large handkerchief, strode to the front of the platform.

"It's a God-damned hot day," the clergyman began.

A thousand pairs of eyes goggled and an electrical shock straightened the crowd erect. Beecher paused, and then, raising a finger of solemn reproof, went on, "That's what I heard a man say here this afternoon!"

He then proceeded into a stirring condemnation of blasphemy and needless to say, took the audience with him.

—Milton MacKaye

Punctuality

1478. If you want a little extra leisure, always be on time for appointments.

1479. Haste turns usually upon a matter of ten minutes too late, and may be avoided by a habit like that of Lord Nelson, to which he ascribed his success in life, of being ten minutes too early.

—Christian Nevell Bovee

Quackery

1480.   It is better to have recourse to a quack, if he can cure our disorder, although he cannot explain it, than to a physician, if he can explain our disease, but cannot cure it.

—CHARLES C. COLTON

Quality

1481.   Good things cost less than bad ones.

—ITALIAN PROVERB

1482.   A company's greatest asset is the quality performance of its employes. An employe's greatest asset is the quality performance of his company.

1483.   In the City of Bagdad lived Hakeem the Wise One, and many people went to him for counsel which he gave freely to all, asking nothing in return. There came to him a young man who had spent much but got little, and said: "Tell me, Wise One, what shall I do to receive the most for that which I spend?" Hakeem answered, "A thing that is bought or sold has no value unless it contains that which cannot be bought or sold. Look for the Priceless Ingredient." "But what is this Priceless Ingredient?" asked the young man.

Spoke then the Wise One. "My son, the Priceless Ingredient of every product in the market-place is the Honor and Integrity of him who makes it. Consider his name before you buy."

Quarrel—Quarrels

1484.   We often quarrel with the unfortunate to get rid of pitying them.

—LUC DE CLAPIERS VAUVENARGUES

1485.   When worthy men fall out, only one of them may be faulty at first; but if strife continue long, commonly both become guilty.

—THOMAS FULLER

Question—Questions

1486. In most quarrels there is a fault on both sides. A quarrel may be compared to a spark, which cannot be produced without a flint, as well as steel. Either of them alone may hammer on wood forever, no fire will follow.

—CHARLES C. COLTON

Question—Questions

1487. The fool wonders, the wise man asks.

—BENJAMIN DISRAELI

1488. A wise question is partial knowledge.

—FRANCIS BACON

Quotation—Quotations

1489. The Devil can cite Scripture for his purpose.

—WILLIAM SHAKESPEARE

1490. A thing is never too often repeated which is never sufficiently learned.

—SENECA

1491. A great man quotes bravely, and will not draw on his invention when his memory serves him with a word as good.

—RALPH WALDO EMERSON

1492. Let every bookworm, when in any fragrant scarce old tome he discovers a sentence, a story, an illustration, that does his heart good, hasten to give it.

—SAMUEL T. COLERIDGE

1493. He that recalls the attention of mankind to any part of learning which time has left behind it may be truly said to advance the literature of his own age.

—DR. SAMUEL JOHNSON

Race relations

1494. America needs the Negro as a constant reminder of the gap between its promise and fulfillment.

—RABBI RICHARD G. HIRSCH

1495. Whenever I hear a man or woman express hatred for any race, I wonder just what is in themselves they hate so much. You can always be sure of this: You cannot express hatred for anything or anybody unless you make use of the supply of hatred within yourself. The only hatred you can express is your own personal possession. To hate is to be enslaved by evil.

—THOMAS DREIER

Reading

1496. To read without reflecting is like eating without digesting.

—EDMUND BURKE

1497. We should be as careful of the books we read as of the company we keep.

1498. To acquire the habit of reading is to construct for yourself a refuge from almost all of the miseries of life.

—W. SOMERSET MAUGHAM

1499. Some read books only with a view to find fault, while others read only to be taught; the former are like venomous spiders, extracting a poisonous quality, where the latter, like the bees, sip out a sweet and profitable juice.

—SIR ROGER L'ESTRANGE

1500. To think without a proper amount of good reading is to limit our thinking to our own tiny plot of ground. The crop cannot be large. To observe only and neglect reading is to deny ourselves the immense value of other people's observations; and since the better books are written by trained observers the loss is sure to be enormous. Extensive reading without the discipline of practical observation will lead to bookishness and artificiality. Reading and observing without a great deal of meditating will fill the mind with learned lumber that will always remain alien to us. Knowledge to be our own must be digested by thinking.

Real estate

1501. It's getting so there are only two kinds of houses on the market—the kind you don't want and the kind you can't afford.

Reality—Realities

1502. Fortune does not change men; it unmasks them.
—MME. SUZANNE NECKER

1503. Fearful as reality is, it is less fearful than evasions of reality ... it is useless to evade reality, because it only makes it more virulent in the end. But instead, look steadfastly into the slit, pin-pointed malignant eyes of reality: as an old-hand trainer dominates his wild beasts.
—CAITLIN THOMAS

Recreation

1504. Work hard but take time to live. Man, the worker, and man, the player, are not two men, but one.
—THOMAS W. LANTZ

1505. Recreation's purpose is not to kill time, but rather to make time live; not to help the individual serve time but to make time serve him; not to encourage people to hide from themselves but to help them find themselves.
—G. OTT ROMNEY

Red tape

1506. One morning when a lieutenant reported for work at the base housing office he found the noncommissioned officer-in-charge, a seasoned master sergeant, searching through every desk drawer and shelf in the office, mumbling under his breath.

"What's the trouble, Sarge, lose something?" asked the lieutenant.

"I don't know what to do, Lieutenant," replied the sergeant. "We run outta forms to order forms with."

—1ST LT. HAROLD D. CRAIG

1507. Red tape is neither new nor a strictly American bureaucratic invention. It is said that there was a time when the windows of Windsor Castle were never washed on the inside and the outside at the same time. The outside of the windows was under the jurisdiction of Woods and Forests while the inside was under the jurisdiction of the Lord Stewards. It took a forced meeting of the two departments before both sides of the windows could be washed on the same day.

Reform—Reforms

1508. Most reformers come from the meddle class.

1509. To reform means to shatter one form and to create another; but the two sides of this act are not always equally intended nor equally successful.

—GEORGE SANTAYANA

Religion

1510. When your religion gets into the past tense it becomes pretense.

1511. Educate men without religion and you make them but clever devils.

—DUKE OF WELLINGTON

1512. Religion converts despair, which destroys, into resignation, which submits.

—LADY BLESSINGTON

Religion

1513. In religion as in friendship, they who profess most are ever the least sincere.

—R. B. Sheridan

1514. If your religion does not change you then you had better change your religion.

—Elbert Hubbard

1515. Better a sincere atheist than a man who says he believes in God but lives as if he didn't.

1516. It is rare to see a rich man religious; for religion preaches restraint, and riches prompt to unlicensed freedom.

—Owen Feltham

1517. Religions are different paths to the same summit: The one which approaches from the East reaches it as well as the one from the West.

—K. Y. Azizuddin

1518. When a man shapes his religion to the contours of his desires, he has in reality, only offered a form of appeasement to his conscience.

—Douglas Meador

1519. A young girl was asked: "Whose preaching brought you to Christ?" She replied: "It wasn't anybody's preaching; it was Aunt Mary's *practicing.*"

1520. Religion does not repose upon a choice of logic; it is the poetry of man's experience, the philosophy of the history of his life.

—Robert Louis Stevenson

1521. Let us accept different forms of religion among men, as we accept different languages, wherein there is still but one human nature expressed. Every genius has most power in his own language, and every heart in its own religion.

—JEAN PAUL RICHTER

1522. Once when inspecting a school, a visitor asked this question of the head teacher: "Where in your day's schedule do you teach religion?"

"We teach it all day long," was the reply. "We teach it in arithmetic, by accuracy. We teach it in language, by learning to say what we mean. We teach it in history, by humanity. We teach it in geography, by breadth of mind. We teach it in handicraft, by thoroughness. We teach it in astronomy, by reverence. We teach it in the playground, by fair play. We teach it by kindness to animals, by good manners to one another, and by helpfulness in all things. We teach it by showing the young that we, their elders, are their friends."

1523. Samuel Taylor Coleridge, the great English poet of the Romantic period, was once talking with a man who told him that he did not believe in giving children any religious instruction whatsoever. His theory was that the child's mind should not be prejudiced in any direction, but when he came to years of discretion, he should be permitted to choose his religious opinions for himself. Coleridge said nothing, but after a while he asked his visitor if he would like to see his garden. The man said he would, and Coleridge took him out into the garden, where only weeds were growing. The man looked at Coleridge in surprise, and said, "Why, this is not a garden! There are nothing but weeds here!"

"Well, you see," answered Coleridge, "I did not wish to infringe upon the liberty of the garden in any way. I was just giving the garden a chance to express itself and to choose its own production."

—REV. E. OWEN KELLUM, JR.

Religion-Science. See Science-Religion

Religious freedom

1524. Of all the blessings which America bestows upon her citizens religious freedom stands as the living monument to her greatness. Without freedom to worship, for each individual to seek God in his own way, the meaning of liberty would be empty indeed.

—SENATOR FRANK CHURCH

1525. Freedom of religion is a positive right. It is a right to *do*, not a right merely to refuse to do. Freedom of worship means the right of the individual to choose and to adhere to whichever religion he prefers. He should be able to join others in religious association in order that together they may express their beliefs, and he should incur no civil penalty because of his religious views.

—MERLIN L. NEFF

Remorse

1526. Remorse is the form that failure takes when it has made a grab and got nothing.

—ELBERT HUBBARD

Reputation

1527. Reputation is precious, but character is priceless.

1528. Many a man's reputation would not know his character if they met on the street.

—ELBERT HUBBARD

1529. An honest reputation is within the reach of all men; they obtain it by social virtues, and by doing their duty. This kind of reputation, it is true, is neither brillant nor startlng, but it is often the most useful for happiness.

—FRANCOIS DE LA ROCHEFOUCAULD

Research

1530. Two professors arrived in a small Mexican town to spend the summer in research. Exasperated at the slow pace of everything, one of them voiced the opinion that the natives did not even know how to tell time. The other professor went walking the next morning and espied a native reclining in the shade of a wall with his faithful burro beside him. To research his partner's opinion, he asked, "What time is it?"

The Mexican reached out and lifted the tail of his burro and said, "9:15." The professor suppressed his astonishment and looked at his watch. Surely enough it was that time. He continued his walk. About an hour later he returned and again asked, "What time is it now?" The Mexican lifted the burro's tail and replied, "10 o'clock."

The professor hurried back to his partner. "We are dead wrong" he reported. "I saw the most amazing thing, a native without a watch who could tell time by his burro's tail."

Both professors hurried back. Neither man nor beast had moved a foot since the previous encounter. When questioned, the man again lifted the animal's tail and announced, "10:45."

"This is beyond belief," cried the second professor. "How can you possibly tell time by that burro's tail?"

"Eet es easy, senors," replied the Mexican. "When I leeft his tail I can see the clock in the town tower."

Resentment

1531.   Resentment seems to have been given us by nature for defense, and for defense only; it is the safeguard of justice, and the security of innocence.

—Adam Smith

1532.   The word "resent" means to feel again. When you continue to think about a hurt and dwell on it, and talk about it, you are in effect refeeling the injury or rehurting yourself. This may cause all sorts of unhappy psychological and emotional reactions. . . . When grievance and hurt are drained off, they will have no opportunity to harden into misunderstanding and hostility.

—Dr. Norman Vincent Peale

Resourcefulness

1533.   When Will S. Taylor and Ernest Watson were on a sketching trip in Italy, they sometimes attracted too large a group of kibitzers—two or three might be tolerated, but no more. Then Taylor hit upon the idea of arising from his sketching stool, removing his hat, and passing it around like a beggar entreating the onlookers with the word *solde* (an Italian small coin). It worked.

1534. During Roman Emperor Nero's regime two officials plotted to kill a noble captive who had insulted them, by having him thrown to the lions in the public arena. However, under Roman law he was entitled to a chance to live if he were lucky enough to draw the right slip of paper from a helmet in which two slips were placed, one marked "no," signifying freedom, the other marked "yes," signifying death. As the time for the drawing drew near, the Roman officials sought to make doubly sure that their victim would not escape by marking both slips "yes," but a friendly guard warned the captive of their action. Taken before his judges to make the drawing, he selected one slip and immediately tore it to bits, saying "I am free." The Romans stared in anger. "One moment—what did your slip say?" they cried. "Read the one which remains," replied the captive as he moved toward the door.

1535. Some people seem to have the knack for turning misfortunes to their advantage. Take, for instance, the farmer who planted a ten acre field of corn. It looked like he would have a bumper crop—until the corn borers got into it.

"Why, in less than two days," he said, "they practically wiped out that whole field. While I sat around feeling sorry for myself, I suddenly got an idea. Why not harvest the corn borers and sell them for fish bait? So I did. And do you know that I made twice as much money selling the corn borers as I would have made off the corn crop if it had matured?"

—Bill Rieger

Responsibility—Responsibilities

1536. One way to keep a man's feet on the ground is to put a heavy responsibility on his shoulders.

—Phoebe Beeber

1537. God educates men by casting them upon their own resources. Man learns to swim by being tossed into life's maelstrom and left to make his way ashore. No youth can learn to sail his lifecraft in a lake sequestered and sheltered from all storms, where other vessels never come. Skill comes through sailing one's craft amidst rocks and bars and opposing fleets, amidst storms and whirls and countercurrents. Responsibility alone drives man to toil and brings out his best gifts.

—Newell D. Hillis

Retirement

1538. You'll need less to live on after you retire, but you'll need it a *whole lot* more.

1539. Retirement is a misnomer. It's really the time for your second career. Time for the old dog to perform new tricks, not to rest and rust.

1540. Exert your talents and distinguish yourself, and don't think of retiring from the world until the world will be sorry that you retire.

—Dr. Samuel Johnson

Retrogression

1541. Keep out of the suction caused by those who drift backwards.

—E. K. Piper

1542. Any time the going seems easier, better check and see if you're not going downhill.

Retrospect

1543. Be careful that your yesterday doesn't fill up too much of today.

1544. The oftener you look back, the quicker you won't get there.

Revenge

1545. A time filled with varied and interesting experiences seems short in passing, but long as we look back. On the other hand, a tract of time empty of experience seems long in passing, but in retrospect short.
—WILLIAM JAMES

Revenge

1546. Revenge converts a little right into a great wrong.
—GERMAN PROVERB

1547. Revenge is like biting a dog because the dog bit you.

1548. If you want to get even with someone—why not start with someone who has helped you.

1549. I will not be revenged, and this I owe to my enemy; but I will remember, and this I owe to myself.
—CHARLES C. COLTON

1550. In ancient days a Philosopher saw a Fool beating his Donkey. "Abstain, my son, abstain, I implore you," said the Philosopher. "Don't you know that those who resort to violence shall suffer from violence?"

"That," explained the Fool, diligently belaboring the animal, "is what I am trying to teach this beast—which has just kicked me."

Doubtless," murmured the Philosopher to himself as he walked away, "the wisdom of fools is no deeper nor truer than ours, but they really do seem to have a more impressive way of imparting it."

1551. One day a little girl in a white frock and with an armful of flowers, passed by a boy who was playing in the dusty street. The sight of that dainty figure stirred the spirit of mischief in the boy's heart and suddenly he threw a handful of dirt at the little girl—it struck the edge of her white dress and fell in a shower upon her white kid shoes. The girl stood still—her face flushed pink. Her lips trembled as if she would cry but instead a smile broke over her face, and taking a flower from the others, she tossed it at the boy who stood waiting to see what she was going to do.

What a victory it would be for us if our hearts were big enough to toss back a smile and a friendly word every time life gave us a hurt!

Revolution—Revolutions

1552. The best security against revolution is in constant correction of abuses and introduction of needed improvements. It is the neglect of timely repair that makes rebuilding necessary.

—RICHARD WHATELY

1553. Martin Luther defied history; Karl Marx interpreted it; and Henry Ford contemptuously ignored it; and all three of them were the architects of revolutions. But revolutions must always be in the making since it is through them that the world moves and society reshapes and purges itself. Every revolution has a sense of history in it somewhere, for history is in itself just as much a revolutionary force as it is a record of the past. The revolution which becomes cruel and horrible begins nearly always with a repudiation of history, or of most of its values. The revolution in which charity tempers the violence of change begins with an assertion of the value of historic continuity.

—ROGER LLOYD

Reward—Rewards

1554. The world has a way of giving what is demanded of it. If you are frightened and look for failure and poverty, you will get them, no matter how hard you may try to succeed. Lack of faith in yourself, in what life will do for you, cuts you off from the good things of the world. Expect victory and you make victory. Nowhere is this truer than in business life, where bravery and faith bring both material and spiritual rewards.

—DR. PRESTON BRADLEY

1555. All acts of thoughtfulness and kindness must spring from the heart for the only reward one is likely to receive is an inner satisfaction. Yet

251

Risk

once in a while under unusual circumstances, a thoughtful kindness does return a rich and tangible reward.

One such legend of American business began on a stormy night in Philadelphia in the Nineties. A man and his wife entered a small hotel after midnight seeking a room. They had no baggage, nor had they made reservations, for the overnight stop was unplanned. They had tried for hours to find accommodations in other hotels, but a convention had taken up all available space.

The clerk on duty could have turned them down with a clear conscience because even his small hotel was also sold out. Perhaps he considered the weather outside, or perhaps the look of weariness on the faces of the couple touched his heart.

"I'll tell you what," he said. "You can have my room, if that is agreeable with you."

They protested at first, not wanting to impose on him, but the clerk's reassurances were so sincere, they could not refuse the offer. The next morning when they paid their bill, the guest thanked him and said, "You ought to be managing the finest hotel in the United States."

Like any of us, the clerk was pleased with the compliment but thought no more of the incident. Some time later he received a round-trip ticket to New York City and an invitation to visit the man to whom he had given his room that rainy night.

William Waldorf Astor was planning to build a new thirteen-story hotel at the corner of 33rd Street and Fifth Avenue. The Waldorf, which later became the Waldorf-Astoria, was to be the finest hotel in the United States. He wanted the clerk, George C. Boldt, to help in the planning and to be its first manager.

Risk

1556. A ship is safe when it is in harbor. But that is not what ships are for.

1557. Who would not have his footsteps show
Must walk in neither mud nor snow.
—From the Chinese

Rivalry

1558. Women do not disapproved of their rivals; they hate them.
—James Parton

252

1559. It is impossible for authors to discover beauties in one another's works: they have eyes only for spots and blemishes.

—Joseph Addison

Romance

1560. She most attracts who longest can refuse.

—Aaron Hill

1561. Generally the woman chooses the man that will choose her.

—Paul Geraldy

1562. In some European countries coffee plays an important role in any romance. The family invites their daughter's suitor to a family dinner. The prospective marriage is discussed in great detail—including the financial aspect. When the time comes for a decision, the family does not say yes or no in deference to the suitor's feelings. Instead the talk ends with coffee. If the coffee is sweetened, the suitor will soon be one of the family. If not, he will have to find a new romance.

Salesmanship

1563. A good salesman *may* be a good orator, but he *must* be a good listener.

1564. Easy sales are like tranquilizers. They wear off. Then the real selling becomes twice as difficult.

1565. A good salesman is somewhat like a key. Sometimes he must have brass. He must always go around poking in the right places. He will always make pockets jingle. Above all he must be able to open a closed door.

—Frank G. McInnis

1566. There are two methods to influence the prospect to buy. One is logical reasoning. The other is suggestion. By logical reasoning, the salesman must persuade and convince the prospect to buy by offering facts why it is wise to buy. By suggestion he plants an idea in the prospect's mind, and this idea ferments and gives him an impulse to buy.

—J. FRANK STRAWN

1567. The salesman is a vitally needed person. He not only presents to the buying public those goods which enable them to enjoy better living, but he also assists the manufacturer, dealer, and shipper in the conduct of their businesses. His optimistic attitude stimulates business and prosperity. He is the front-line fighter against pessimism and business depressions.

—CLARENCE A. KELLEY

1568. Salesmen move forward with the times. When one product becomes outmoded, they switch to another. Salesmen replaced the broom with the vacuum cleaner, the ice box with the refrigerator and the horse and buggy with the automobile. Each change brings progress for them and their careers. Tomorrow's products and the opportunities they will bring are waiting for the young men and women who are getting started now.

1569. The old stereotype of the salesman as a brash, fast-talking drummer is becoming obsolete. The new breed is polished, educated, carefully trained. Often he's not called a salesman at all but a "professional representative," "customer specialist," "company representative." And his function is not simply to sell but to service and counsel customers as well. ... This new type of company representative is a purveyor of information about his products as well as of the products themselves. He not only knows his customer's needs but actually, and often by invitation, helps to create those needs.

1570. When Henry Ford purchased a very large life insurance policy for himself, the Detroit newspapers blazoned the fact, since the amount was so large and Mr. Ford was so prominent.

One of the articles was read by an old friend of Ford who happened to be in the insurance business. Being surprised completely by the purchase, since he had not heard Ford was in the market for insurance, this friend went to see Mr. Ford and asked him if the story was really true. Ford replied that it most certainly was. The friend asked why the policy wasn't bought from him since he was a personal friend and had been in the insurance business for many years. Henry Ford's simple reply was, "You never asked me."

Salutation

1571. A woman who was hard of hearing found herself seated next to a distinguished clergyman at a banquet who was also a college professor with a Ph.D. In spite of his talents, he was not inclined to engage freely in conversations with strangers at social gatherings. The woman had tried several starts without success when she suddenly had an idea.

Smiling her best she said, "I am a little puzzled about how to address you. Should I call you Reverend Dodds, Professor Dodds, Doctor Dodds, or just plain Mr. Dodds?"

"Just call me anything you like," he replied genially. "Some of my best friends call me an old fool."

"Oh," she replied, not hearing correctly but anxious to be pleasant, "those people really know you, don't they?"

Scandal

1572. Scandal breeds hatred; hatred begets division; division makes faction, and faction brings ruin.

—Francis Quarles

1573. The tale-bearer and the tale-hearer should be both hanged up, back to back, one by the tongue, the other by the ear.

—Robert South

School—Schools

1574. Tradition is what schools get when they don't want to build new buildings.

Science

1575. The public school is the common denominator of our much cherished democratic way of life. It is in the public school that the concept of equal educational opportunity for all has its seedbed. The public school is the "rock of ages" for those who would build on a solid educational foundation. The public school is a shelter from a stormy blast for the weary, wayworn retarded child. The public school is the fountain of youth for all those who would sup at her store of knowledge. The public school is the major American stronghold where an acceptable level of conduct is taught, demanded and maintained. Our society—all races, colors, creeds, and classes—turn to the public school for leadership and guidance.

—Blaine M. Madison

Science

1576. The only things left for science to control are women and the weather.

1577. Science is a first-rate piece of furniture for a man's upper chamber, if he has common sense on the ground floor.

—Dr. Oliver Wendell Holmes

1578. The more science we have, the more we are in need of wisdom to prevent its misuse. The imminent tragedy of the contemporary world is written in the fact that positivistic modern culture has magnified science and almost completely emancipated itself from wisdom.

—Mortimer J. Adler

Science—Religion

1579. Science, sometimes regarded as abettor of irreligion, now frequently paves the way to faith. Scientists are the first to admit that they have loosed in the world forces which are safe only in the hands of devout and reverent men.

1580. Stated in the simplest terms, science is but a sense of curiosity about life, religion is a sense of reverence for life, literature is a sense of wonder at life, art is a taste for life, while philosophy is an attitude toward life, based on a greater or lesser, but always limited, comprehension of the universe as far as we happen to know it.

—LIN YUTANG

1581. The true scientist lives by faith. Each day he goes into his laboratory in search of truth, believing what he cannot prove. He has the will to believe in the absence of absolute certainty and couples it with action in accordance with his belief.

Religious faith is concerned with ultimates—the purpose and goal of life. True religion is the vision of another and better world—invisible but eternal—holding the higher standards and values that give richness and meaning to life. Faith is truly a great adventure.

—DONALD M. GRAHAM

Season—Seasons

1582. What's good about March? Well, for one thing, it keeps February and April apart.

1583. Mother Nature is a wonderful woman, but she's no acrobat. She still can't jump from summer to winter without a fall, nor from winter to summer without a spring.

Seating assignments

1584. *A Plea For Understanding*
Man has climbed Everest
Conquered the seas
Brought cruel tyrants
To their knees
Spanned raging rivers
With bridges of steel
And built endless roads
For the automobile.
Yet these are puny, prosaic feats,
Compared to assigning everyone seats.

—ANONYMOUS

257

Secret—Secrets—Secrecy

1585. The man who has no secrets from his wife either has no secrets or no wife.

—GILBERT WELLS

1586. He who trusts a secret to his servant makes his own man his master.

—JOHN DRYDEN

1587. A secret is too little for one, enough for two, and too much for three.

—JAMES HOWELL

1588. There are some occasions when a man must tell half his secret, in order to conceal the rest.

—LORD CHESTERFIELD

1589. It is said that he or she who admits the possession of a secret has already half revealed it. Certainly it is a great deal gained towards the acquisition of a treasure, to know exactly where it is.

—WILLIAM GILMORE SIMMS

Security

1590. You get the short end of the bargain when you trade opportunity for security.

1591. Too many people are thinking of security instead of opportunity. They seem more afraid of life than death.

—JAMES F. BYRNES

Self-appraisal

1592. Self-portraits usually are colored.

1593. Never to talk about oneself is a very refined form of hypocrisy.
—Friedrich Wilhelm Nietzsche

1594. To expect more than your mother expected of you is expecting too much.
—William Feather

1595. The man who knows his worth respects his fellow man because he respects himself first. He does not boast; is not self-seeking; nor does he force his personal opinion on others.
—Harry M. Banfield

1596. When Abraham Lincoln was a candidate for President of the United States, someone asked him about his aspirations to that high office. He answered that he did not fear his opponents, "But," he said, "there is a man named Lincoln of whom I am very much afraid. If I am defeated, it will be by that man."
—Rev. Dillard S. Miller

1597. Give us, O. Lord, the vision to see our own faults first, the wisdom to appreciate how offensive they may be to others, the understanding to know how difficult it may be to correct them, the courage to try in spite of it, the strength to persist long after we would like to give up, and the humility to give You a share of the credit when we do succeed.

Self-assurance

1598. For they can conquer who believe they can.
—Virgil

1599. Men who have excessive faith in their theories or ideas are not only ill-prepared for making discoveries; they also make poor observations.
—Claude Bernard

Self-confidence

1600. If a man has faith in his power, he can wait.

—ELBERT HUBBARD

1601. The strength that comes from confidence can be quickly lost in conceit.

1602. The good opinion of others is wasted on those who lack faith in themselves.

1603. The man who has confidence in himself inspires confidence in others. They give him the opportunity to prove what he can do.

Self-control

1604. No man is free who cannot control himself.

—PYTHAGORAS

1605. The person who laughs outside when he is crying inside, who wears a smile on his face when there are tears in his heart, has mastered the art of all arts—self-control.

1606. No horse gets anywhere until he is harnessed. No steam or gas ever drives anything until it is confined. No Niagara ever is turned into light and power until it is tunneled. No life ever grows great until it is focused, dedicated, disciplined.

—DR. HARRY EMERSON FOSDICK

Self-deception

1607. The first and worst of all frauds is to cheat oneself. All sin is easy after that.

—SAMUEL BAILEY

1608. It is as easy to deceive one's self without perceiving it as it is difficult to deceive others without their finding it out.

—François de La Rochefoucauld

Self-denial

1609. The more a man denies himself, the more he shall obtain from God.

—Horace

1610. It's easier to make money than save it. The latter involves self-denial.

1611. The worst education which teaches self-denial is better than the best which teaches everything else, and not that.

—John Sterling

Self-discipline

1612. Like most writers, Don Marquis, humorist and columnist, procrastinated shamefully before putting pen to paper, but he had his own method of disciplining himself. A friend once asked him: "How do you ever manage to get today's work done?" "That's simple," replied Marquis, "I pretend it is yesterday's."

1613. The man imbued with self-confidence wastes no time worrying about what others may think, or listening to the doubts and fears of the timid ones. He decides what he wants to do, determines that he can do it, and then goes to work to prove to himself that he is right.

—*Nuggets*

1614. It is an established fact that the men and women who have reached a high degree of success in the great things of the world, who are examples worthy of emulation, have been and are people who have studied themselves. They learned how to strengthen their weak points, cultivate their capabilities and arouse their latent talents and energies by self-discipline; and through their efforts to become something worthwhile in life have developed strong characters which enabled them to reach the top of the ladder in their particular lines.

1615.   The French novelist, Émile Zola, is said to have set himself the task of writing four pages of finished material each day. He continued this practice for many years, and while one of his daily stints considered alone does not seem much, he presented the world with many interesting volumes before his life ended.

Zola had no employer standing over him while he worked. He performed an honest day's work each day through self-discipline. It is true that he found the work which was congenial to him, but it is even more important that he worked assiduously at it. He wrote and revised, added and deleted, because like most great authors he was never fully satisfied with the early drafts of anything he wrote. Small wonder that he became one of the most widely read authors of his time.

Self-doubt

1616.   Great men suffer hours of depression through introspection and self-doubt. That is why they are great. That is why you will find modesty and humility the characteristics of such men.

—Bruce Barton

1617.   A person who doubts himself is like a man who would enlist in the ranks of his enemies and bear arms against himself. He makes his failure certain by himself being the first person to be convinced of it.

—Alexandre Dumas

Self-improvement

1618.   Keep proving your worth by improving it.

1619.   We gain nothing by being with such as ourselves; we encourage each other in mediocrity. I am always longing to be with men more excellent than myself.

—Charles Lamb

1620. Failure to hit the bull's-eye is never the fault of the target. To improve one's aim, one should seek to improve himself.

1621. Always dream and shoot higher than you know you can do. Don't bother just to be better than your contemporaries or predecessors. Try to be better than yourself.
—WILLIAM FAULKNER

1622. The initiative for self-development must come from the individual, since no one can force him to improve himself. This means you must be a self-starter in charting your course for the future.

1623. A man's work is in danger of deteriorating when he thinks he has found the one best formula for doing it. If he thinks that, he is likely to feel that all he needs is merely to go on repeating himself ... so long as a person is searching for better ways of doing his work he is fairly safe.
—EUGENE O'NEILL

Self-interest

1624. Who thinks only of himself is hopelessly uneducated. He is not educated, no matter how instructed he may be.
—NICHOLAS MURRAY BUTLER

1625. The world will always be governed by self-interest; we should not try to stop this; we should try and make the self-interest of cads a little more coincident with that of decent people.
—SAMUEL BUTLER

Selfishness

1626. If I am not for myself who will be for me? But if I am for myself alone what am I? If not now—when?
—RABBI HILLEL

Self-love

1627. It is to be doubted whether he will ever find the way to heaven who desires to go thither alone.

—OWEN FELTHAM

Self-love

1628. Love thyself last.

—WILLIAM SHAKESPEARE

1629. Self-love is not so vile a sin as self-neglecting.

—WILLIAM SHAKESPEARE

1630. Self-love is often rather arrogant than blind; it does not hide our faults from ourselves, but persuades us that they escape the notice of others.

—DR. SAMUEL JOHNSON

1631. Socrates was asked by a disciple: "Why is it that you tell everybody who wants to become your disciple to look into this pond here and tell you what he sees?"

"That is very simple, my friend," answered the sage. "I am ready to accept all those who tell me they see the fish swimming around. But those who see only their own image mirrored in the water are in love with their Ego. I have no use for them."

Self-praise

1632. The man who sings his own praise invariably sings a solo.

1633. The most silent people are generally those who think most highly of themselves.

—WILLIAM HAZLITT

1634. The trouble with singing one's own praise is that he seldom gets the right pitch.

264

Self-reliance

1635. No man should part with his own individuality and become that of another.

—WILLIAM E. CHANNING

1636. He who thinks he can find within himself the means of doing without others is much mistaken; but he who thinks that others cannot do without him is still more mistaken.

—FRANÇOIS DE LA ROCHEFOUCAULD

Self-respect

1637. The truest self-respect is not to think of self.

—HENRY WARD BEECHER

1638. When people do not respect us we are sharply offended; yet deep down in his private heart no man much respects himself.

—MARK TWAIN

1639. When all is said and done, it is the strength and wisdom that comes from within, not that which is imposed from without that justifies us in our own eyes and in the eyes of the world. If we have that we can face the world upon our own ground and go forward into the future in freedom. Here is something truly indestructible.

—JOHN O'LONDON

Sensitivity

1640. The heart that is soonest awake to the flowers is always the first to be touched by the thorns.

—THOMAS MOORE

1641. There are moments when petty slights are harder to bear than even a serious injury. Men have died of the festering of a gnat bite.

—CECIL DANBY

1642. Some people constantly complain of wounded pride, are perpetually being humiliated, resent the way they are treated. Some of them admit they are sensitive. The real trouble, however, usually is not sensitiveness, but vanity. The cure is the cultivation of a larger measure of humility. The world loves to take the high-and-mighty nobody down a peg. Courteous manners inspire courteous treatment. Snobbishness incites retaliation. If you are supersensitive and find yourself frequently subjected to treatment you resent, try to change your own attitude to one of courtesy and humility—and watch how the world's attitude towards you and your outlook towards the world will change for the better. It doesn't pay to allow vanity to make you unhappy and to interfere with your development and progress.

—B. C. FORBES

Sentiment—Sentiments

1643. All the beautiful sentiments in the world weigh less than a single lovely action.

—JAMES RUSSELL LOWELL

1644. In the life of a nation ideas are not the only things of value. Sentiment also is of great value; and the way to foster sentiment in people, and to develop it in the young, is to have a well-recorded past and to be familiar with it. . . . A people that studies its own past and rejoices in the nation's proud memories is likely to be a patriotc people, the bulwark of law and the courageous champion of right in the hour of need.

—JOSEPH ANDERSON

Separation

1645. When loving hearts are separated, not the one which is exhaled to heaven but the survivor, it is, which tastes the sting of death.

—JOSEPH JOUBERT

1646. When two loving hearts are torn asunder, it is a shade better to be the one that is driven away into action, than the bereaved twin that petrifies at home.

—CHARLES READE

Seriousness

1647. It is not so important to be serious as it is to be serious about the important things. The monkey wears an expression of seriousness which would do credit to any college student, but the monkey is serious because he itches.

—ROBERT M. HUTCHINS

1648. Seriousness is not a virtue. It would be a heresy, but a much more sensible heresy, to say that seriousness is a vice. It is really a natural trend or lapse, because it is the easiest thing to do. It is much easier to write a good *Times* article than a good joke in *Punch*.

For solemnity flows out of men naturally, but laughter is a leap. It is easy to be heaven; hard to be light. Satan fell by the law of Gravity.

—G. K. CHESTERTON

Sermon—Sermons

1649. The average man's idea of a good sermon is one that goes over his head and hits a neighbor.

1650. A good sermon should not only comfort the afflicted—but afflict the comfortable.

1651. A New York clergyman once offered this suggestion to anyone who felt drowsy during a sermon: "Lift both feet off the floor and keep them elevated two inches. All desire to sleep will disappear."

Shame

1652. Shame may restrain what law does not prohibit.

—SENECA

1653. I consider that man to be undone who is insensible to shame.

—PLAUTUS

Sharing

1654. Nothing is truly infamous, but what is wicked; and therefore shame can never disturb an innocent and virtuous mind.

—Bishop Sherlock

1655. Be assured that when once a woman begins to be ashamed of what she ought not to be ashamed of, she will not be ashamed of what she ought.

—Livy

Sharing

1656. To rejoice in the prosperity of another is to partake of it.

—William Austin

1657. A man is happy who has sufficient for his own needs plus a surplus to share with others—provided that he does.

1658. No one is happy or free who lives only for himself. Joy in living comes from immersion in something one recognizes to be bigger, better, worthier, more enduring than himself. True happiness and true freedom come from squandering one's self for a purpose.

—Carl W. McGeehon

Silence

1659. Silence never yet betrayed anyone!

—Conte de Ravarol

1660. The cruelest lies are often told in silence.

—Robert Louis Stevenson

1661. Some people would say more if they would talk less.

1662. It can show a fine command of language to say nothing.

1663. To sin by silence when they should protest makes cowards out of men.

—Abraham Lincoln

1664. Silence, when nothing need be said, is the eloquence of discretion.

—Christian Nevell Bovee

1665. Not everyone who has the gift of speech understands the value of silence.

—Johann Kaspar Lavater

1666. As we must account for every idle word, so must we for every idle silence.

—Benjamin Franklin

1667. To avoid trouble and insure safety, breathe through your nose. It keeps your mouth shut.

1668. Smart people speak from experience; smarter people, from experience, don't speak.

1669. It is not the stillness of the tongue that matters but the silence of the heart.

1670. When sober what you said when you were drunk; that will teach you to keep your mouth shut.

—Ernest Hemingway

1671. Silence is the voice of the convinced; loudness is the voice of those who want to convince themselves.

—Dagobert D. Runes

Silence

1672. Silence is golden when someone is playing Chopin, or when the thrush is singing. But when there is really cause for something to say, silence is sheer stupidity.

1673. If you keep your mouth shut long enough, somebody is bound to suspect that you have more than the usual amount of common sense.

1674. One might as well keep his mouth shut: If he talks about himself he is a bore and if he talks about others he is labelled a gossip.

1675. Nature, which has given us one organ for speaking, has given us two for hearing, that we may learn that it is better to hear than to speak.

—Nabi Effendi

1676. He knows not how to speak who cannot be silent; still less how to act with vigor and decision. Who hastens to the end is silent; loudness is impotence.

—Johann Kaspar Lavater

1677. Nothing more enhances authority than silence. It is the crowning virtue of the strong, the refuge of the weak, the modesty of the proud, the pride of the humble, the prudence of the wise, and the sense of fools. To speak is to... dissipate one's strength; whereas what action demands is concentration. Silence is a necessary preliminary to the ordering of one's thoughts.

—Charles de Gaulle

1678. When William Rainey Harper was starting a new university in the West (the University of Chicago), he asked Amos Alonzo Stagg to meet him in New Haven where he offered him the job of heading the new physical education department, with faculty status—a new idea at that time—and a salary of $1500 a year.

The idea sounded so fabulous to Stagg that he was stunned into speechlessness. Harper misinterpreted this silence and said, "I think I can stretch it to $2000." With that Stagg's jaws became really locked. So Harper continued, "You're the one I want and somehow or other I'll manage to get you $2500." Stagg managed to recover his tongue and accepted and forever thereafter told the story to show how he made $1000 by keeping his mouth shut.

—As told by the late Judge Hugo M.
Friend of the University of Chicago
Class of 1905

1679. Some men of history won fame because they didn't talk much. They said little and did much. These men were not morose or unsocial. They were simply not loquacious.

George Washington was one of the silent men of our American scene. He talked when it was necessary, was not hesitant when directions were to be given or advice sought, but the famed Virginian was not given to small talk, nor noted as a conversationalist.

Lincoln had his silent hours when he appeared to be withdrawn from the social chatter about him, and was not of the mind to relate incidents of old Indiana and Illinois days. He had his brooding periods, which on occasion were shrouded in deep melancholy.

Calvin Coolidge had a reputation as a silent president, sparing of speech and loving laconic expressions. But when he was in the mood and of a mind to talk, the Vermonter did not lack for words.

Simplicity

1680. There is nothing quite so complicated as simplicity.
—Charles Poore

1681. When a thought is too weak to be simply expressed, it is clear proof that it should be rejected.
—Luc de Clapiers Vauvenargues

Sin—Sins

1682. Bad men hate sin through fear of punishment; good men hate sin through their love of virtue.

Slander

1683. It is certain we all think too much of sin. We are not damned for doing wrong—but for not doing right.

—Robert Louis Stevenson

1684. As no roads are so rough as those that have just been mended, so no sinners are so intolerant as those that have just turned saints.

—Charles C. Colton

Slander

1685. To persevere in one's duty and to be silent are the best answers to calumny.

—George Washington

1686. The proper way to check slander is to despise it; attempt to overtake and refute it, and it will outrun you.

—Alexandre Dumas

1687. Those who, without knowing us, think or speak evil of us, do us no harm; it is not us they attack, but the phantom of their own imagination.

—Jean de La Bruyère

1688. A great deal depends upon a man's courage when he is slandered and traduced. Weak men are crushed by detraction, but the brave hold on and succeed.

—H. S. Stevens

Smile—Smiles

1689. The smile that masks your feelings comes from the brain; the smile that expresses your feelings springs from the heart.

1690. Nothing on earth can smile but man. Gems may flash reflected light, but what is a diamond-flash compared to an eye-flash and a mind-flash. Flowers cannot smile; this is a charm that even they cannot claim. It is the prerogative of man; it is the color which love wears, and cheerfulness and joy—these three. It is a light in the window of the face, by which the heart signifies it is at home and waiting. A face that cannot smile is like a bud that cannot blossom, and dries up on the stalk. Laughter is day and sobriety is night, and a smile is the twilight that hovers gently between both.

—HENRY WARD BEECHER

1691. *The Value of a Smile*

A smile creates happiness in the home, fosters good will in business—and is the countersign of friends.

It is rest to the weary, daylight to the discouraged, sunshine to the sad, and Nature's best antidote for trouble.

Yet it cannot be bought, begged, borrowed, or stolen, for it is something that is no earthly good to anybody until it is given away!

And if someone is too tired to give you a smile, just give him one of yours anyway. For nobody needs a smile as much as those who have none left to give.

—AUTHOR UNKNOWN

Solitude

1692. The happiest of all lives is a busy solitude.

—VOLTAIRE

1693. Half the pleasure of solitude comes from having with us some friend to whom we can say how sweet solitude is.

—WILLIAM JAY

1694. A man must keep a little back shop where he can be himself without reserve. In solitude alone can he know true freedom.

—MICHEL E. de MONTAIGNE

1695. For the most part I do the thing which my own nature drives me to do. It is embarrassing to earn so much respect and love for it.... I live in that solitude which is painful in youth but delicious in the years of maturity.

—ALBERT EINSTEIN

1696. It is easy in the world to live after the world's opinion; it is easy in solitude to live after your own; but the great man is he who, in the midst of the crowd, keeps with perfect sweetness the independence of solitude.

—RALPH WALDO EMERSON

Space, Outer. See **Outer space**

Speech, Freedom of

1697. I have always been among those who believed that the greatest freedom of speech was the greatest safety, because if a man is a fool, the best thing to do is to encourage him to advertise the fact by speaking.

—WOODROW WILSON

1698. If all mankind minus one were of one opinion, and only one person were of the contrary opinion, mankind would be no more justified in silencing that one person, than he, if he had power, would be justified in silencing mankind.

—JOHN STUART MILL

1699. Without free speech no search for truth is possible; without free speech no discovery of truth is useful; without free speech progress is checked and the nations no longer march forward toward the noble life which the future holds for man. Better a thousandfold abuse of free speech than denial of free speech. The abuse dies in a day, but the denial slays the life of the people, and entombs the hope of the race.

—CHARLES BRADLAUGH

Speechmaking. See **Public speaking**

Spelling

1700. There is something wrong in an educational system which does not recognize that some human beings are born with an incapacity to spell.

—ROBERT LYND

1701. An old gentleman who did not have a telephone wanted to order two geese from the butcher. Not wanting to go down in person, he decided to write a note and let the first youngster who passed his house take it for him.

In composing the note, he first wrote: "Please send me two gooses." Reading that over he decided it wasn't correct and tore the note up. On his second trial, he wrote: "Please send me two geeses." This, he decided, was not correct either. For a while he was nonplussed.

Finally, he hit upon a solution. He wrote, "Please send me a goose." After signing his name, he added a postscript: "Send another one along with it."

Spending

1702. The dollar that's been told where to go does a much better job than the one that just went.

1703. According to one psychologist many people who over-spend have never grown up, and are afraid they won't get something if they have to wait.

1704. The man who squanders his money is never, for that reason, held in high repute. If a wastrel is in control in any line of business he is unlikely to hold executive office long. Only in the case of government, though it, too, is supposed to be a responsible organization, is a clearly unproductive spending policy regarded with tolerance hard to justify on any reasonable basis.

—FELIX MORLEY

Sports

1705. To many football fans the pint after touchdown is the most important part of the game.

1706. Football occupies the same relation to education that a bullfight does to farming.

—ELBERT HUBBARD

Statistics

1707. In grandpappy's day the country could be talked into a depression. With modern progress, it now can be statisticized into one.

1708. When we say that some event is a probability, we are usually trying to predict the future. When we say that something is a statistic, we are usually trying to describe the past. For instance, before a novice skier plunges down an expert slope he's merely a probable accident victim. After he has been carried away from the bottom he is a statistic.

Probability and statistics have always had this close relationship. Statistics, as records of past events, give us confidence that the future will remain consistent with the past.

They are always the most interesting questions which can be answered only by "probably," or "maybe," or "perhaps," or "sometimes."

Status quo

1709. No statue was ever erected to the memory of a man or woman who thought it was best to let well enough alone.

1710. You cannot at present change your surroundings. Whatever kind of life you are to live must be lived amid precisely the experience in which you are now moving. Here you must win your victories or suffer your defeats. No restlessness or discontent can change your lot. Others may have other circumstances surrounding them, but here are yours. You had better make up your mind to accept what you cannot alter. You can live a beautiful life in the midst of your present circumstances.

—J. R. MILLER

Strategy

1711. The best strategy is always to be very strong, first generally, then at the decisive point.

1712. Though fraud in all other actions be odious, yet in matters of war it is laudable and glorious, and he who overcomes his enemies

276

by strategem is as much to be praised as he who overcomes them by force.

—Niccolo Machiavelli

Stupidity

1713. Genius may have its limitations but stupidity is not thus handicapped.

—Elbert Hubbard

1714. He is stupid, like all heartless people. For ideas do not come from the head but from the heart.

—Heinrich Heine

1715. Whenever a man does a thoroughly stupid thing, it is always from the noblest of motives.

—Oscar Wilde

Submission

1716. A few conquer by fighting, but it is well to remember that more battles are won by submitting.

—Elbert Hubbard

1717. The marvel of all history is the patience with which men and women submit to burdens unnecessarily laid upon them by their government.

—William E. Borah

Substitute—Substitutes—Substitution

1718. Of all the substitutes, a substitute speaker is the worst.

—Kin Hubbard

1719. Substitutes are not acceptable to the mature mind which desires the thing itself.

—Robert Louis Stevenson

Success

1720. The road to success is always under construction.

1721. If at first you do succeed, don't take any more chances.
—KIN HUBBARD

1722. He met success like a gentleman and disaster like a man.

1723. To climb to the top and not lose your balance is not easy.

1724. Success is the progressive attainment of an intelligent goal.

1725. The secret of success is to be forever pushing without seeming to be.

1726. Success wins glory, but it kills affection, which misfortune fosters.
—ROBERT LOUIS STEVENSON

1727. The secret of success in life is known only to those who have not succeeded.
—JOHN CHURTON COLLINS

1728. Success comes to those who make the greatest profit from the fewest mistakes.

1729. You will never get ahead of anyone as long as you are trying to get even with him.

1730. It takes time to succeed, because success is merely the natural reward for taking the time to do anything well.
—JOSEPH ROSS

1731. The first law of success is to establish a goal in life; the second law is to work toward it.

1732. Success has a way of coming in a hurry after you have endured a long haul of plodding along slowly.

1733. Chance may sometimes help, and sometimes provoke, a success; but must never rule, and rarely allure.

—JOHN RUSKIN

1734. For those who start at the bottom, the top is always a long climb; but for those who start at the top, the bottom is often but a short fall.

1735. Don't be in a hurry to succeed. What would you have to live for afterwards? Better make the horizon your goal; it will always be ahead of you.

—GEORGE BERNARD SHAW

1736. A woman has two chances to a man's one of becoming a success. If she can't get what she wants by being smart, she can usually get it by being dumb.

1737. The secret of a happy and successful life is to be content with the abilities God gave you and discontented with the use you make of them.

—BURTON HILLIS, c *Better Homes & Gardens*

1738. Success is living in a manner that insures immortality which in turn, is not life after death, but rather the continuation of life in the memory of people.

—DR. MORRIS FISHBEIN

1739. The difference between getting somewhere and nowhere is the courage to make an early start. The fellow who sits still and does just what he is told will never be told to do big things.

—CHARLES M. SCHWAB

1740. Success is feminine and like a woman; if you cringe before her, she will override you. So the way to treat her is to show her the back of your hand. Then maybe she will do the crawling.

—WILLIAM FAULKNER

1741. Success is the sum total of little obstacles surmounted. If you are too conscious of the opposition, or if you wait for cooperation, you are licked. But if you will use everything that resists you by putting it to work to propel you, there isn't a thing you cannot accomplish.

—W. F. W. WRATTEN

1742. Wealth, notoriety, place, and power are no measure of success whatever. The only true measure of success is the ratio between what we might have done and what we might have been on the one hand, and the thing we have made and the thing we have made of ourselves on the other.

—H. G. WELLS

1743. A man is successful when he refuses to slander even his enemies; when he does not expect to get paid for everything he does; when he does not wait until tomorrow to do the things he might do today; when he is loyal to his employer and to his associates; when he intelligently cooperates with others, and is tolerant in thought and deed.

1744. If a man consistently prefers honor to wealth, truth to trickery, kindness to covetousness, modesty to vaingloriousness, service to recognition, humility to grandeur, usefulness to material reward—that man wins the sort of success in life that no slumping markets can rob him of. If the material rewards come also, well and good; he will know how to use them. If they do not, it matters little.

1745. A man who is a success never has to prove it. The reason why spectacular spenders throw their money around so conspicuously is because they are trying to prove to others—and to themselves—that they are successful. What they are really demonstrating is their spiritual poverty. Success—the real, not the flashing kind—can never be measured by bank balances; money measures only prosperity. Success is a matter of character.

1746. It is a mistake to suppose that men succeed through success; they much oftener succeed through failure. By far the best experience of men is made up of their remembered failures in dealing with others in the affairs of life. Such failures in sensible men incite to better self-management, and greater tact and self-control, as a means of avoiding them in the future.

—SAMUEL SMILES

1747. Ty Cobb attributed his success in baseball to a letter written to him by his father.

Ty played 37 games with the Augusta Club of the South Atlantic League. He hit a mere .237 and was released. When he wrote his father he received a curt answer, a brief note which read: "Don't come home a failure."

Cobb immediately signed with Anniston, Alabama, in the Southeastern League. He made good, hitting .370. The following spring Augusta gave him another chance which he didn't muff. Cobb went on to become recognized as the greatest baseball player in history, with the most hits, runs and stolen bases. He was made a member of the Baseball Hall of Fame in 1936.

—*Friendly Adventurer,* WINTER 1962

Suffering

1748. If you suffer, thank God!—it is a sure sign that you are alive.

—ELBERT HUBBARD

1749. To have suffered, nay—to suffer, puts a keen edge on what remains of the agreeable. This is a great truth and has to be learned in the fire.

—ROBERT LOUIS STEVENSON,
Letter to William Archer

Supply and demand

1750. A city in Italy fines couples for love-making on benches along a beachwalk. Many offenders and accumulating fines made it necessary, recently, for officials to meet and decide what to do with the money. Yup, you guessed it! They're buying more benches.

1751. The farmer raised two chickens and sold them to a city man and with the proceeds bought two shirts. The city man now had two chickens and the farmer two shirts.

A planner advised the farmer to shorten up on supply so as to increase the price. Accordingly the farmer raised but one chicken and took it to the market, selling it for the price of two—but when he bought a shirt it cost him twice as much as formerly.

The city man had one chicken and the farmer one shirt. This is called the more abundant life?

Suspicion

1752. Ambition and suspicion always go together.
—Georg Christoph Lichtenberg

1753. Suspicion is rather a virtue than a fault, as long as it doth as a dog that watcheth, and doth not bite.
—George Savile (Marquis of Halifax)

Tact

1754. Talent without tact is only half talent.
—Horace Greeley

1755. A wise man sees as much as he ought, not as much as he can.
—Michel E. de Montaigne

Taxation

1756. Temporary taxes outlast permanent waves.

1757. To tax and to please, no more than to love and to be wise, is not not given to men.

—Edmund Burke

1758. The general rule always holds good that in constitutional states liberty is a compensation for the heaviness of taxation; in despotic states the equivalent for liberty is the lightness of taxation.

—Charles de Secondat Montesquieu

Taxes

1759. There's this to be said about taxes—if the taxpayer is alive, he's kicking.

—Vesta M. Kelly

1760. A government that gives you everything you want usually takes everything you have.

1761. The difference between a taxidermist and a tax collector is that the taxidermist takes only your skin.

—Mark Twain

1762. There is nothing sinister in so arranging one's affairs as to keep taxes just as low as possible. Nobody owes any public duty to pay more than the law demands. Taxes are enforced exactions, not voluntary contributions. To demand more in the name of morals is mere cant.

—Learned Hand

1763. A man who cannot be acquainted with me, taxes me; looking from afar at me, he ordains that part of my labor shall go to this or that whimsical end—not as I, but as he happens to fancy. Behold the consequences. Of all debts, men are least willing to pay taxes. What a satire is this on government! Everywhere they think they get their money's worth, except for these.

—Ralph Waldo Emerson

Teacher—Teachers

1764. A good teacher widens the gap of accomplishment between the most able and the least able children in her class; a great teacher widens this gap while greatly increasing the accomplishments of the least able.

1765. A teacher is happiest when everyone understands the lesson, saddest when there is a huge stack of smudgy tests to correct, slowest when the bell-to-go rings, fastest when no one is ready for the test, yet, nicest when you've just decided to hate her, and the most longwinded when keeping you after school.

1766. If a doctor, lawyer or dentist had 40 people in his office at one time, all of whom had different needs, and some of whom didn't want to be there and were causing trouble, and the doctor, lawyer or dentist, without assistance had to treat them all with professional excellence for nine months, then he might have some conception of the classroom teacher's job.

—Donald D. Quinn

1767. Insight or knowledge of oneself is a prerequisite to happiness in teaching. The happy teacher is the well-adjusted teacher. He gets along with others because he gets along with himself. He knows and accepts himself. Against this background of self-knowledge and self-acceptance he sees his purpose in life and his work in the classroom is a consistent effort to achieve that purpose.

—George J. Turner

Teaching

1768. The art of teaching is the art of assisting discovery.

—Mark Van Doren

1769. The word "teaching" is basically misleading. Schools cannot really teach; they can only instill a desire for learning.

—Byron J. Nichols

1770. The whole art of teaching is only the art of awakening the natural curiosity of young minds for the purpose of satisfying it afterward.
—ANATOLE FRANCE

1771. A teacher who can arouse a feeling for one single good action, for one single good poem, accomplishes more than he who fills our memory with rows of natural objects, classified with name and form.
—JOHANN WOLFGANG VON GOETHE

1772. Carlyle once received a letter from a young man which read like this: "Mr. Carlyle, I wish to be a teacher. Will you tell me the secret of successful teaching?" Carlyle immediately wrote back: "Be what you would have your pupils be. All other teaching is unblessed mockery and apery."

Teen-age—Teen-agers

1773. There's nothing wrong with teen-agers that trying to reason with them won't aggravate.
—FRANKLIN P. JONES

1774. In the lexicon of teen-agers, parents are the sum of the squares on both sides of the family.

1775. Too many teen-agers who think marriage will be a solution to their problems find out that marriage itself can be a problem.

1776. Teen-agers are what they are because the affluent American economy can afford them. What appears as rebellion to teachers and other adults actually is a disagreement between the generations as to the stage at which the adolescent may enter the adult world.
—*The Shape of Education for 1962-3*

Temper

1777. Nothing cooks your goose as quickly as a boiling temper.

1778. Our temper gets us into trouble and our pride keeps us there.
—ARNOLD H. GLASOW

Texas—Alaska

1779. With all due respect to Texas and Alaska, the biggest state on the map today is the state of confusion.

1780. "I think the children are old enough now," the Texan whispered to his wife. "Let's tell them about Alaska."

1781. Nothing, it seems, makes Alaskans more happy than the fact that their state exceeds Texas in size. In a restaurant in Nome, this sign hangs on the wall: "Clam Chowder, 50¢. Texas-size bowl, 25¢."

1782. Although Alaska now is the largest state in the Union, Texas still boasts the largest bank lobby, not only in the United States but in the world. The lobby of Houston's newest bank covers one and a half acres.

1783. Senator E. L. Bartlett of Alaska was twitting House Speaker Sam Rayburn of Texas about the fact that Alaskan statehood has reduced Texas to second rank in size.
"If you don't keep quiet," Rayburn warned, "a few Texans will come to your state and throw a cocktail party. When they get through using your ice, you'll be smaller than Rhode Island."
—WALTER TROHAN

1784. Senator John G. Tower (R-Tex) reports that a Texan and an Alaskan were debating the size and importance of their states on a journey by steamer along the Alaskan coast. The Texan was yielding no ground, insisting that the Lone Star State conceded first place in nothing— size, scenery, products or advantages.

As they debated an iceberg loomed ahead. The Texan stopped, studied it a moment, then conceded: "Well, I've got to admit you've got bigger ice cubes."

—WALTER TROHAN

1785. Shortly after Alaska achieved statehood a Texan visited the new state to see if things were really bigger than in Texas. Browsing around Fairbanks, he noticed a farm-supply warehouse stocked with huge stacks of chicken wire. The Texan spoke to one of the warehousemen.

"In Texas the chickens are so big," the Texan laughed, "that chicken wire won't hold them. We don't have any use for chicken wire in Texas."

"That's not chicken wire," the Alaskan replied. "That's mosquito netting."

—RUSSELL NEWBOLD

Thanksgiving Day

1786. On Thanksgiving Day let's count our blessings as thoughtfully as we count our calories.

—HERB LYON

1787. For the true meaning of Thanksgiving, let us not search our surroundings; let us search our hearts.

1788. Thanksgiving is a time for accepting from God's hand what He gives to us. It means that not only do we become thankful when things obviously are good and to our taste and to our liking—anybody can do that—but it also means accepting from God all that He gives.

—REV. LOWELL M. ATKINSON

1789. It is the spirit of Thanksgiving that has the meaning; not the mere preparation for a feast in which so many engage. The simplest fare can be full of meaning and gratitude. Thanksgiving should become a habit on our part, and *every day* we should thank our Creator for the many blessings that are ours. We should be thankful for the privilege of living in a free land, with endless choices for service and happiness. What other nation in the world has placed on its coins the words: "In God We Trust"?

1790. *Proclamation of Thanksgiving*

It has pleased Almighty God to prolong our national life another year, . . . to favor as well our citizens in their homes as our soldiers in their camps, and our sailors on the rivers and seas, with unusual health. He has largely augmented our free population by emancipation and by immigration, while he has opened to us new sources of wealth, and has crowned the labor of our workingmen in every department of industry with abundant rewards. Moreover, he has been pleased to animate and inspire our minds and hearts with fortitude, courage, and resolution sufficient for the great trial . . . into which we have been brought by our adherence as a nation to the cause of freedom and humanity. . . .

Now, therefore, I . . . do hereby appoint and set apart the last Thursday in November next as a day which I desire to be observed by all my fellow-citizens, wherever they then may be, as a day of thanksgiving and praise to Almighty God, the beneficent Creator and Ruler of the Universe. And I do further recommend to my fellow-citizens aforesaid, that on that occasion they do reverently humble themselves in the dust, and from thence offer up penitent and fervent prayers and supplications to the great Disposer of events for a return of the inestimable blessings of peace, union, and harmony throughout the land which it has pleased him to assign as a dwelling-place for ourselves and for our posterity throughout all generations.

—ABRAHAM LINCOLN, 1864

Theory

1791. Man must always in some sense cling to the belief that the unknowable is knowable, otherwise speculation would cease.

—JOHANN WOLFGANG VON GOETHE

1792. A theoretical physicist may develop an accurate formula for the curve of a baseball in flight, but it takes a pitcher years of practice to control the curve.

—CHARLES F. KETTERING

Thinking

1793. One thought driven home is better than three left on base.

1794. Thinking is like loving and dying. Each of us must do it for himself.

—John Ruskin

1795. If our best thoughts come from others, where do they get theirs?

Threat—Threats

1796. He threatens who is afraid.

—French proverb

1797. King Philip of Macedon wrote a threatening letter to the rulers of Sparta, and said:
"If once I enter your territories, I will destroy you all, never to rise again."
The Spartans replied in a letter which contained only one word—IF.

—Plutarch

Thrift

1798. The one person you have to watch if you're going to save money is yourself.

1799. Getting rich is not so difficult. First, learn how to make money faster than you can spend it. From there on, it's quite easy.

1800. Economy has frequently nothing whatever to do with the amount of money being spent, but with the wisdom used in spending it.

—Henry Ford

1801. Economy no more means saving money than it means spending money. It means, the administration of a house; its stewardship; spending or saving, that is, whether money or time, or anything else, to the best possible advantage.

—Josiah Royce

1802. Thriftlessness often fosters cowardice. Thrift inspires courage. Shiftless persons rarely have much backbone. They are so dependent upon others for assistance that often they cannot assert themselves to preserve their self-respect. Their wasteful habits sap their self-reliance, their self-assurance. The thrifty individual, on the other hand, has learned to stand on his own feet. He has learned how to take care of himself, how to manage his affairs, how to provide against emergencies. Therefore, he is little inclined to submit to uncalled for indignities. Nor is he afraid to take reasonable risks. His financial backlog gives him courage. And without courage few successful careers have been built up. Thus we arrive at the formula: Thrift develops courage; courage develops success.

—B. C. Forbes

Time

1803. Time is money few spend wisely.

—Arnold H. Glasow

1804. Time is a dressmaker specializing in alterations.

—Faith Baldwin

1805. Time is not an enemy unless you try to kill it.

1806. Time does not become sacred to us until we have lived it.

1807. It's better to know the importance of a minute than the value of a dollar.

1808. There would be a lot more work done if we weren't living in such a clock-eyed world.

1809. Time is a man's most precious possession—his most precious commodity. To take a man's time, is to take a portion of his life. To give a man some of your time is to give him a portion of yours.
—Margaret E. Mulac

1810. Time may be said to be lost when it is not devoted to some good, useful purpose, or when opportunities of improvement are neglected. We ought to squeeze the most out of our time when we consider that it is short, irrecoverable, uncertain, committed to our trust for which we shall have to give account.

1811. We all complain of the shortness of time, and yet we have much more than we know what to do with. Our lives are spent either in doing nothing at all, or in doing nothing to the purpose, or in doing nothing that we ought to do; we are always complaining our days are few, and acting as though there would be no end of them.
—Seneca

Tit for tat

1812. The robbed that smiles steals something from the thief.
—William Shakespeare

1813. The famous playwright could not place him.
"Chevalier? Chevalier?" he repeated. "What is it you do, young man? I'm afraid I'm not familiar with your work."
To an actor, this was an unforgivable offense. Instead of being offended, however, Chevalier was relieved.
"I'm glad to hear that," he said. "I'm not familiar with your work, either. Now we can start on even terms."

1814. Many years ago a new neighbor moved next door to the great Florentine artist, Botticelli. The man was a weaver. He installed eight looms, which made an annoying noise and shook the walls of the house. The artist called on the weaver to protest, but the latter scoffed at Botticelli and said a man could do anything he wanted to do in his own home.

Noting his wall was higher than his neighbor's, the artist had a huge stone balanced precariously on the top of the wall. The weaver stopped work and rushed over to protest. The artist simply reminded the weaver, "A man can do anything he wants to in his own home." The weaver began to see the artist's problem with considerable understanding.

Toast—Toasts—Toasting

1815. May the most you wish for be the least you get!

1816. May we live to learn well ... and learn to live well!

1817. Love to one, friendship to many, and goodwill to all!

1818. Here's to the New Year—may you *use* it in good health.

1819. Here's to happy times ... may they come often and stay longer!

1820. May the roof above never fall in and the folks below never fall out.

1821. May the years treat you kindly ... and your friends follow suit.

1822. Here's to the ladies ... they need no praise ... they speak for themselves!

1823. Here's to friendship ... the wine of life; let's drink *of* it and *to* it!

1824. Happy are we met, happy have we been;
Happy may we part and happy meet again!

1825. President John F. Kennedy, at a luncheon for members of Congress, gave a new twist to an old toast. The Congressmen lifted their glasses "To the President of the United States." The President responded by lifting his glass, "To the People of the United States."

Tolerance

1826. I believe with all my heart that civilization has produced nothing finer than a man or woman who thinks and practices true tolerance.
—FRANK KNOX

1827. The most lovable quality that any human can possess is tolerance. Tolerance is the vision that enables us to see things from another person's point of view. It is the generosity that concedes to others the right to their own opinions and their own peculiarities. It is the bigness that enables us to let people be happy in their own instead of our way.

Tomorrow

1828. Tomorrow is two days late for yesterday's job.

1829. It is foolish to fear tomorrow—if it comes it will be today.

1830. Every tomorrow has two handles. We can take hold by the handle of anxiety or by the handle of faith.

Traffic, Automobile

1831. Horsepower was a lot safer when the horses had it.

1832. Better be patient on the road than a patient in the hospital.

293

1833. Never gamble in heavy traffic. The cars may be stacked against you.

1834. Drive as if you were early for an appointment with the Internal Revenue Service.

1835. Women have a wonderful sense of right and wrong, but little sense of right and left.
—Don Herold

1836. An automobile can help you see the world, but it's up to you to decide which world.

1837. Too much of the world is run on the theory that you don't need road manners if you drive a five-ton truck.

1838. A highway intersection is one place where it does not pay to call the other fellow's bluff.

1839. In Tokyo the taxicab drivers are required to affix photos of their wives to the windshields of their cabs. The company believes they will drive more carefully if reminded of their loved ones.

1840. Aptitude and attitude are the two things that add up to safe driving. Skill is important but the motorist with the right *attitude* is the one with the safest driving record.
—Carol Lane

1841. A Chinese student was riding in an auto with one of our western speed-demons one day. The driver saw a train coming, and said: "Unless we beat that train across we shall be delayed three minutes." He stepped on the gas, and made it, with only seconds to spare. When they were safely across, the Oriental said quietly: "Now, what are you going to do with the three minutes?"

Travel

1842. Travel makes a wise man better but a fool worse.

—THOMAS FULLER

1843. Being on a ship is being in a jail, with the chance of being drowned.

—DR. SAMUEL JOHNSON

1844. People travel to faraway places to watch, in fascination, the kind of people they ignore at home.

—DAGOBERT D. RUNES

1845. It is hard to understand people who travel miles to enjoy scenery, then litter it with rubbish.

1846. Americans who flock together abroad tend to develop nationalism rather than patriotism. One should not, like a snail, carry one's country on one's back. Its place should be in the heart, invisible but present.

—IRENA WILEY

1847. Foreign travel ought to soften prejudices, religious or political, and liberalize a man's mind; but how many there are who seem to have travelled for the purpose of getting up their rancor against all that is opposed to their notions.

—CHARLES B. FAIRBANKS

Trouble—Troubles

1848. Trouble is the molehill; worry is the mountain.

295

Truth

1849. The entrances to trouble are wide, but the exits are narrow.
—William Feather

1850. The way out of trouble is never as simple as the way in.

1851. The size of your troubles usually depends on whether they are going or coming.

1852. Trouble, like the hill ahead, straightens out when you advance upon it.

Truth. See also **Veracity**

1853. As things change the truth changes.
—Robert Beverly Hale

1854. It is seldom as hard to tell the truth as it is to hide it.

1855. A man had rather live a hundred lies told of him, than one truth which he does not wish to be told.
—Dr. Samuel Johnson

1856. I shall never be influenced by any consideration but one: Is it the truth as I know it—or better still, feel it? If so, shoot, and let the splinters fly where they may.
—Eugene O'Neill

Tyranny

1857. The only tyrant I accept in this world is the "still small voice." within me.
—Mohandas K. Gandhi

Unhappiness

1858. Why fly from the unhappy? Their state makes us more sensible of the value of the happiness we possess.

—Leckinska Stanislaus

1859. Men who are unhappy, like men who sleep badly, are always proud of the fact.

—Bertrand Russell

Unselfishness

1860. No man can live happily who regards himself alone, who turns everything to his own advantage. Thou must live for another if thou wishest to live for thyself.

—Seneca

1861. No one is happy or free who lives only for himself. Joy in living comes from immersion in something one recognizes to be bigger, better, worthier, more enduring than he himself is. True happiness and true freedom come from squandering one's self for a purpose.

—Carl W. McGeehon

Vacation—Vacations

1862. The marvelous part of a vacation is that it makes you feel good enough to go back to work and so poor you have to.

1863. Most people take a vacation to forget everything and sure enough when they reach their destination and unpack they discover they have.

1864. A vacation is when you pack seven suitcases, four children, two aunts, a mother-in-law, two dogs and a parakeet and say, "It's good to get away from it all."

Valentine Day

1865. Valentine Day is for the young in heart regardless of their age.

1866. St. Valentine's Day is an ancient festival of love tokens. There were three St. Valentines who were martyred, but little is known about them. The association of the day with love affairs is thought to have originated in Europe during the Middle Ages, for the people believed the birds chose their mates on that day.

In ancient Rome during the Lupercalia, boys and girls chose their mates for the year, and swains gave their sweethearts gifts on that day. So going steady is really an old custom.

Variety—Varieties

1867. He that sips of many arts drinks of none.
—Thomas Fuller

1868. Sameness is the mother of disgust, variety the cure.
—Petrarch

Veracity. See also **Truth**

1869. Who lies for you will lie against you.
—Russian proverb

1870. A half-truth is the most cowardly of lies.

1871. Remember: one lie does not cost *one* truth but *the* truth.
—Friedrich Hebbel

1872. A liar begins with making falsehood appear like truth, and ends with making truth itself appear like falsehood.
—William Shenstone

1873. It is hard to believe that a man is telling the truth when you know that you would lie if you were in his place.
—H. L. Mencken

1874. If I accustom a servant to tell a lie for *me*, have I not reason to apprehend that he will tell many lies for *himself*.
—Dr. Samuel Johnson

Verbosity

1875. In multitudes of words surely some mistakes.
—Chinese proverb

1876. Lincoln's Gettysburg Address contains 266 words. The Ten Commandments contain 297 words. The Bill of Rights contains 557 words. But a federal agency needed 26,911 words for an order reducing the price of cabbage.

Vocabulary

1877. A man's thinking is exact only to the degree that he has words to make it so. We can think in nothing but words. When our words run out, we come to the end of our thinking; all we can do is to repeat ourselves.
—Elmer G. Letterman

1878. Did you know that you have three vocabularies—one for reading, one for speaking and one for writing? They are never the same and the one that lags the farthest behind is your writing vocabulary. Recognizing words when you read them is one thing. Saying them is another. And writing them is something else because, for one reason, writing involves your knowledge of spelling.
—Leslie J. Nason

Vocation

1879. It is well for a man to respect his own vocation whatever it is. and to think himself bound to uphold it, and to claim for it the respect it deserves.
—Charles Dickens

1880. Fountain pen manufacturer, Lewis E. Waterman, began his business career as an insurance agent. At one time, after working on a client for several weeks, he persuaded the man to take out a large policy.

Waterman called on him with the contract ready for signature. He placed it on the desk and took a fountain pen from his pocket. As he opened it, it began to leak and ink ran over the contact.

Waterman hurried back to his office for another policy form. By the time he returned, however, the man had changed his mind. Waterman was so disgusted that he gave up the insurance business then and there and devoted his time to the development of a reliable fountain pen.

—E. E. Edgar

Vote—Votes—Voting

1881. It's impolite to ask the average person for whom he'll vote, but you can easily find out by asking him which candidate he thinks is going to win.

1882. The entire power of a democracy rests in the vote. With it, citizens affirm their faith in the ability and integrity of incumbent office holders—or "throw the rascals out." If the vote is not used by a large percentage of the people, then rule by a minority is invoked—and the corruptors of government are expert at organizing minority votes. So, from lazy citizenship comes corruption. From corruption comes political confusion. And from confusion comes the death of freedom. The working parts of any machine will mold and rust with lack of attention and disuse. Political machinery is no different. And if the secret ballot, the most vital part of our Republic's political machinery, is allowed to corrode for lack of use, then the whole process of free government will soon grind to a halt.

—Lou Colbert

War

1883. War doesn't determine who is right—only who is left.

1884. In his search for world peace mankind has stuck to his guns.

1885. War is what results when one country takes steps to defend itself from another country that is taking steps to defend itself.

1886. In war, as in life, it is often necessary, when some cherished scheme has failed, to take up the best alternative open, and if so, it is folly not to work for it with all your might.

—Winston Churchill

War—Peace

1887. In peace, sons bury their fathers; in war, fathers bury their sons.

—Herodotus

1888. In a sense no one ever wins a war. Both the winner and the loser are improverished, and peace treaties have so often proved to be the seedbeds of later conflicts. Fighting has never solved anything.

1889. The time has come to realize that the only way armaments will be reduced and a more peaceful world created is to deal with what causes wars and armaments. Every war has come from conflicting political ambitions, when one country insists on imposing its ambitions on an opposing one. Just as there can be no peaceful life in our own country without constant compromise, constant give and take, there cannot be peaceful adjustments in international life without a similar accepted process. Until the people of our own country and the world understand that, wars are going to continue.

Weakness

1890. A weak mind is like a microscope, which magnifies trifling things but cannot receive great ones.

—Lord Chesterfield

Wealth

1891. You cannot run away from a weakness; you must some time fight it out or perish; and if that be so, why not now, and where you stand?
—Robert Louis Stevenson

Wealth

1892. It's hard to get rich in a small town—everybody's watching.

1893. The real measure of our wealth is how much we should be worth if we lost our money.
—John Henry Jowett

1894. Those who dream of wealth without work should wake up to the fact that work is wealth.

1895. To be wealthy, a rich nature is the first requisite and money but the second.
—Robert Louis Stevenson

1896. Riches do not exhilarate us so much with their possession as they torment us with their loss.
—Gregory the Great

1897. Real wealth comes to the man who learns that he is paid best for the things he does for nothing.

1898. The only way for a rich man to be healthy is, by exercise and abstinence, to live as if he was poor.
—William Temple

1899. Riches without charity are worth nothing. They are a blessing only to him who makes them a blessing to others.
—Henry Fielding

1900. It is easier to dream about the good we would do if we had more money than it is to do what we can with what we have.

1901. Concentration of wealth will never be a problem as long as we have those three great institutions for redistributing it: taxes, wives and offspring.

1902. Wealth in itself is neither good nor bad, and the mere possession of wealth is neither good nor evil. It is what one does with his wealth, it is how one uses it, that really matters.

—DR. C. M. REVES

1903. No one is richer than another. Everything depends on what one does with what he has. Each day is full of riches for the man who knows how to appraise its opportunities—and has done the necessary planning to be able to grasp them.

1904. To suppose, as we all suppose, that we could be rich and not behave the way the rich behave, is like supposing that we could drink all day and stay sober.

—LOGAN PEARSALL SMITH

1905. It is true that we might do a vast amount of good if we were wealthy, but it is also highly improbable; not many do; and the art of growing rich is not only quite distinct from that of doing good, but the practice of the one does not at all train a man for practicing the other.

—HENRY DAVID THOREAU

1906. Many years ago Rudyard Kipling made a commencement address at McGill University in Montreal. He said one striking thing which deserves to be kept in remembrance. He was warning the students against an overconcern for money, or position, or glory. He said "Someday you will meet a man who cares for none of these things. Then you will know how poor you are."

—HALFORD E. LUCCOCK

Wisdom

1907. Wisdom is the power to put our time and our knowledge to the proper use.

—Thomas J. Watson

1908. I doubt the wisdom of being too wise: and I see much wisdom in some folly.

—Elbert Hubbard

1909. We must attain wisdom as we go upstairs—one step at a time.

—Tsze-kung

1910. We are made wise not by the recollections of our past, but by the responsibilities of our future.

—George Bernard Shaw

1911. The beginning of wisdom is the realization that the thing you are anxious about today won't seem important tomorrow.

1912. A fool always accuses other persons; a partially wise man, himself; a wholly wise man, neither himself nor others.

—Johann Herder

Wit and humor

1913. To be witty is not enough. One must possess sufficient wit to avoid having too much of it.

—Andre Maurois

1914. Humor is an affirmation of dignity, a declaration of man's superiority to all that befalls him.

—Romain Gary

1915. Wit is a mighty tart, pungent ingredient, and much too acid for some stomachs.

—WASHINGTON IRVING

Witness—Witnesses

1916. Although invisible, there are always two witnesses present at our every action: God and our conscience.

1917. Law is a strange thing. It makes a man swear to tell the truth, and every time he shows signs of doing so some lawyer objects.

Woman—Women

1918. The average woman likes to be put on a pedestal—but not out of reach.

1919. They talk of professional women. Personally I have never met an amateur.

—WINSTON CHURCHILL

1920. Feminine arithmetic is somewhat inexact; yet many a gal who cannot add can certainly distract.

Word—Words

1921. If you think the words "night" and "evening" have the same meaning, note the different effect they have on a gown.

1922. The word *aliment* means food; this traces to the Latin *alo*, "nourish." So the way most of our divorce laws are written now, if a wife sues for release from her bonds, she expects alimony, which, etymologically, is really "eating money."

Work

1923. Someone has said that all living is just learning the meaning of words. That does not mean the long ten-syllable words we have to look up in the dictionary. The really great words to master are short ones—work, love, hope, joy, pain, home, child, life, death.

1924. The meaning of words often depends upon how you say them. On their honeymoon a bridegroom whispered to his one and only, "If an atom bomb exploded today, you would be the last person I would think of." She kissed him lovingly in response. Ten years later when he shouted the same words at her, she hit him with a plate.

1925. Back in Mark Twain's day, one of the finest words in our language was "square" ... You gave a man a square deal if you were honest. And you gave him a square meal when he was hungry. You stood four-square for the right, as you saw it, and square against everything else. When you got out of debt, you were square with the world. And that was when you could look your fellow man square in the eye.

Then a lot of strange characters got hold of this honest, wholesome word, bent it all out of shape and gave it back to our children. Convicts gave it the first twist. To them a *square* was an inmate who would not conform to the convict code. From the prisons it was flashed across the country on the marijuana circuit of the bopsters and hipsters. Now everyone knows what a *square* is. He is the man who never learned to get away with it. A Joe who volunteers when he doesn't have to. A guy who gets a kick from trying to do something better than any one else can.

—CHARLES H. BROWER

Work

1926. Thou, O God, dost sell us all good things at the price of labor.

—LEONARDO DA VINCI

1927. Work is everybody's birthright. To youth it brings hope; to middle-age, confidence; and to the aged, repose.

—EUGENE P. BERTIN

1928. No man needs sympathy because he has to work, because he has a burden to carry. Far and away the best prize that life has to offer is the chance to work hard at work worth doing.

—THEODORE ROOSEVELT

1929. The law of work does seem utterly unfair—but there it is, and nothing can change it: the higher the pay in enjoyment the worker gets out of it, the higher shall be his pay in money also.

—MARK TWAIN

World, The

1930. It's not enough to save the world—we must make the world worth saving.

1931. The thing that matters today is to be aware of the fact that the world is not moving toward self-destruction, but that all men, in spite of all revolutions, wars, cataclysms, and natural catastrophes, are headed toward a new reality, that the gates of the future, as one says rhetorically, are open.

—LEONARDO RICCI

Worry—Worries

1932. Worry pulls tomorrow's cloud over today's sunshine.

1933. Worry cannot change the past, but it can ruin the present.

1934. It cannot be said that worry doesn't do any good. Experience teaches us the contrary. The fact is that the things we worry about just don't happen.

1935. A man who never worries either has not the character and the mentality necessary, or he just does not care. He may think he has some sort of Epicurean philosophy that rises above the worry level, but chances are he is just plain selfish, or just plain no good. Worry is merely a cue to do something about that which concerns us and requires action.

Worthlessness

1936.   No man is completely worthless—he can always serve as a horrible example.

1937.   There are two kinds of men who never amount to much— those who cannot do what they are told, and those who can do nothing else.

Writing.   See also **Authorship**

1938.   The purpose of writing is to hold a mirror to nature, and too much today is written from small mirrors in vanity cases.

—John Mason Brown

1939.   There's no wound deeper than a pen can give,
It makes men living dead, and dead men live.

—John Taylor

Youth

1940.   A good man dies when a boy goes wrong.

1941.   I am not young enough to know everything.

—James M. Barrie

1942.   Youth is a mirror which reflects all the blemishes of adult society.

—Knute Larson

1943. A new broom sweeps well, but an old one is best for the corners.

—OLD SAYING

1944. Don't let young people confide in you their aspirations; when they drop them, they will drop you.

—LOGAN PEARSALL SMITH

1945. People who wonder where this younger generation is headed would do well to consider where it came from.

1946. Young men are fitter to invent than to judge; fitter for execution than for counsel; and fitter for new projects than for settled business.

—FRANCIS BACON

1947. When the young behave badly it is because society has already behaved worse. We have the teen-agers, like the politicians and the wars, that we deserve.

—J. B. PRIESTLEY

1948. It is, perhaps, a good thing that youth does not know that most of its dreams will never come true. For, unless the young believed they could accomplish miracles, they never would try. And it is only by trying to do the impossible that humanity gets a little farther along with each new generation.

1949. Youth ends when we perceive that no one wants our gay abandon. And the end may come in two ways: the realization that other people dislike it, or that we ourselves cannot continue with it. Weak men grow older in the first way, strong men in the second.

—CESARE PAVESE

1950. Youth is not a time of life ... it is a state of mind. It is not a matter of ripe cheeks, red lips and supple knees; it is a temper of the will, a quality of the imagination, a vigor of the emotions; it is a freshness of the deep springs of life.

Youth means a temperamental predominance of courage over timidity, of the appetite for adventure over love of ease. This often exists in a man of fifty more than a boy of twenty.

Nobody grows old merely living a number of years; people grow old only by deserting their ideals. Years wrinkle the skin, but to give up enthusiasm wrinkles the soul. Worry, doubt, self-distrust, fear and despair ... these are the long, long years that bow the head and turn the growing spirit back to dust.

Whether seventy or sixteen, there is in every being's heart the love of wonder, the sweet amazement of the stars and star-like things and thoughts, the undaunted challenge of events, the unfailing child-like appetite for what next, and the joy and game of life.

You are as young as your faith, as old as your doubt; as young as your self-confidence, as old as your fear; as young as your hope, as old as your despair.

In the central place of your heart there is a wireless station; so long as it receives messages of beauty, hope, cheer, courage, grandeur and power from the earth, from men and from the infinite, so long are you young.

When the wires are all down and the central place of your heart is covered with the snows of pessimism and the ice of cynicism, then are you grown old indeed and may God have mercy on your soul.

—Samuel Ullman

Youth—Age

1951. The old know what they want; the young are sad and bewildered.

—Logan Pearsall Smith

1952. If youth could trade some of its enthusiasm to age for some of its caution, both would be better off.

1953. Youth is so sure the rules have changed. Age is sure they haven't. Youth feels it knows how far it can go. Age is deeply aware of the danger. Youth feels it can apply the brakes in time. Age knows it isn't always so.

—Richard L. Evans

SUBJECT INDEX

(Numbers in the index refer to selections in the text, not to page numbers.)

A

Ability—Abilities, *1*, *2*, 278, 339, 417, 1763
Ability, Physical, 417
Absence, *3–5*, 713, 927, 1319
Absent-mindedness, *6*, *7*
"Absent-tea-ism," 54
Absolute, 996
Abstinence, *8*, *9*, 1295, 1897
Absurdity—Absurdities, 295, 1333
Abundant life, 1750
Abuse—Abuses, *10*, 282, 805, 1295, 1552
Accident—Accidents, 532, 739, 1707
Acomplishment—Accomplishments *11*, *12*, 416, 1094, 1459, 1763
Accord, 423
Accountant—Accountants, 13, 14
Accounting, *13*, *14*, 1809
Accuracy, 1522
Accusation—Accusations, 141, 1911
Ache—Aches, 1117
Achievement—Achievements. See also *Accomplishment*, *15*, *16*, 212, 628, 739, 848, 1355, 1433
Acid—Acids, 173, 1914
Acorn—Acorns, 808
Acquiescence, 83
Acquisitiveness, 1071
Acrobat—Acrobats, 1583
Action, *17–21*, 148, 428, 493, 960, 1394, 1581, 1770
Activity, 518
Actor—Actors, 1812
Adjustment—Adjustments, 184, 202, 1093
Admiration, 79
Adolescence, *22*, *23*
Adolescent—Adolescents, 1775
Adult—Adults, 1775
Adult Society, 1941

Ad valorem tax, 480
Advancement, *24*, *25*, 872
Advantage—Advantages, 71, 447, 1535, 1783, 1859
Advent, 240
Adventure—Adventures, 115, 830, 1098, 1949
Adversity—Adversities, *26–29*, 428, 685, 709, 718, 1277
Advertisement, Newspaper, 1143
Advertiser—Advertisers, 30
Advertising, *30–32*, 579
Advice, *33–35*, 428, 639, 1009, 1011, 1012, 1171, 1386, 1945
Advocacy, 134
Aeronautics, 49
Affectation, *36*
Affection—Affections, 720, 1148, 1269, 1725
Affluence, 1775
Africa, 266, 638
Age, *37–40*, 453, 921
Aggravation—Aggravations, 285
Aggressiveness, 259, 579
Aging, *41–49*
Agreement—Agreements, 160, 423
Aim—Aims, 611, 1619
Air, 784
Airplane—Airplanes, 167
Alarm clock—Alarm clocks, 219, 252
Alaska, State of, *50*, *51*, 1778–1781
Alaska—Texas. See *Texas—Alaska*
Alaskan State Song, 50
Albany, New York, 1439
Alcoholic liquor, 467, 1704
Alertness, 49, 515
Alfalfa, 633
Alimony, 1921
Allegheny Mountains, 1438
Allegiance, 1065
All-embracing, 18

Subject Index

Alley—Alleys, 797
Ally—Allies, 451
Altar—Altars, 899
Alteration—Alterations, 1803
Altercation—Altercations, 1819
Alternative—Alternatives, 697, 1885
Amateur—Amateurs, 1918
Ambassador—Ambassadors, 150
Ambition—Ambitions, 52, 53, 162, 307, 599, 632, 649, 1402, 1595, 1751, 1888
Ambulance—Ambulances, 859
Amend—Amends, 1196
America—American—Americanism, 54–57, 204, 424, 457, 475, 477, 656, 665, 824, 963, 1033, 1140, 1175, 1339, 1388, 1405, 1494, 1775, 1845
American Federation of Labor, 1034
American tradition, 56
Amputation—Amputations, 90
Amusement—Amusements, 115, 1207
Analysis—Analyses, 1071
Anarchy, 1051
Ancestor—Ancestors, 60
Ancestry, 58–61
"Ancient institution," 310
Angel—Angels, 218, 244, 1415
Anger, 62–71, 158, 423, 769
Animal—Animals, 245, 1503, 1522
Animal lover—Animal lovers, 457
Anniston, Alabama, 1746
Anomaly—Anomalies, 989
Ant—Ants, 588
Antagonist—Antagonists, 354
Antibiotic—Antibiotics, 633
Anticipation, 922
Antidote—Antidotes, 1690
Anti-Utopia, 260
Anxiety—Anxieties, 72, 73, 238, 399, 1199, 1214, 1829
Apathy, 699
Apparel, 1207, 1249
Appearance—Appearances, 74, 75, 378, 901, 1247
Appeasement, 1518
Appetite, 1041, 1207
Applause, 110, 199, 1010, 1223
Apple—Apples, 476
Appointment—Appointments, 253
Appreciation, 76, 77, 579, 702
Appreciation, Art, 130
Apprehension—Apprehensions, 72, 238, 1294

Approbation, 78, 79
Approval, 78, 79
April, Month of, 1582
Aptitude, 1839
Arab—Arabs, 457, 1289
Arbitrariness, 828, 1040
Arbitrator—Arbitrators, 599
Archaeologist—Archaeologists, 925
Architect — Architects — Architecture, 80-82, 1055
Archives Building, U.S., 1331
Arena—Arenas, 1534
Argument—Arguments, 83-88, 280 1071
Arithmetic, 1522
Arithmetic, Feminine, 1919
Arizona, State of, 572
Arlington National Cemetery, 1439
Armament—Armaments, 1883, 1888
Army—Armies, 188
Army, German, 166
Arrival, 904
Arrogance, 316, 1206, 1629
Arrow—Arrows, 770
Arrow, Poisoned—Arrows, Poisoned, 379
Art, 89-95, 1040, 1097, 1220, 1232, 1580
Art appreciation, 130
Art, Modern, 96, 97
Arteries, Hardening, of, 1251
Artificiality, 1500
Artificial teeth, 331
Artisan—Artisans, 1304
Artist—Artists, 899, 944, 1304, 1813
Ash—Ashes, 307
Aspiration—Aspirations. See also Ambition, 98, 99, 479, 1148, 1220, 1595, 1943
Assassin—Assassins, 960
Asset—Assets, 515, 985, 1149
Assistance, 585, 847
Associate—Associates, 281, 599, 1742
Assyrian, 652
Astronomer—Astronomers, 618
Astronomy, 1522
Atheism, 100, 101, 535, 823, 1515
Athens, Greece, 345
Athletic coach, 417
Atom—Atoms, 102
Atom bomb, 1923
Atomic age, 102, 103
Atom-splitting, 102
Attachment—Attachments, 57
Attainment—Attainments, 1030

Subject Index

City—Cities, *261, 262*
Civic duty, *263, 264*
Civilization, 99, 137, *265, 266*, 935, 1015, 1069, 1363, 1444, 1825
Civil liberty—Civil liberties, 343
Clam chowder, 1780
Class—Classes, 182
Classroom, 1766
Class warfare, 1446
Cleaver—Cleavers, 415
Clergyman—Clergymen, 1571, 1650
Cleveland, Ohio, 1439
Cleverness, *267*, 993
Climate, 581
Clock, 127, 231
Clock, Alarm, 219
Cloth, 1067, 1428
Clothes—Clothing, 116, 137, 349, 1067, 1207, 1249
Clothier, 1438
Cloud—Clouds, 139, 1931
Coach—Coaching, 417
Coach, Athletic, 417
Coachman—Coachmen, 308
Co-authorship, 113
Cobweb—Cobwebs, 941
Cocksuredness, 195
Cocktail party, 1782
Coddling, 229
Coercion, *268, 269*, 1052
Coffee, 1562
Coffee break—Coffee breaks, 54
Coffin—Coffins, 555
Coffin-maker—Coffin-makers 555
Cohesiveness, 986
Coincidence—Coincidences, *270*
Coin, Gold—Coins, Gold, 822
Collaboration, 113
College—Colleges, *271–273*, 1113
College degree—College degrees, 273
College freshman—College freshmen, 274
College graduate—College graduates, 273
College student—College students, 1645
Color—Colors, 471
Columbia University, 917, 1043
Columnist, 1611
Comfort, 1271, 1649
Commandments, Ten, 161
Commencement exercises, *274, 275*, 917
Commendation, 79
Commentary—Commentaries, 39
Committee—Committees, *276*, 394

Common cause, 1186
Common denominator, 1575
Commonplace, 77
Common sense, 1577, 1672
Communism, *277–279*
Companion—Companions, 714
Companionship, 942, 1692
Comparison—Comparisons, *280, 281*, 317
Compassion, 1139, 1144
Compatibility, 1431
Compensation, 158, *282, 283*, 932
Competition, 1071, 1392
Complaint—Complaints, 174, 263, *284, 285*, 357, 520, 1810
Complicate—Complicated, 14
Compliment — Compliments — Complimentary, *286–288*, 842, 929, 1001, 1038, 1289
Compromise—Compromises, *289–291*, 609, 1108, 1443, 1888
Compulsion, 184, 299
Compulsory education, 477
Compunction, 359
Computer—Computers, 487
Concealment, 267, 300, 1036, 1289, 1587
Conceit, *292, 293*, 796, 1600
Concentration, 791, 1013, 1676
Concession—Concessions, 526, 1826
Conciseness, 159–161
Conclusion—Conclusions, 601
Concord, New Hampshire, 1439
Condescension, *294, 295*
Conductor, Train, 1240
Conference—Conferences, *296, 297*
Confidence, 150, *298–300*, 388, 392, 450, 718, 1244, 1362, 1600, 1707, 1926
Confidence, Misplaced, 298
Conflict, 1343
Conformity, 208, *301, 302*, 1247
Confusion, 290, 1040, 1120, 1472, 1881
Confusion, State of, 1778
Congress, U.S., 1126, 1143, 1213, 1824
Conjecture, 1790
Conqueror—Conquerors, 373
Conquest, 369, 1030, 1597, 1715
Conscience, 279, *303–308*, 456, 467, 1013, 1414, 1419, 1518, 1856, 1915
Consent, 78
Consequence—Consequences, 619, 1111

316

Subject Index

Educational system—Educational systems, 1699
Efficiency, 599, 1189, 1227, 1370
Effort, 16, 119, 210, *485–487*, 628, 649, 772, 957, 1259, 1290, 1433, 1947
Ego, 1630
Egotism, *488, 489*
Egyptian, 824
Eiffel Tower, 49
Election—Elections, 1388
Electric light bulb, 1378
Electric power, 265
Electrification, 1468
Elegance, 321
Elf—Elves, 248
Eloquence, 109, *490–492*, 1476, 1663
Embalming, 704
Embarrassment, 1694
Emergency—Emergencies, 741, 1801
Emotion—Emotions, 848, 866, 1013, 1340, 1374, 1949
Emotional stability, 580
Employe relations, 599
Employer-Employe, 394, *493–501*, 1614, 1742
Employment, 454, *502–506*, 801, 1102
Emporia, Kansas, 917
Emptiness, 366
Emulation, 1613
Encouragement, 356, 628, 875, 933
Endeavor—Endeavors, 649
Endurance, 27, 157, *507, 508*
Enemy—Enemies, 297, 311, 329, 339, 380, 382, 398, 461, *509–515*, 636, 674, 1243, 1549, 1616, 1711, 1742, 1804
Energy, 893
Energy, Conservation of, 952
Engagement, Marriage, 6
Engineer—Engineers—Engineering, *516, 517*, 610
England, 54, 241, 1019, 1143
English, 204, 520, 1231
Englishman—Englishmen, 204, 1388
Enjoyment, 9, 532, 701
Enlightenment, 1144
Ennui, *518–520*
Enslavement, 1495
Enterprise—Enterprises, 71, *521, 522*
Entertainment, 32, 930
Enthusiasm, 47, 173, 416, *523–525*, 615, 1949, 1951

Entrance—Entrances, 1848
Envy, 164, 283, *526–533*, 847, 872, 1005, 1006, 1269, 1786
Epicurean philosophy, 1934
Epigram—Epigrams, 892
Epiphany Eve, 247
Epitaph—Epitaphs, *534–577*
Equality, *578–580*, 805, 921, 1339, 1575
Equal protection, 805
Equal rights, 653
Equilibrium, 909
Error—Errors, 19, 100, 328, 599, 634
Erudition, 1367
Escape, 342, 467, *581–583*, 694, 893
Escapism, 1292
Esteem, 720
Estray—Estrays, 1366
Eternity, *584*, 858, 1126, 1178, 1344
Ethics, 902
Ethics, Code of, 991
Europe, 266, 331, 1143, 1562, 1865
Evasion—Evasions, *585*, 1503
Evening gown, 1249
Everlastingness, 1301
Evidence, 619, 1013
Evil, 479, *586, 587*, 630, 805, 1269, 1495, 1686
Evil spirit—Evil spirits, 870
Example—Examples, 211, 270, 282, *588–593*, 639, 1311, 1613, 1935
Exasperation, 892
Excess—Excesses—Excessiveness, 474, *594, 595*, 1295
Exchange, 702, 745
Excommunication, 1143
Excuse—Excuses, 214, 428, *596, 597*
Executive—Executives, *598, 599*, 633, 1162, 1251, 1703
Executive, Business, 186, 498
Exemption, Tax—Exemptions, Tax, 138
Exercise, Physical, *600, 601*, 638
Exhaustion, 1469
Exhilaration, 1259
Exile—Exiles, 378
Exit—Exits, 1848
Exoneration, 981
Expectation—Expectations, 212, 886, 922
Expedient—Expedients, 522
Experience, 483, *602–606*, 921, 1094, 1105, 1247, 1445, 1520, 1545, 1667
Experiment—Experiments, 139, 1002

Subject Index

Flower—Flowers, 244, 625, *661–663*, 911, 1187, 1271, 1430, 1551, 1639, 1689
Flower box—Flower boxes, 1349
Focus, 1605
Folly, 75, 122, 334, 370, 902, 1907
Food—Foods, *664*, *665*, 1207, 1296, 1921
Fool—Fools, 79, 85, 336, 366, 643, *666*, *667*, 757, 982, 1051, 1386, 1403, 1487, 1550, 1676, 1696, 1841, 1911
Foolhardiness, 334
Foolishness, 75, 122, 334, 1269
Foot—Feet, 358, 364, 938, 1042, 1328
Football fan—Football fans, 1704, 1705
Footscraper, 1221
Footstep—Footsteps, 1557
Force, 299, 416, 646, 1711
Forebear, 61, 891
Forecast-Forecasts, 374
Foreman—Foremen, 198
Foresight, 1214
Forest—Forests, 1120
Forget—Forgetting—Forgetfulness, 428, *668–670*, 806, 1020, 1397
Forgiveness, 311, 333, 428, *671–683*, 1166, 1268
Form, Government—Forms, Government, 1231
Formula—Formulae, 1137, 1791, 1801
Fortitude, *684–686*
Fortune, *687–689*, 1502
Forward-looking, 15, 1332
Fossil—Fossils, 361
Foundation—Foundations, 894
Fountain pen, 1879
Fraction—Fractions, 842
Fragrancy, 1374
France, 1019, 1143
Frankincense, 248
Frankness, 321, *690*, *691*, 741
Fraud—Frauds, 592, 1606, 1711
Freedom, 248, 362, 370, 377, 653, *692–702*, 801, 1044, 1077, 1516, 1638, 1657, 1693, 1696, 1697, 1860, 1881
Freemasons, 1143
Freezer—Freezers, 125
Fremont, Ohio, 1439
French, 457, 520, 610, 638, 823, 824, 1231, 1614
French government, 610
Frenchman—Frenchmen, 1228

Freshman, College—Freshmen, College, 274
Friday—Fridays, 1143
Friend—Friends, 26, 46, 117, 153, 154, 215, 293, 311, 329, 388, 398, 436, 446, 461, 510, 511, 583, 601, 636, 674, 873, 1243, 1261, 1377, 1381, 1690, 1692, 1820
Friendless, 690, 1020
Friendship, 379, 436, 458, *703–721*, 1148, 1433, 1513, 1816, 1822
Fright, 1554
Frost, 632
Fruit—Fruits, 663, 665
Frustration, 791, 1101
Frying pan, 694
Furrow—Furrows, 312
Futility, 1287
Future, The, 150, 357, 462, 603, 637, *722–726*, 1033, 1287, 1364, 1385, 1446, 1494, 1577, 1621, 1707, 1909, 1932

G

Gain—Gains, 283
Gallows, 344
Gambler—Gamblers—Gambling, 519, *727–730*, 1832
Ganges River, 784
Garage—Garages, 81
Garden—Gardens—Gardening, *731*, *732*, 1523
Gas—Gassing, 1468, 1605
Gem—Gems, 161, 1689
General—Generals, 199
General Motors Corp., 610
General Welfare, 802
Generosity, 580, 725, *733–736*, 758, 767, 1068, 1096, 1208, 1826
Geneva Bible Society, 136
Genius, 357, *737*, *738*, 1521, 1712
Gentleman—Gentlemen, 432, *739–741*, 1721
Genuineness, *742*, *743*
Geography, 1522
German, 824, 1228
German army, 166
Germany, 242, 1019
Gettysburg Address, Lincoln's, 161, 1875
Gibbet—Gibbets, 344
Gift—Gifts, 150, 286, 702, *744–749*, 1402

Subject Index

Log cabin, 1438
Logic, 1520, 1566
London, England, 860
London, Port of, 1379
London Times, The, 1143
Loneliness, 399, 599, *1116–1200*
Lone Star State, 1783
Longevity, 12, 418, *1121–1123*
Longitude, 139
Long-windedness, *1124–1126,* 1764
Loom—Looms, 1813
Loquacity, 1677
Lord Stewards, 1507
Lord's Prayer, The, 161
Loss—Losses, 283, 340, *1127, 1128*
Loudness, 1670, 1675
Love, 4, 5, 44, 117, 230, 280, 379, 399, 440, 455, 599, 628, 847, 899, 997 1128, *1129–1139*, 1166, 1214, 1238, 1309, 1317, 1344, 1404, 1694, 1749, 1793, 1816, 1865
Loyalty—Loyalties, 55, 162, 458, 720, *1140, 1141,* 1227
Loyalty, Idealogical, 291
Loyalty, Political, 1229
Luck, 275, 363, 601, *1142, 1143,* 1287, 1365
Lupercalia, 1865
Luxury, 9, 228, 321, 751, 1207

M

Machine—Machines,, 118, 516, 517, 1144
Machine age, *1144*
Machinery, 1425
Magi, 238, 247
Magic, 32
Magician—Magicians, 417
Magistrate—Magistrates, 373, 800, 1010, 1016
Magnet—Magnets, 1264
Magnification, 395, 1889
Majority—Majorities, 804, 1405
Malaria, 610
Malice, *1145,* 1340
Mallet—Mallets, 197
Mambo Boys, 1019
Man—Men, 101, 220, 373, 425, 648, *1146–1148*
Man—Woman, 1006, 1133, *1149–1159,* 1225, 1561
Management, 1033, *1160–1162*

Management, Business, 182
Management, Executive, 599
Management—Labor, 182
Manager, Baseball, 142
Mandolin—Mandolins, 240
Mankind, 34, 121, 164, 791, 921, 953, 1247, 1415, 1697, 1883
Manners, *1163, 1164*
Manners, Good, 1522
Manufacturer—Manufacturers, 1567
Manuscript—Manuscripts, 1357
Marble, 1211
March, Month of, 1582
Marion, Ohio, 1439
Marketing, 599
Market place, 592, 1120
Marriage, 6, 270, 331, 451, 452, *1165–1176,* 1774
Married life, *1177, 1178*
Martyr—Martyrs, 1352
Martyrdom, 469, 1865
Mason—Masons—Masonic, 1055, 1143
Masonic Lodge—Masonic Lodges, 1143
Massacre—Massacres, 188
Massage—Massages, 1045
Master—Masters, 115, 444, 831
Master-Servant, 1585
Mate—Mates, 1165
Material possession—Material possessions, 1274
Mathematics, 1071
Matter, 279
Maturity, *1179–1182*, 1694
McGill University, 1905
Meadow—Meadows, 323
Meaning—Meanings, 1040
Meanness, 1208
Measles, 1132
Measurement—Measurements, 192, 1256
Mechanic—Mechanics, 1055, 1304
Mechanical energy, 1444
Meddle—Meddling, 1508
Medical profession, *1183, 1184*
Medicine—Medicines, 29, 421, 1207
Mediocrity, 301, 1021, 1392, 1396, 1618
Meditation, 1500
Meekness, 652
Meeting—Meetings, *1185*
Melancholia, 169, 1678
Melody—Melodies, 1415
Memorial—Memorials, 1186
Memorial Chapel, 1475

328

Memorial Day, *1186, 1187*
Memory—Memories, 383, 721, 891, 1154, 1320, 1491
Mental attitude—Mental attitudes, 417, 506
Mental health, *1188, 1189*
Mental hospital—Mental hospitals, 1156
Mentality, 1934
Mental peak, 48
Mental power, 48
Mental prayer, 1427
Merchandise, 989
Mercilessness, 188
Mercurial thermometer, 1143
Mercy, 957, 1014
Merit, 58
Mexico, 1530
Microscope—Microscopes, 618, 1889
Middle age, 330, 606, 1311, 1926
Middles Ages, 330, 1865
Military power, 1213
Millstone—Millstones, 1172
Mind, The, 49, 77, 130, 279, 338, 406, 476, 479, 481, 484, 580, 785, 817, 868, 922, 945, 1045, 1138, 1188, 1269, 1328, 1366
Mind, Breadth of, 1522
Mind, Change of, 910, *1190, 1191*, 1268
Mind, Peace of, 940, *1192*
Mind, State of, 1119, 1229, 1949
Minister—Ministers, 255–257, 828
Minority report—Minority reports, 276
Minority rule, 1881
Miracle—Miracles, 1137, 1947
Mirror—Mirrors, 1937, 1941
Mischief, 715, 1551
Misdemeanor—Misdemeanors, 331
Miser—Misers, 1004
Misery—Miseries, 52, 1498
Misfortune—Misfortunes, 1139, *1193, 1194*, 1535, 1725
Mishap—Mishaps, 1194
Misnomer—Misnomers, 1539
Missionary—Missionaries, 167
Misstep—Missteps, 187, 1458
Mistake—Mistakes, 392, 397, 428, 452, 643, 970, *1195–1199*, 1339, 1727, 1874
Mistress—Mistresses, 115
Mistrust, 450
Misunderstanding, 599, 1532

Model—Models, 947
Moderation, 804, 840
Moderator—Moderators, 599
Modern age, *1200*
Modesty, 53, 364, 820, *1201, 1202*, 1407, 1615, 1676, 1743
Molehill—Molehills, 1847
Mona Lisa, 94
Monday—Mondays, 252
Money, 162, 163, 171, 172, 282, 383, 976, 984, 1003, 1094, 1182, *1203–1210*, 1467, 1702, 1703, 1744, 1802, 1892, 1894
Money-saving, 127
Monkey—Monkeys, 1646
Monologue, 1416
Monotony, 301
Month—Months, 175
Montpelier, Virginia, 1439
Montreal, Canada, 1905
Monument—Monuments, 215, 469, 820, *1211*
Moon, 606
Moon, New, 310
Moral control, 302
Moral power, *1212, 1213*
Moral principle—Moral principles, 522
Moral standard—Moral standards, 628
Morale, 1045
Morality, 963
Morality, Political, 1339
Morality, Social, 1339
Morals, 701, 1040, 1761
Mores, 846
Morning—Mornings, 220
Moroseness, 1678
Mortality, 952
Mosquito—Mosquitoes, 610
Mosquito netting, 1784
Mother—Mothers, 558, 1275, 1309
Mother-Child, 1593
Motherhood, *1214, 1215*
Motion, 93, 440, 1145, 1361, 1714
Motorcyclist—Motorcyclists, 859
Motorist—Motorists, 1839
Mountain, 1474, 1847
Mount Clemens, Michigan, 892
Mount Everest, 1584
Mount Vernon, Virginia, 1439
Mourning, 864, 1187, *1216, 1217*
Mouse—Mice, 95, 417, 1042
Mousetrap—Mousetraps, 31

Servant—Servants, 444, 831, 1004, 1585, 1873
Service, 170, 867, 1118, 1209, 1433, 1743
Setback—Setbacks, 1287
Settlement—Settlements, 772
Sew—Sewing, 576, 1002
Sewing machine, 1002
Sex, 169
Shadow—Shadows, 188, 445, 824, 951, 966, 1404
Shame, 975, 1289, 1367, *1651–1654*
Sharing, 6, 288, 628, 1020, *1655–1657*
Sheep, 1435
Shelf—Shelves, 1506
Shepherd—Shepherds, 238, 749, 1080
Shiftlessness, 1801
Ship—Ships, 602, 686, 989, 1258, 1537, 1556, 1842
Ship captain, 1379
Shirt—Shirts, 1750
Shoe—Shoes, 247, 599, 1165
Shoemaker—Shoemakers, 1373
Shoes, High-heeled, 331
Shortcoming—Shortcomings, 682
Short cut—Short cuts, 1364
Shortening, 1124
Shortstop, Baseball, 142
Short story—Short stories, 1098
Shoulder—Shoulders, 76, 839, 1111, 1536
Shrewdness, 1363
Shrink—Shrinking, 1297
Shuttlecock—Shuttlecocks, 624
Shyness, 911
Sickness, 188, 283, 628, 851
Sightseer—Sightseers, 358
Signature—Signatures, 1879
Signpost, 828
Silence, 78, 149, 285, 431, 716, 769, 1222, 1632, *1658–1678,* 1684
Simile—Similes, 280
Simplicity, 160, 791, *1679, 1680*
Sin—Sins, 365, 587, 1166, 1317, 1606, 1662, *1681–1683*
Sincerity, 741, 954, 1413, 1513, 1514
Sing—Singing, 169
Sinner—Sinners, 1139, 1683
Sister—Sisters, 540
Size—Sizes, 161, 1783
Skate—Skating, 971
Skepticism, 1199

Skier—Skiers, 1707
Skill—Skills, 119, 339, 417
Skin, 47, 1760
"Skollies," 1019
Slander, *1684–1687,* 1742
Slave—Slaves, 60, 377, 699
Slavery, 702, 1230, 1443
Sleep—Sleeping, 391, 806, 995, 1003, 1125, 1650, 1858
Slipper—Slippers, 7, 247
Small talk, 1678
Small town—Small towns, 1891
Smartness, 1735
Smile—Smiles, 183, 662, 686, 876, 1069, 1271, 1551, 1604, *1688–1690,* 1811
Smoke—Smoking, 285, 574, 594
Snail—Snails, 1845
Snake—Snakes, 438
Snare—Snares, 387
Snobbery, 1641
Snow, 22, 1215, 1557
Snowflake—Snowflakes, 240
Sobriety, 1669, 1689
Social attitude—Social attitudes, 405
Socialism, 278
Social life, 1244
Social order, 182
Social pressure, 846
Social problem—Social problems, 1446
Social responsibility, 1186
Social structure, 628
Social success, 314
Social virtue—Social virtues, 1051, 1529
Society, 179, 479, 800, 973, 1553, 1946
Soldier—Soldiers, 166, 1070, 1187, 1789
Soldier's pack, 693
Solitude, *1691–1695*
Solo—Solos, 1631
Song—Songs, 50, 876
Song, Love, 280
Soot, 285
Sophistication, 742
Sorrow—Sorrows, 238, 628, 721, 768, 1317
Soul, The, 47, 100, 116, 230, 533, 554, 587, 618, 652, 724, 768, 791, 916, 949, 1005, 1045, 1138, 1164, 1247, 1344, 1949
Sound, 130
South Africa, 1019
South America, 638
South Atlantic League, 1746

Subject Index

Theory—Theories, 1381, 1598, *1790, 1791*
Thermometer, Mercurial, 1143
Thief—Thieves, 1811
Thinking, 17, 428, 668, 1119, 1220, 1500, *1792–1794,* 1876
Thirst, 519
Thorn—Thorns, 1101, 1639
Thoroughness, 1523
Thought—Thoughts, 148, 152, 172, 203, 230, 282, 649, 834, 849, 1036, 1163, 1176, 1302, 1361, 1374, 1389, 1676, 1680, 1792, 1949
Thought, Freedom of, 696
Thoughtfulness, 766, 1214, 1555
Threat—Threats, 1123, *1795, 1796*
Three "R's," 1357
Thrift, 155, 380, 428, *1797–1801*
Thriftlessness, 1801
Thrush, 1671
Thunder, 818
Ticket, Railroad, 772
Tide, 971
Tiger—Tigers, 417
Time, 5, 128, 201, 599, 956, 1450, *1802–1810,* 1906
Time-killing, 1505
Timepiece, 1530
Time-saving, 127, 941
Time-stealing, 152
Time-telling, 1530
Time-wasting, 597
Time-watching, 1807
Timidity, 1214, 1612, 1949
Tit for tat, *1811–1813*
Toast—Toasts—Toasting, *1814–1824*
Tobacco merchant—Tobacco merchants, 574
Today, 16, 462, 1280, 1543, 1742
Togetherness, 1007
Tokyo, Japan, 1838
Tolerance, 311, 599, 701, 1013, 1268, 1274, 1703, 1742, *1825, 1826*
Tomboy—Tomboys, 1357
Tomorrow, 412, 462, 534, 572, 722, 1333, 1448, 1449, 1742, *1827–1829*
Tongue—Tongues, 1573, 1668
Tooth—Teeth, 552, 1042
Tornado, 632
Touchdown—Touchdowns, 1704
Tower—Towers, 1531
Tower of London, 82

Town clock, 263
Toy—Toys, 115, 242
Toy shop—Toy shops, 82
Trade unionist—Trade unionists, 181
Tradition—Traditions, 656, 1140, 1574
Traffic, Automobile, 188, 557, *1830–1840*
Tragedy—Tragedies, 175, 452
Trail—Trails, 593
Trail-blazing, 593
Train—Trains, 772
Train conductor, 1240
Trainer, Animal, 1503
Training, 119
Tranquility, 1137, 1410
Tranquilizer—Tranquilizers, 1564
Transient, 714
Transition, 371
Translation—Translations, 1372
Travel, 649, 904, 946, *1841–1846*
Traveler—Travelers, 364, 1434
Treasure—Treasures, 1289, 1588
Tree—Trees, 593, 808, 1305
Tribe—Tribes, 1229
Tribesman—Tribesmen, 1229
Trick—Tricks, 922, 1539, 1743
Trifle—Trifles, 637, 1247, 1889
Triumph—Triumphs, 369, 969
Trouble—Troubles, 195, 206, 283, 440, 686, 1017, 1028, 1066, 1690, 1765, *1847–1851*
Trumpet—Trumpets, 1176
Trust, 619
Truth, 776, 1013, 1148, 1285, 1409, 1581, 1698, 1743, *1852–1855,* 1916
"Tsotsies," 1019
Tune—Tunes, 1060
Tune—Tuning, 28
Turbulence, 939
Turkey, 364
Tutor—Tutors, 1009
Tuxedo, 108, 1249
Twilight, 1689
Tyranny, 115, 362, 609, 700, 702, 1072, 1285, *1856*
Tyrant—Tyrants, 115, 362, 636, 1584

U

Ugliness, 91, 130, 1208, 1289
Umbrella—Umbrellas, 977
Uncertainty—Uncertainties, 374, 882, 1199

AUTHOR AND SOURCE INDEX

(Numbers in the index refer to selections in the text, not to page numbers.)

343

Author and Source Index

Harris, Rev. Obadiah, 481
Harrison, Elizabeth, 356
Havighurst, Robert J., 1019
Hawthorne, Nathaniel, 838, 1211
Haynes, Donald, 702
Hazlitt, William, 322, 355, 522, 704, 929, 1632
Head, Murdock, 846
Hebbel, Friedrich, 1870
Heine, Heinrich, 1713
Hemingway, Ernest, 1669
Herder, Johann, 1911
Herodotus, 1886
Herold, Don, 1460, 1834
Hesburgh, Theodore, 1309
Hess, John D., 1110
Hichens, Robert, 583
Higdon, Harry J., 1365
Hill, Aaron, 1560
Hillel, Rabbi, 1625
Hillis, Burton, 1736
Hillis, Newell D., 1537
Hinton, John, 882
Hippocrates, 1183
Hirsch, Rabbi Richard G., 1494
Hoffer, Eric, 182, 694, 963
Holmes, Carl, 1020
Holmes, Ernest, 523, 611, 615
Holmes, John Haynes, 452
Holmes, Dr. Oliver Wendell, 40, 196, 1366, 1577
Home, Henry, 199, 306, 711
Hoover, Herbert, 652, 960, 1048
Horace, 58, 726, 1607
Hostetter, B. Charles, 1215
Howard, John A., 859
Howe, Rev. N., 1349
Howell, James, 1586
Hubbard, Elbert, 46, 494, 826, 1514, 1526, 1527, 1599, 1705, 1712, 1715, 1747, 1907
Hubbard, Kin, 1717, 1720
Hughes, Charles Evans, 426
Hughes, Edwin Holt, 803
Hunt, Richard M., 1474
Hunting, Gardner, 1355
Hutchins, Robert M., 966, 1052, 1646
Huxley, Aldous, 314
Huxley, Thomas H., 695

I

Irving, Washington, 1914

J

Jackson, Andrew, 805
Jackson, Gordon, 1118
Jackson, Robert, 162
James the Sixth, 374
James, William, 936, 1545
Jay, William, 1692
Jefferson, Thomas, 801, 1466
Jerrold, Douglas, 310
Johnson, Philip, 1339
Johnson, Dr. Samuel, 8, 71, 281, 295, 388, 579, 624, 640, 716, 825, 939, 1177, 1270, 1300, 1493, 1540, 1629, 1842, 1854, 1873
Johnson, Stewart B., 16
Jones, Franklin P., 1772
Jones of Nayland, 334
Joubert, Joseph, 222, 643, 1260, 1644
Jowett, John Henry, 1892
Jung, Carl, 1404

K

Kant, Immanuel, 913
Keller, Helen, 60
Kelley, Clarence A., 1567
Kellum, Rev. E. Owen, Jr., 1523
Kelly, Vesta M., 1758
Kempis, Thomas à, 414
Kennedy, Bishop Gerald, 258
Kettering, Charles F., 205, 1258, 1791
Kierkegaard, Sören, 696, 883, 1418
Kinney, Agnes M., 1066
Knox, Frank, 1825
Kraus, Karl, 116
Kytle, Jack, 313

L

La Bruyère, Jean de, 184, 758 775, 794, 864, 1150, 1158, 1686
La Follette, Robert M., 259
Lake, Kirsopp, 619
Lamb, Charles, 1618
Lambert, Constance, 1218
Landor, Walter Savage, 359
Lane, Carol, 1839
Langland, William, 507
La Noue, François de, 158
Lantz, Thomas W., 1504
Lao-tzu, 798
Lapp, Charles L., 747
Large, John Ellis, 304

Author and Source Index

INDEX TO NAMES AND PERSONALTIES
REFERRED TO IN THE TEXT

*(Numbers in the index refer to selections
in the text, not to page numbers.)*

Index to Names and Personalties Referred to in the Text

Index to Names and Personalties Referred to in the Text